Practical
Stone Masonry

This book is dedicated to

the memory of the late

BILL HOLLAND

sometime Foreman Mason, York Minster

A man of fearlessly individual opinion,

to whom so much is owed

Practical Stone Masonry

P. R. HILL
Stone Consultant

AND

J. C. E. DAVID
Setter-out, York Minster

 Routledge
Taylor & Francis Group

LONDON AND NEW YORK

First published in the United Kingdom 1995 by
Donhead Publishing Ltd

This edition published 2013 by Routledge
2 Park Square, Milton Park, Abingdon, Oxon OX14 4RN
711 Third Avenue, New York, NY 10017

Routledge is an imprint of the Taylor & Francis Group, an informa business

⊙ ISBN13   978 1 873394 14 4 (hbk)

A CIP catalogue for this book is available from the
British Library

Typeset by Carnegie Publishing, Preston

Contents

Preface

This book is intended for use by working masons and apprentices, and those engaged in planning and supervising such works. The emphasis is directed towards masonry techniques used in the repair and preservation of stone buildings, for it is in this area that the majority of traditional masonry skills are practised today. Few new buildings are now of solid, dressed stone, although many of the techniques and other information presented here apply equally to new and repair work of a traditional nature. Neither stone cladding nor the hanging of solid stonework on steel frames are covered.

Anyone writing on the technical aspects of masonry must have in mind the book which for many years has been the stone masons' bible: *Modern Practical Masonry* by E. G. Warland, first published in 1929. Warland presented a picture of a highly mechanized trade, where machinery was essential to keep down costs and help stone to compete more effectively with other materials, the mason being used only for those details which could not be done by machine. He was writing at a time when the traditional stone trade was strong and in a position to compete with new materials such as concrete. Even steel-framed buildings were being clad in solid stone rather than with a veneer of thin slabs. Warland's book was a successor to *Practical Masonry* by W. R. Purchase, published in 1895, in which machinery is not mentioned but banker work is given only nine pages, as apprentices would have been expected to receive most of their training directly from a skilled mason. Most of the contents of both books are concerned with the geometry and setting-out of masonry details, and are directed entirely towards new work, which is infinitely simpler than repair work.

The chapter headings in this book are not dissimilar to those in Warland, but the content has a very different direction. Since the 1950s, both the commercial and educational emphasis has been on new techniques and methods of using stone and, although there has been a revival in the stone trade since the 1960s and 1970s, and many stone buildings are being repaired instead of demolished, there is a large gap in the understanding of traditional masonry by those supervising such contracts. There is little educational material directed towards high-class repair work for the benefit of the apprentice mason. Much of the literature on the care of stone buildings has been directed towards preserving 'as found' rather than repairing, or has been written by those often having only the smallest understanding of the craft of the stone mason. This book aims to fill that gap by presenting, in an accessible form, the essentials of setting-out, working and fixing for repairs, as it is these skills which form the core of the mason's trade. While it is essential for the mason to have some understanding of other aspects of the repair of historic buildings, such as cleaning and surface treatments, techniques and philosophies are constantly changing, and only broad outlines are given here. In every case suggestions for further reading are included.

It is not only masons, and particularly apprentice masons, who can learn from this book. All those concerned in the specifying and supervising of stonework, and those whose primary interest is the conservation, in its widest sense, of ancient buildings, can learn much from these pages. A knowledge of basic geology, causes of decay and methods of cleaning, can be learned, and in much greater detail, from other works. However, a full and practical description of what is, or more importantly should be, involved in full-size setting-out from existing detail and subsequent working and repair cannot be found elsewhere at the time of writing. A careful reading and understanding of Chapters 4 and 5 will give the architect an appreciation of what can be achieved by the masonry trade, something which is almost completely lacking at present. By the same token, the mason should read Chapter 12, where the problems of supervision and some idea of the conflicting schools of thought among those in overall charge of the maintenance of building are considered. From the banker, or the architect's office, the world can appear to be a very simple place. It is far from it, and the gap in understanding between the theoretician and the practitioner must be bridged.

Any mason today must have an awareness of the possibilities for conservation of stone as an alternative to replacement. Conservators have multiplied since the 1970s and, as a result, many buildings are maintained using conservation rather than masonry techniques. While it is unfortunately true that many conservators come from an academic rather than a trade background and have seen their skills as being superior, the conservator should be seen as an ally rather than an enemy. This book is not the place to discuss the wide range of conservation techniques available but the mason should be aware of them and the bibliography lists some introductory material.

Although today the interest in masonry skills is greater than for many years, some entrants see it as a rather romantic trade. Nothing could be further from the truth; it could be summed up as heavy, dusty and dirty, and, at times, tedious to say the least. There is little romance about fixing high on a scaffold in the teeth of a bitter east wind. Many of the romantics depart at this point, the time spent on training them being a loss to the trade. On the other hand, many large masonry firms are now producing worked stone from rough block to finished product entirely by the use of computer-controlled machinery. There is nothing wrong with that, and for new building work it is an economical and sensible way to run a business. It can be less satisfactory for repair work, where the startling accuracy stands out amid the mediaeval human frailty. Also, there is the temptation to simplify mouldings to ensure that they can be worked by machine, which is not the best way to conserve an old building.

The craft of the mason can only be learned and maintained by diligence and persistence over many years. It takes eight or ten years to make a useful all-round mason. It is then that the heavy, dirty work begins really to pay off in terms of job satisfaction. Both the factors in the previous paragraph militate against the long-term training of the traditional mason who, despite all the new machinery, is still the most vital element in the maintenance of stone buildings.

The authors should not be seen as opposed to machinery in the stone trade; anything which reduces tedious roughing-out is most welcome. But there is a place for everything, and there is a danger that the banker mason will disappear from the scene. Add to these factors the attitude of those conservationists who would rather see a building crumble to dust rather than intervene and, when the need for truly skilled traditional masons arises, they may not be there. There are already too many so-called masons who are nothing of the sort but whose work is accepted because there is no one else, or because no one knows any better. The chapter covering supervision should help to rectify the last point.

The standards set down in the following pages for setting-out, working and fixing stone may seem unreasonably high, but they are readily achievable and there seems little point in describing less than the best traditional trade practice.

This book, written from practical experience, thus serves to satisfy a number of aims:

- To provide an up-to-date summary of the best traditional trade practice for the benefit of the apprentice mason, including both banker work and fixing.
- To give for the first time a practical explanation of the methods of setting-out stonework from basic techniques to complex features.

- To look at the practical aspects of replacement of stone as a means of preserving a building.
- To give practical guidance to architects and others without masonry skills on what is involved in, and what is and is not acceptable in the way of specifications and workmanship.

A resumé of the state of training of masons draws attention to some of the potentially serious shortcomings of the current system that is now taking over from traditional apprenticeships. Allowing a total tolerance of 2 mm when working mouldings is hardly aiming for high standards in training.

The majority of references are to limestone and sandstone; the techniques for working granites form almost a different trade. Many dimensions are given in Imperial as well as metric measure. This has been done, after careful thought, because Imperial is still very widely used in the trade, because it fits very well with work on buildings which were designed and built in that measure, and because it is in many ways more useful. The cubic foot is still the most widely understood and the most practical measure of the volume of stone. It is not for nothing that French masons use their own foot (usually of 300 mm).

Both authors are trained stone masons writing on the basis of their practical experience of working, fixing, setting-out and supervision. All the examples and techniques described in this book are based directly on this experience.

Kevin Calpin has very kindly contributed Chapter 13 on training.

P. R. H.
J. D.

Acknowledgements

The authors are grateful to the following for advice and assistance.

Mr S. Boyle, Stone mason, formerly of York Minster and the cathedral of St John the Divine, Washington, DC; Realstone Ltd, Wingerworth, Chesterfield, for information and discussions on computerized setting-out and computer-controlled machinery; Atkins and Partners, Frances Street, Doncaster, for information on the Intergraph Micro-Station CAD program; Mr D. N. Isherwood RIBA, of Sunderland, Peacock & Associates, Clitheroe, for discussions on supervision and specifications; Mr S. Mills, Health and Safety Officer, York Minster Stoneyard, for advice on health and safety matters; Mr A. Swift, Department of Geology, Leicester University, and Mrs V. M. Croll, for advice on geological matters; Mrs J. Watkinson for checking the bibliography and for proof-reading much of the typescript; Mr R. Winterton of Robin Winterton Stonemasons, Beaverdyke, Clifton, York, for comments on Chapter 4; and the Dean and Chapter of York for permission to include Figures 4.1– 4.4, 4.7– 4.10, 7.1, 7.4, 7.7 and 8.3.

Mrs S. David has given invaluable assistance, and Figures 6.1, 6.2 and 6.5– 6.9 were prepared by Mr A. Smith of the City of Lincoln Archaeology Unit.

Mr I. Ward of Boden & Ward, Stonemasons, very kindly read a draft of the text, and made a number of very valuable comments and suggestions for improvement.

By way of conversation and example, many stonemasons have contributed indirectly towards this book but, for advice and discussions on every aspect of the trade over very many years, the authors acknowledge the particular influence of Mr B. Boden, Boden & Ward, Stonemasons, Flore, Northampton, Mr G. Butler BEM, Head Carver, York Minster Stoneyard, and Mr M. O'Connor, Foreman Mason, Lincoln Cathedral.

All errors and omissions remain the responsibility of the authors. References throughout the text to the male gender are to be understood as including the female.

1

An Architectural History of the Trade

The craft of the stone mason is one of the oldest, and has been subject to continuous development since man first dragged a few boulders together to form a shelter. It must have been quickly realized that by knocking off awkward angles, using another piece of stone as a hammer, boulders could be made to fit together better. Pounding a large boulder with a smaller, perhaps harder boulder was the first means of shaping stones; examples have survived in Britain in the form of standing stones erected as temples. Of these, the best known example is Stonehenge, in which the outer circle is made up of local sarsen stone shaped by pounding to give tolerably rectangular uprights, with tenons onto which mortised lintels are fitted. Stonehenge was built and rebuilt between 3000 and 2000 BC.

A thousand years earlier, metal tools were being used in Egypt for shaping the stone of the pyramids. As iron was unknown to the builders, the chisels were of copper, perhaps hardened to some extent by hammering or by the addition of arsenic. Accuracy of working was important to the Egyptians: on the Great Pyramid an archaeologist has noted that 'the mean variation of the cutting of the stone from the straight line and from a true square is but 0.01" on a length of 75" up the face . . .'. Both the pyramids and the associated temples were, however, relatively unsophisticated structures in artistic terms; they were works of civil engineering rather than graceful architecture.

Western architecture owes a great deal to the influence of the Greeks. The last half of the first millennium BC saw the beginnings of the great works of Greek architecture, of which the Parthenon is perhaps the best known example. Here, sophisticated features of design with which we are familiar today came into use, showing an awareness of optical illusions and a knowledge of geometry: the columns taper towards the top with a curved outline (entasis), without which they would appear to be concave; columns are inclined inwards to the centre line of the building, to prevent the appearance of leaning outwards; architraves rise slightly in the centre to avoid the appearance of sagging. Statues and high relief carvings of a quality rarely surpassed, and the use of mouldings and other geometric enrichment all testify to the skill and ability of the Greek masons and carvers.

Although the arch was known to the Greeks, they made little use of it in their public buildings. The Romans, on the other hand, showed an imaginative use of arches in almost all their building and civil engineering. An understanding of the principles of structural engineering, the accurate working of stone, and the development of concrete, led to some of the greatest works of building known in the ancient world. The huge amphitheatre in Rome, known as the Colosseum, rises in three great tiers of arches, with the widespread use of concrete vaults throughout. Aqueducts crossed wide, deep valleys; the Pont du Gard in southern France rises some 49 m (160'), with main arches of 24 m (80') span, to carry the water channel 275 m (900') across the valley. Careful design and accurate working of the stone was essential to the Romans, and much of their work was carried out with tools and techniques which differ little from those in use today. There is, however, no evidence that they developed the use of templets for working mouldings, which seem to have been worked at least partly *in situ* and which in consequence tend to vary in section. Multiple pulley blocks on large cranes were used to raise the stones, the motive power being provided either by hand winches or treadwheels. It should be said that, while the remains of many Roman buildings survive in Britain, most of them were built by the army for military use and the quality of the workmanship is generally poor. The army was capable of good work but rarely bothered.

Following the collapse of the Roman empire in the west, around AD 400–450, the tradition of building in dressed stone in Britain seems to have fallen into disuse. The early Saxon invaders were builders in timber, and masonry building was reintroduced by the later Saxons in the ninth and tenth centuries as an importation from the continent, especially France and Normandy. Techniques seem to have been basic: mouldings tended to be simple, often consisting of a single chamfer, and mullions were of a roughly columnar or baluster form. Small window openings were often bridged with two inclined slabs, although the arch proper was used over larger openings. Very often, both arches and other features were built using material robbed from the standing remains of Roman buildings.

The arrival of the Normans in 1066 led to a great expansion of building in stone. Their economic power and central organization meant that money could be found for the great churches and castles which sprang up, often using imported stone such as that from Caen in Normandy. Much use was made of the axe for dressing this soft stone, especially for ashlar, but at all times the mallet and chisel was used for the more delicate work. Norman architecture, however, more usually known today as Romanesque, was generally heavy in appearance and not renowned for the accuracy of working: joints were wide and details often clumsily executed. Some of the carving, however, although tending to be shallow by later standards, is superb. Where stone vaults were used, they were semicircular barrel vaults, requiring thick walls with relatively small windows for their support.

As the Norman style progressed, techniques were refined and architecture became lighter in appearance. The pointed arch appeared during the twelfth century. At first it was used alongside the round arch but was later used on its own in the style known as Gothic. Mouldings became thinner and more complex with deep undercutting, which was (and is) not easy to work. The use of the pointed arch spread to vaulting. This was now based on arched ribs which took the thrust to specific points on the walls, which were stiffened by deep buttresses. The space between the buttresses became almost redundant in terms of structural stability and windows became bigger. At this stage, known as the Early English period of Gothic, the windows were tall and sharply pointed. A pair of windows set under a single head had a blank space between the two arches, and gradually this was pierced to give the beginnings of tracery, which developed during the thirteenth century into what is known as the Decorated period.

By this time, all the techniques of the masonry trade today were in use: full-size setting-out of tracery and other features was an essential part of the process; templets were in universal use (made from thin boards); and stone was often ordered from the quarry ready worked, either to templets supplied or to stock patterns. The trade had become a large, well-organized business.

When looking at mediaeval building, it is worth bearing in mind that the stonework was usually painted, often outside as well as inside. Even the elements of mouldings were frequently picked out in alternating colours: red, green and blue were among the favourites. The effect, to modern eyes, must have been startling in the extreme.

As the Early English period gave way to the Decorated, and the Decorated to the Perpendicular, mouldings became simplified and easier to work, with less undercutting. At the same time, the amount of carved and moulded stonework grew: internal wall surfaces were covered with blank tracery panels, exterior buttresses were similarly decorated, with gablets and finials set on pentagons, hexagons and octagons. Setting-out was becoming increasingly complex as the master masons flexed their geometrical and technical skills, and as a result, the skills of the banker mason were extended perhaps further than ever before or since.

During the fifteenth and sixteenth centuries, the ornateness of the Perpendicular period, with its fan vaults and elaborate wall treatments, often showed simpler forms at the same time. Windows might be square headed, with simple chamfers in place of multiple mouldings, and pillars might be unmoulded octagons. These latter features, together with the four-centred arch, were typical of the Tudor style of the first half of the sixteenth century, when most of the major new buildings were secular rather than religious.

It was during the sixteenth century, however, that the greatest change for 400 years occurred. The pointed or Gothic style was abandoned in favour of the rebirth, or Renaissance, of the classical styles of Greece and Rome. Flat pilaster buttresses, pediments, round-headed windows and a generally square look to buildings became the rule. Ornament, where it existed, was restrained, not to say severe, and symmetry was all important. Lavish ornament reappeared briefly in the seventeenth century in the flowering of the Baroque style, with huge wavy scrolls, flying figures and much gilding of interiors. This in turn gave way to the more restrained Georgian style of Renaissance architecture; many of the major public buildings in this country are in this imposing and dignified style.

Later styles of architecture have mostly been variations on earlier themes. The Victorians, for example, returned to a form of the Gothic style for their churches and, up to the outbreak of the Second World War, when building in solid stone was virtually abandoned, public buildings were developments of Renaissance work. Any solid stone used in new building today is almost invariably hung on steel frames.

This necessarily brief summary of the changing styles of architecture in England is included in order to give the stone mason some feeling of the history of his craft and the extent to which his work influenced, and was influenced by, the building styles. All stone buildings, large or small, were worked and built by stone masons, using the tools and techniques which are still the basis of the craft today.

For 800 years trade practice has been passed on, both verbally and by example, from master to apprentice in a continuous line. The disruption of that process in recent years has contributed to the present decline in standards. Technological advances are welcome, but the lessons and standards of the past must be remembered and implemented if the present trend is to be reversed.

2

Health and Safety at Work

'Health and safety at work' does not mean just a vague responsibility of employers to ensure that their employees are protected from obvious and immediate dangers in the workplace. Specific requirements are set out in Regulations made under the Health and Safety at Work Act 1974 (hereafter 'the Act'), and these lay a duty on the employee as well as the employer to ensure that risks to employees, the public and the environment are recognized, identified and minimized so far as is practicable.

It is not possible within the scope of this book to cover detailed aspects of these Regulations as they apply to the stone mason, but general points can be made, and a note of relevant legislation and general reading matter is given in the bibliography. Nothing should be read as being a definitive statement of current law.

It is essential that everyone employed in the masonry trade should be fully aware of health and safety requirements for all situations. For the stone mason these may include, among others, the use of forges, working on scaffolds, loading and unloading lorries, use of saws and other machinery, general manual handling of heavy objects, mechanical hoisting, handling lime, cement and adhesives, stone cleaning, polishing and consolidation, as well as the routine, but clearly potentially dangerous, everyday working of stone. Some of the risks are identified in the following chapter as the activity is discussed but each situation must be formally considered on site in relation to the particular circumstances. The existence of a risk may be defined simply by the nature of the material being handled, or it may be a matter of some judgement. The seeking and taking of informed advice will make the judgement more certain and the risks less hazardous. The Health and Safety Executive must be seen as a friend rather than an enemy and its help, which is freely available, sought in every case of doubt.

DUTIES OF EMPLOYERS

Section 2 of the Act says, among other provisions, that:

1. It shall be the duty of every employer to ensure, so far as is reasonably practicable, the health, safety and welfare at work of all his employees.
2. Without prejudice to the generality of an employer's duty under the preceding subsection, the matters to which that duty extends include in particular:
   (a) The provision and maintenance of plant and systems of work that are, so far as is reasonably practicable, safe and without risks to health;
   (b) Arrangements for ensuring, so far as is reasonably practicable, safety and absence of risks to health in connection with the use, handling, storage, and transport of articles and substances;
   (c) The provision of such information, instruction, training, and supervision as is necessary to ensure, so far as is reasonably practicable, the health and safety at work of his employees;
   (d) So far as is reasonably practicable as regards any place of work under the employer's control, the maintenance of it in a condition that is safe and without risks to health, and the provision and maintenance of means of access to and egress from it that are safe and without such risks;
   (e) The provision and maintenance of a working environment for his employees that is, so far as is reasonably practicable, safe, without risks to health, and adequate as regards facilities and arrangements for their welfare at work.

The above general provisions have been amplified by a series of Regulations covering specific aspects of health and safety. It should be noted that the Act applies equally to self-employed persons, who are regarded as both employer and employee. Provision is also made for the protection of the public; section 3 of the Act says, among other provisions, that:

1. It shall be the duty of every employer to conduct his undertaking in such a way as to ensure, so far as is reasonably practicable, that persons not in his employment who may be affected thereby are not thereby exposed to risks to their health or safety.
2. It shall be the duty of every self-employed person to conduct his undertaking in such a way as to ensure, so far as is reasonably practicable, that he and other persons (not being his employees) who may be affected thereby are not thereby exposed to risks to their health or safety.
3. In such cases as may be prescribed, it shall be the duty of every employer and every self-employed person, in the prescribed

circumstances and in the prescribed manner, to give to persons (not being his employees) who may be affected by the way in which he conducts his undertaking the prescribed information about such aspects of the way in which he conducts his undertaking as might affect their health or safety.

DUTIES OF EMPLOYEES

Section 7 of the Act says, among other provisions, that it shall be the duty of every employee while at work:

1. To take reasonable care for the health and safety of himself and of other persons who may be affected by his acts or omissions at work.
2. As regards any duty or requirement imposed on his employer or any other person by or under any of the relevant statutory provisions, to co-operate with him so far as is necessary to enable that duty or requirement to be performed or complied with.

It is important to remember that it is not only employers who are liable to prosecution for failure to observe the provisions of the Act and Regulations. The employee is also liable at law for failure to observe his duties under the Act and successful prosecutions of employees are far from unknown. An employee can also be dismissed for failure to observe safety instructions.

Where personal protective equipment is issued (see below), it must be worn in all appropriate circumstances.

Active risk reduction

It is thus the duty of both employer and employee to take all reasonable steps to reduce the risks involved in any work undertaken. The employer in particular has a duty to eliminate, so far as possible, operations which might give rise to risks and, where risks cannot be eliminated, to take steps to minimize those risks.

To this end, there is a formal procedure to be followed, as laid down in Regulation 3(1) of the Management of Health and Safety at Work Regulations 1992, under which a full assessment of the risks likely to arise in any operation must be made.

RISK ASSESSMENT

Risk assessment is carried out by the employer either directly or with advice from a suitable external assessor. The in-house assessor should be a competent person (usually the Safety Officer), experienced in the work being assessed. The employees also have a part to play in that they are likely to be familiar with particular problems and may have practical advice to offer in their resolution.

Making the assessment

The assessment must be 'suitable and sufficient', and may be general, covering the range of normal work undertaken (such as everyday work in the banker shop) or specific to a particular operation (such as a newly opened site or part of a site). The depth of detail will depend on the nature of the operation, the degree of risk and the duration of the operation. The assessment must be carried out in respect of the operatives, anyone in close proximity and the environment. The purpose of the assessment is not merely to identify the risks but to indicate such action as is practicable in order to eliminate or at least minimize those risks.

The following study of the everyday operation of working stone in a typical workshop environment will serve as an example of how risk assessment highlights the large number of potential dangers in a situation, and suggests some risk-reduction actions. It is not only obvious physical dangers which must be considered, but also the effect of chemicals and other substances covered by the Control of Substances Hazardous to Health Regulations 1992 (COSHH). The phrase 'hazardous substances' does not refer just to obvious chemicals such as hydrofluoric acid and well-known hazardous substances such as blue asbestos. It covers any materials used in the workplace, from lime and diesel oil to the dust from grinding wheels, and the adhesive used to stick back a missing corner. All these substances can have an adverse effect on health.

The study given below is neither exhaustive nor detailed but emphasizes the potential hazards that can lurk in a banker shop. A banker shop is not seen by the average mason as a particularly dangerous place, but a formal, written risk assessment will very clearly show the risks to which a mason is exposed every working day.

The suggestions for avoidance of and minimizing risks are given in general terms only, as this is not the place to give a detailed exposition on the application of the Regulations. Information sheets giving details of the risks involved in various processes, and the current standards for exposure to hazardous substances as well as the current standards for protective equipment are published by, among others, the Building Employers' Confederation, the Stone Federation, and the Health and Safety Executive. Such information is reissued at intervals as appropriate. Readers are advised to familiarize themselves with this and other literature in the bibliography.

Activity/equipment and potential risk

Stone dust – health hazards of dust inhalation and respiration.

Noise – especially from use of pneumatic tools and other power tools.

Lighting – eye strain due to incorrect type/position of light fittings.

Flying debris – damage to eyes and body from flying stone chips, from individual and adjacent masons.

Grinding wheels – inhalation of dust from wheel, damage to eyes from sparks and fragments of wheel and tool, bursting of wheel.

Adhesives – inhalation of solvent vapours, skin contact.

Compressed air – air embolism from contact with skin (especially open wounds), sudden disturbance of dust and debris affecting lungs and eyes.

Falling objects – stone, tools.

Obstructions – stones, stone debris, tools and movable equipment left on floor, power and pneumatic cables and lines.

Mechanical hoisting – falling stone.

Risk reduction action

Work out of doors, dust extraction equipment, respirator/mask. Consider wet working of stone.

Provide ear defenders, sound deadening wall coverings.

Modify to suit individual requirements.

Provide safety goggles, adjust position of bankers and/or direction of working.

Provide respirator/mask and goggles; wheels to be checked, fitted and dressed only by qualified personnel.

Provide respirator/mask, gloves and overalls for large quantities, improve ventilation.

Never use air line to blow dust from clothing or work, maintain all fittings to reduce risk of accidental separation. Never play the fool with compressed air.

Ensure that stone is stable on banker (especially when propped to adjust working surface), ensure that the banker is stable and sufficient for the size of stones being worked, ensure tools are not left on banker when not being used. Provide safety footwear.

Keep floor swept of skelps at frequent intervals, keep gangways clear at all times, put away all equipment when not in use. Make adjacent masons aware of cables in use.

Ensure that safe working load of lifting tackle is not exceeded, maintain tackle in good order, make attachments to hoist in proper manner, handle split-pin lewis with care, ensure that drilled lewis holes are clean. Never stand with any part of the body beneath load.

Manual lifting and turning of stone – falling stone, trapping of fingers, toes, spinal and general muscle injury.	Do not lift stones that are too heavy. Where two or more people are involved plan movements in advance and only one person should co-ordinate the activity. Use chain blocks or other mechanical hoist where possible.
Pneumatic hammer – noise, vibration damage to joints and blood vessels in hands ('white finger').	Wear ear defenders, wear anti-vibration gloves, do not use pneumatic tools continually.
Angle grinders – excessive dust and noise, wheel disintegration.	Wear ear defenders, goggles and respiratory protection. Use with due regard to position of other masons, possible need for additional dust extraction/ventilation. Avoid use of worn wheels and working with excess pressure.
General use of power tools – electric shock, sprains due to jamming of drills, etc.	Inspect all power tools and cables before use for obvious signs of damage, maintain in accordance with instructions, use 110 V equipment or residual current device (RCD).

As an example of the sort of detail that must be considered under COSHH, there are maximum standards of exposure to stone dust (which may contain silica, calcium carbonate, calcium oxide, magnesium oxide, ferrous oxide, ferric oxide and aluminium oxide) against which a respirator/mask must be worn, the mask (at the time of writing) being to BS 6016 type 1, 2 or 3 depending on the volume of dust present, expressed in milligrams per cubic metre of air. All COSHH risks should be assessed in respect of skin contact, eyes, lungs, swallowing and open wounds.

Scope of risk assessment

Risk assessment should be made in respect of each activity undertaken, either as a general activity, as the normal run of work in the banker shop, or for specific works which are out of the ordinary. In this respect, it should be noted that each new scaffold is a new working situation and should be assessed accordingly. In the same way, the introduction into the banker shop of a 2 tonne stone where 100 kg stones are the norm presents a new situation which must be assessed accordingly. The assessment should not be a last minute undertaking, but made with sufficient time to consider all aspects of the work.

All employees should be made aware of the risk assessment for their normal everyday work as well as for new situations.

Recording the assessment

Once made, the assessment must be recorded in writing and made known to all personnel concerned. The only exception is where fewer than five people are employed, although the assessment must still be carried out and made known but need not be recorded in writing, and where the risk is low and short term, and recording in writing would be excessive. For the self-employed and for firms with fewer than five employees, it can often be worthwhile to make a written record of the assessment at least from time to time. A formal procedure can highlight risks which a verbal asesssment might overlook, and the record can be useful for accident investigation and for routine visits of safety inspectors.

Acting on the assessment

As we have seen, the risk assessment is not made in isolation from reality, or for form's sake, simply to identify the risk and then forget about it. Once a risk, potential or actual, has been identified, action must be taken to deal with it. This does not end with warning an employee that lifting a heavy stone might trap his fingers or hurt his back: active steps must be taken.

The first principle is to eliminate the risk. In the case of lifting, the provision of a chain block will save a strained back and eliminate that risk. It will of course introduce other risks, for example, trapping the fingers between the chain and the pulley (it may sound unlikely but it has happened), but the risk is lower and can be more easily guarded against.

It may not, of course, be possible to use a mechanical lifting device as may be the case when fixing in an awkward place. In this situation, the addition of another person to the gang for half an hour might reduce the risk. Every avenue must be explored before accepting that the risk has to remain.

There may be more than one way of protecting against injury. Handling lime and cement can cause dermatitis and skin burns, which can be very severe. A less serious effect can be painful drying and cracking of the skin, especially between the fingers. The traditional way of dealing with this has been the issue of gloves. In York in 1499 gloves were issued to the masons 'for the settyng'. However, gloves are not always convenient to work in and modern barrier creams can provide alternative protection. Equipment that is not seen as appropriate for a particular purpose will not be used, regardless of the law.

Two simple examples are given above of how risk reduction may be approached. The principle to be followed is that an identified risk must be eliminated whenever 'reasonably practicable' and, where this is not possible, the effect must be guarded against by the provision of suitable personal protective equipment.

RECORDING AND REPORTING OF ACCIDENTS

All injuries and accidents occurring in the workplace must be recorded with details of the occurrence and any consequences. Any injury to an employee which results in absence from work for more than 3 days must be notified to the Health and Safety Executive (HSE) on the prescribed form. Analysis of the Accident Book may highlight areas where previously unidentified or apparently minor risks are causing repeated accidents, and action can be taken to eliminate or minimize these risks.

In addition, under the Reporting of Injuries, Diseases and Dangerous Occurrences Regulations 1985 (RIDDOR), all fatal and serious injuries, and any of the specified dangerous occurrences must be reported without delay (normally by telephone) to the HSE. Serious injuries include loss of limb, most bone fractures, loss of sight and admission to hospital for over 24 hours. Dangerous occurrences include failure of lifting tackle, collapse or partial collapse of a scaffold over 5 m, and high collapse of a wall or floor in a place of work. The scene of a serious accident or dangerous occurrence should be left untouched until it has been investigated.

Certain prescribed diseases and occupational conditions, including white finger, must also be reported in writing to the HSE.

Full details of conditions and occurrences that are covered by the Regulations are listed in the HSE booklet on RIDDOR given in the bibliography.

PERSONAL PROTECTIVE EQUIPMENT

Personal protective equipment (PPE) is anything which protects the person from hazards, and includes such items as hard hats, overalls, masks and gloves. PPE must be issued free by the employer (and replaced as necessary) in circumstances where risks to health and safety cannot be eliminated, and where site rules demand its use to guard against potential as well as actual risks. The use of PPE is a legal requirement for everyone including the self-employed and visitors.

PPE should not be taken home without permission. Overalls contaminated by blue asbestos are an obvious risk to the health of others. However, lesser risks of contaminated PPE also exist and it should be left on site, preferably in a place reserved for its storage.

CONSTRUCTION (DESIGN AND MANAGEMENT) REGULATIONS (1994)

These Regulations, generally referred to as CDM, are coming into effect at the time of writing. They impose new duties in relation to the management of health and safety throughout the stages of most construction projects, including demolition.

CDM places new duties on five key parties: the client, the designer, the planning supervisor, the principal contractor, and contractors of the self-employed. Broadly speaking, these duties are to ensure that there is adequate planning of health and safety management even before the contractor is appointed, that resources are available to deal with health and safety matters, that risks are designed out of the project so far as reasonably practicable, that information about risks on site are made available to everyone concerned, including employees, that adequate training has been given, and that a health and safety file is maintained and made available to contractors who may come on to the site in future during maintenance, repair or renovation.

These form only a sample of the duties imposed by the Regulations, and it is essential that everyone involved in the design and management of construction work should be fully aware of their responsibilities. To this end, there is a wide range of literature available from the Health and Safety Executive, a selection of which is given in the bibliography.

3

Stone: Its Nature and Problems

GEOLOGY

The subject of geology is wide ranging and complex. What is given here is a very brief introduction to the topic, sufficient to give the stone mason an appreciation of the origin of stones, their nature and their basic classification. Suggestions for further reading are given in the bibliography.

Building stones used in this country are of the following three types: igneous, sedimentary and metamorphic.

Igneous

Igneous rocks are either intrusive or extrusive. Intrusive rocks came originally from well below the outer solid crust of the earth (the lithosphere) and were forced towards the surface as a liquid magma. They are largely made up of silicates and classified according to the percentage of silicon dioxide; those with a high proportion are known as acid rocks and contain quartz, a crystalline form of silica. Those with a low proportion of silicon dioxide are referred to as basic or ultra-basic rocks. The difference in silica content between acid and basic rocks is not necessarily very great: acid rocks contain upwards of 65 per cent, and basic rocks between 45 and 55 per cent. These figures are approximate.

In addition to their chemical make-up, igneous rocks vary according to the position in the earth at the time of cooling. When forced to the surface by volcanic activity, they are known as volcanic rocks and may occur either in sheets which have poured out onto the earth's surface, or in dykes where they have been forced to the surface through a fissure. They cooled rapidly, forming a fine-grained material. *Basalt* is probably the best known volcanic rock which has been used in this country for building.

When the magma has cooled within the lithosphere, it forms plutonic rock, which, because it cooled slowly, has a coarser grain. Of the acid rocks of this type, *granite* is by far the commonest in use. A similarly formed but basic rock is *gabbro*.

Extrusive rocks were formed above the surface of the earth as a result of volcanic activity. An example is *tuff*, a solidified volcanic ash. This has not been widely used in this country for building, although large deposits in other parts of the world have been extensively used. It is also a pozzolanic material used in the making of mortar (see below, Chapter 9).

Sedimentary

Sedimentary rock is formed chiefly by erosion of older rocks by organic deposits and by precipitation of chemical elements from overlying water. The principal sedimentary rocks used by stone masons are sandstones and limestones. Each type can be further subdivided according to composition.

The main component of *sandstones* is quartz in the form of grains held together by a cementing material the nature of which has a major influence on the weathering properties of the stone. Typical sandstones are made up of rounded grains of quartz, whereas gritstones have angular grains and tend to be rather coarser. The difference between sandstone and gritstone results from the ways in which the grains were transported (by wind or water), and the distance they travelled before finally being deposited: the greater the distance, the smaller and rounder the grains. Some varieties of gritstone are referred to as *millstone grit*, their angular grains having made them particularly useful in flour mills.

The most durable sandstones are those in which the cementing material is silica. When the grains and the *siliceous cement* are thoroughly combined, the stone is extremely hard and difficult to work. This type of stone is known as quartzite, of which a good example is the *sarsen* stone used for the construction of much of Stonehenge. Most of the durable sandstones and gritstones have silica as the chief cementing agent, with the addition of other material.

The cement may also contain oxides of iron, either red oxide or brown hydrated oxide, and is then known as *ferruginous cement*. The oxides may be present alone or combined, and they have an obvious effect on the colour of the stone. Calcium carbonate (lime), in the form of calcite, gives a *calcareous cement*. Small amounts of this in the make-up of the stone may make the stone a little easier to work but have little effect on the resistance to weathering. Where calcite is the major component of the cement, the stone is referred to as a *calcareous sandstone*. The calcite is subject to attack by carbon dioxide in rain-water and, especially in poorly compacted stones, may have a short life. *Argillaceous cements* are of a clayey nature and as such do not give a durable stone.

The various types of cementing material may be combined. Thus, stones with a chiefly siliceous cement may be distinctively coloured by a proportion of ferruginous cement and many of the most durable sandstones have a small proportion of calcareous cement.

The chief constituent of *limestones* is calcium carbonate (which may take the form of fossil remains of marine or freshwater organisms), lime (which is precipitated from the water), or small rounded grains (oölites) (which have formed around shell fragments, grains of sand or other material). The cementing material is usually calcium carbonate but may be siliceous.

The most widely used and best known limestones are from the Jurassic beds known as the Greater and Inferior Oölites. The names refer to their postion, the Greater being later than, and thus higher than, the Inferior and most emphatically have no bearing on their quality. Some confusion is caused because Oölite refers to the geological age and stones from the Oölite series are not necessarily oölitic in nature.

The limestones from the Oölite series occur from *Portland* in the south of England to *Ancaster* in the North Midlands. Oölite does occur north of this but in relatively small deposits. Most of this stone contains fossils as well as oölites, the proportion of which may vary according to the particular bed within the quarry. A few, such as *Ketton*, have an easily visible oölitic structure with large grains and no apparent fossils, while in others, such as *Weldon*, shell fragments make up the majority of the stone.

Some limestones are made up very largely of complete fossils, which not only give a pleasing appearance but are capable of taking a high polish. Typical of these are *Purbeck*, *Alwalton*, and *Frosterly* 'marbles', which are not true marbles: Purbeck and Alwalton are from the Oölite series, and Frosterly is a Carboniferous limestone. Purbeck, although most commonly used as slabs and columns, has often been worked into tracery and carvings. Highly fossiliferous stone appearing above or between the beds of many building stones will often take some degree of polish and is often known as ragstone, distinguished by the name of the building stone, e.g. Hornton Rag. Ragstones are not usually easy to work. They should not be confused with Kentish rag, which is a specific grey–green sandy limestone used for hammer-dressed walling.

Magnesian limestones from the Permian series are largely made up of calcium magnesium carbonate (dolomite). They are usually fine-grained stones, which lend themselves to the working of fine detail and weather extremely well except in a polluted atmosphere. It is very unwise to mix them with other limestones, on which they can have a destructive effect (see below, p. 19).

The Carboniferous limestones are also used for building, but are not generally used unless only very simple working is required. Their use has generally been confined to walling with other stone used for the dressings. A limestone which is still being formed visibly is *tufa*, where water seeping through some limestones precipitates calcite. It is sponge-like in appearance with many small or large cavities which make it very light in weight; this property has made it of significant use in the past for vaulting and the cavities also give it insulating properties.

Gypsum is made up of calcium sulphate laid down by evaporation. When occurring in large fine-grained blocks, it is known as *alabaster* and much used for carved work. Many mediaeval tomb effigies were carved from alabaster quarried and worked in the Nottingham area. It is very soft, capable of being easily scratched with the finger nail, and very susceptible to water damage.

Metamorphic

Metamorphic rocks are those in which the original structure has been altered (metamorphosed) by heat or pressure. For practical purposes, only two metamorphic rocks are important: marble and slate.

Marble began as limestone, in which, after heating under pressure, the calcium carbonate has been changed into calcite crystals. Pure calcium carbonate yields a white marble such as Carrara, while the presence of other minerals gives a coloured or figured marble. The best marbles have been produced by heat and pressure on a large scale as a result of major movements. The heat resulting from volcanic intrusions (such as basalt dykes) forms a coarser material, often known simply as recrystallized limestone. At the time of writing, there are only two true marbles being quarried commercially in the British Isles, Ledmore in Scotland and Connemara in Eire.

Slate is formed from clay deposits which have been subjected to high pressure and heating over a long period. The effect of this is not only to harden the clay, but also to realign the flakes of mica and other minerals into planes of cleavage at right angles to the pressure. It is along these planes, which normally have no relationship to the original bedding planes, that the slate can easily be split. Some slates, most notably Westmorland (Cumbrian) Green, are formed not from clays but from volcanic ash (tuff).

True slates should not be confused with highly laminated sand-stones and limestones (such as Collyweston), which can be split along the narrow bedding planes into thin flags for use as a roofing material. They are invariably very much thicker than slate and are known as stone slates.

THE WEATHERING AND DECAY OF STONE

All stone, as soon as it is quarried, begins to suffer from the various agents of decay. The process may be extremely slow, so that chisel marks may still be clear after hundreds of years, or it may be rapid, calling for replacement in less than 50 years. The slow and gradual loss, over several centuries, of a millimetre or two from the face of a stone is not a matter for concern. What does matter is a continuing and rapid loss, or a sudden change in the rate of loss, even if the actual loss is not great. There are a great many possible causes and it is not always possible to identify the cause with any certainty, but a simple process of elimination will very often provide the answer.

The first cause to be looked at is the characteristics of the stone itself, both the general stone type and of an individual suspect stone in particular.

The matrix

As noted above, an argillaceous matrix binding the grains together is not likely to give a long-lasting stone. The clay is relatively easily washed out by rain-water, releasing the grains to cause rapid and visible decay. This can be a serious matter, as the decay is likely to continue at the same rate until the stone is destroyed. Similarly, the matrix in a calcareous sandstone will be attacked by rain-water, releasing the grains, which fall as a sandy deposit.

Clay beds

Many stones have thin clay beds between the beds of solid stone. They are usually no more than 1 or 2 mm thick, between stone beds half a metre or more thick, and can be avoided when the stone is sawn. In some stones, however, the clay beds may be thicker and occur more frequently. Weathering will rapidly produce a charac-teristically furrowed appearance where the soft beds have eroded much faster than the stone. Unless the erosion has gone very deep into the stone, there is not likely to be a major problem in an ashlar wall; the rate of erosion will slow down to some extent as the softer beds are protected under the overhang of the stone beds. Where such stone is used in an arch or other load-bearing element, or an overhanging feature, the danger of collapse is more serious. Clay beds occur in both limestone and sandstone.

All sedimentary stone varies within a given quarry bed, owing to the precise conditions under which it was laid down. This means that, within a single stone, there will be harder and softer beds which may not be immediately apparent but which will react differently to weather conditions. Physical erosion caused by wind-blown sand, as well as an increase in the effect of damage caused by soluble salts (as described below), may attack these softer beds and, to a limited extent, give an effect not unlike that of rain acting on clay beds.

Shakes

Stone often has naturally occurring cracks as a result of earth movement. The cracks usually run across the beds. They are often so fine as to be virtually invisible but they can constitute a source of weakness. They are known variously as shakes or vents. When the stone is being worked, they can usually be detected by a dead sound when the stone is tapped with a hammer but occasionally they reveal themselves only when the stone is partly worked. If they do not approach the face of the stone, they may do no harm and can safely be ignored. Sometimes the cracks may be filled with calcite, which has the effect of sealing them; opinion varies as to whether calcite veins are likely to have an adverse effect on the weathering properties of the stone. The type of stone also affects this point – magnesium limestone often shows these veins standing out from a weathered surface with no ill-effect on the stone at all.

Cracks may also result from the stone being quarried with the use of high explosive, which is likely to result in cracks that run in all directions through the stone. It is not advisable to use stone quarried in this way or when high explosive has been used near to a face from which building stone is being extracted.

Incompatibility

Some stone types can be incompatibile with each other. Sandstones can be affected by rain-washings from all types of limestone. Magnesium or calcium sulphates, produced from the limestone by sulphur-based acids in the air, are deposited on the sandstone and attack it as described below. This may be seen where a block of limestone used to repair a sandstone wall will tend to produce a hollow 'shadow' of itself on the sandstone. If the sandstone is placed above the limestone, the problem does not occur. Ordinary limestones can be attacked in the same way by washings from magnesium limestone, although, as with limestone attacking sandstone, there is sometimes no problem at all. However, it is unwise to mix any of the three types of stone in a building.

It is noted in detail in the chapters on setting-out and supervision that stone should normally be laid on its natural bed or, in special circumstances, edge bedded. Face bedding is liable to lead to delamination of the stone, either gradually or in scales or sheets from 5 to 20 mm thick. Failure due to face bedding is usually easy to recognize, especially in highly laminated stone, but there may be another reason for the loss of the face.

Contour scaling

This is a phenomenon occurring on both ashlar and mouldings, where the face becomes detached in scales or sheets which follow the profile of the stone rather than a bedding plane. Research is still being carried out into the precise cause but it appears to be due to atmospheric pollution. In simple terms, it seems that the pores of the stone become blocked with calcium sulphate deposited by rain-water, which prevents the stone from breathing. Repeated heating and cooling, and wetting and drying, builds up stresses which lead to a fracture of the stone behind the face. This may cause stones that are perfectly sound in appearance suddenly to lose 5–10 mm from the face. In the initial stages, the face of the stone will sound hollow when tapped.

A minor loss of material from the face of the stone may be due to poor workmanship. Working the stone too heavily or with blunt tools may lead to localized damage to the matrix, which, under the influence of the weather, may lead to premature loss of 1 or 2 mm from the surface. This is most undesirable but there is no evidence that it has a long-lasting effect on the life of the rest of the stone.

Cracking

Ironwork

Major cracks appearing in stone may have a number of causes. Large spalls appearing on the face or even cracks right through the stone are likely to be caused by the presence of iron cramps or dowels. Rust, or iron oxide, occupies a larger volume than the iron, and the expansion causes the stone to burst. Strangely, although the adverse effect of iron on stone has been known for at least 500 years, its use has continued almost to the present day. Various attempts have been made to prevent rusting, such as wrapping in lead sheet, painting with bitumen and trying to ensure that the iron was kept well back from the face, but success has rarely been achieved. The only cure is to remove all iron when discovered and to use non-ferrous alternatives. Galvanized steel is not an acceptable substitute. Even so, it is important to ensure that cramps and dowels are kept towards the centre of the stone. They introduce a rigidity to the structure, and any movement they are intended to resist may burst the stone if they are set too close to the face or joints.

Settlement

Cracks running through several stones are more likely to be the result of settlement. The effect is made worse by the use of hard mortars which do not allow for movement. In the north transept of York Minster there is a remarkable deformation of the stone courses but with hardly a crack through any stone. The soft lime mortar has accommodated the movement and allowed gentle settlement to take place.

Frost

A number of cracks occurring across the face of a stone may be the result of frost damage. This happens when the stone is saturated with water and ice, which has a volume about 10 per cent greater than water. Ice forms deep in the pores and exerts an enormous pressure, which is sufficient to burst the stone. Frost damage is most common on exposed elements such as cornices and at the base of buildings where water is drawn up from the ground. The use of a frost-resistant stone will usually prevent this. Frost damage can also exaggerate the presence of small cracks existing in the stone, such as may result from blasting in the quarry. It should be noted that, generally speaking, stones with larger pores tend to resist frost damage better than those with fine pores.

Unsuitable mortar

The use of too hard a mortar both for bedding and pointing can have an adverse effect on stone. If the mortar is too dense and strong, soluble salts are unable to evaporate through the joints, and instead become concentrated in the stone and either cause or accelerate decay (see below for salt decay). The remedy is to cut out the old, hard mortar and repoint to a depth of at least 50 mm with a more suitable mix as suggested in the chapter on mortar. Brushing-off the face of the pointing when partly set removes the smooth surface left by the pointing key and aids evaporation through the joint.

Salt decay

Undoubtedly the most common and most destructive agent of decay is soluble salts forming crystals in and on the stone. *Efflorescence* is the term used to describe the appearance of salt crystals on the face of a building. It resembles a whitish mould growth, which, while unsightly, generally does no harm, the salts being washed away by rain. Crystallization occurring in the pores of the stone is known as *cryptoflorescence*. This, after repeated wetting and drying cycles, exerts pressure which leads to mechanical damage to the structure of the stone. The damage so caused is characterized by the formation of a powdery surface, often accompanied by blistering of the surface. As with frost damage, it is fine-pored stones which are most at risk from cryptoflorescence, especially among the limestones.

Sandstones tend to attract dirt in the areas exposed to weather, whereas limestones tend to remain clean in the rain-washed areas and dirty in the protected areas. Dirt is of itself disfiguring rather than dangerous; it is the constituents of the dirt which matter. If the dirt contains salts, hard, impervious skins of sulphate may be formed, beneath which salt decay will continue unobserved. Blisters can be formed, which fall away to reveal cavities that are sometimes very large.

Salt damage is often seen on the inside of buildings, particularly around windows, caused by the evaporation of salts as water is drawn through the stone by heating of the interior. The effect is often very pronounced on the glazing line of leaded lights, and seems to be the result of the high rates of heating and cooling at this point; many salts become liquid when the temperature rises and crystallize when the temperature falls. Many salts will dissolve without direct wetting; the humidity in the atmosphere is often sufficient to dissolve the salts, which recrystallize when the humidity falls.

The salts most often encountered are sodium sulphate, potassium sulphate, calcium sulphate and, in coastal areas and along roadsides, sodium chloride (common salt).

Some of the more common sources of damaging salts are: concrete and cement mortar, bricks (used above and as a backing for masonry), limestones, sea- and road-salt, washing powder, other household cleaning agents, and sulphur in the atmosphere. Salt damage around the base of a building may be caused by salts from the soil being drawn up into the stonework.

QUARRYING

The stone mason is not normally involved with the quarrying of stone but it is useful to have a broad outline of the techniques of quarrying sedimentary stone.

Quarrying rubble stone

Methods of quarrying vary according to the nature of the stone and the purpose to which it is to be put. Rubble stone for the building of *random rubble* walls (Figure 3.12) is usually taken from thin beds [100–200 mm (4–8″)] of sandstone or limestone which occur either as part of the overburden above the solid beds, or between larger beds. Many small cottages, farms and barns have been built from stone simply picked off the fields. This easy availability is one reason why rubble was used so extensively in the past. Today it is often taken out with a dragline or a JCB, when it will either break into manageable pieces as it is lifted, or can be broken down by a blow from the bucket. Further reduction is with a heavy hammer, and awkward corners dressed off at the time of building using the walling hammer. The hydraulic guillotine is often used today in place of the walling hammer.

Hand-dressed *squared rubble* is used much less than formerly, owing to its high labour content and the widespread use of high-speed circular saws. Pitched-face walling stones sawn to bed heights are a convenient way to use off-cuts but the result bears little resemblance to traditional squared rubble (see Figures 3.9 and 3.10). If excessive cost is to be avoided, the best source is second-hand stone. Where its use is called for, beds of 150–300 mm (6–12″) are to be preferred, quarried in much the same manner as random rubble. Where the stone is hard or the beds are thick, it may need to be extracted using the method described below for block stone.

Quarrying block stone

Extracting stone in large blocks suitable for sawing down to pre-determined sizes ('dimension stone') calls for rather more organization and skill, although machinery may have a smaller part to play. The overburden is stripped mechanically to reveal the upper surface of the solid bed, which may be horizontal or at an angle, depending on whether earth movements have taken place since the stone was deposited. The bedding plane of the stone depends not on the angle at which the stone is lying but on the sedimentary strata.

In most cases, shrinkage of the sediments and general movement in the earth will have introduced cracks, known as joints, which run at right angles to the bedding and to each other. So long as these are reasonably widely separated they are a help rather than a disadvantage, as they often give blocks of manageable size without further splitting. However, they are rarely ideal and their size must be reduced before extraction, using plug and feathers (Figure 3.1).

The plug is a tapered steel bar which is driven into a drilled hole between two feathers, tapered slips of steel which are thicker at the bottom than the top. This means that the plug and feathers together are parallel in elevation, thus exerting pressure for the full length of the feathers. The name feathers is derived from their curled end, which prevents them being carried down into the hole. The holes are drilled in a straight line, between about 150 and 300 mm (6–12″) apart – the distance depends on the nature of the stone, as does the depth to which they are drilled. Shallow holes can produce a clean break in the right sort of stone, especially if the bed height is small, but it is essential that the hole is deeper than the length of the plug. If the plug hits the bottom of the hole, it is liable to fly out with unnerving speed. The plugs are driven home with a heavy hammer in repeated sequence until the block splits, normally in a very regular break. Any awkward angles or poor breaks are straightened up with the scappling hammer, a heavy hammer with one square face and one with a short point. The pick, with two short heavy points, and the spalling hammer with concave cutting faces are also used.

Figure 3.1 Plug and feathers.

Plugs and feathers are also used to split the stone along the bed if the bed heights are too great for easy extraction. They are also useful for splitting blocks in the masons' yard and can be an aid to cutting out stone in a building where, owing to poor access or other reasons, there is difficulty is working with a hammer and punch, or power tools.

Plugs and feathers are classified by the diameter of the hole, ranging from 15 to 50 mm (⅝″– 2″); the smaller sizes are more likely to be of use away from the quarry.

The technique is an ancient one but is still in use with little change over the centuries apart from the use of air-powered drills rather than hammer and jumper drill. Hydraulic wedges are used in some quarries but their economic use depends on the formation of the stone as well as the size of the quarry. Some of the best known building stones are quarried with very simple tools and just a few people.

Especially in small quarries and yards, the softer limestones are sometimes still cut with a large, two-handed cross-cut saw, known as a fishbelly from the shape of its blade. An untoothed blade can also be used, with sand and water run into the cut to provide the cutting medium.

Owing to the increasing demand for road stone and hardcore, many quarries formerly used for building stone are now being worked with high explosive, designed to bring down large quantities of rock in small pieces. This usually renders the stone adjacent to the blast unfit for building stone, as apparently sound pieces are liable to be full of minute cracks which will encourage rapid weathering, even if the stone stays in one piece on the banker.

There is one exception to the ban on the use of explosive. For many years some massively bedded sandstones have been quarried with the aid of small charges to split blocks which may be many tonnes in weight. However, the essential difference is that the explosive is a small charge of black powder just sufficient to split the stone without doing any damage. Black powder is a low explosive that gives a small shock to the stone rather than having a shattering effect.

The above refers to the quarrying of sedimentary stone. Granites are frequently quarried with the thermic lance, and diamond-impregnated wire saws are used in many quarries, especially marble quarries, where the beds are large enough to make this an economical method of extraction.

SELECTION OF STONE FOR REPAIRS

From the point of view of durability and appearance, it is important to use a stone which, if not identical to the original, is very closely matched. With a building of any age it is quite likely that the original quarry (even if known precisely) has long since closed or disappeared. Finding a suitable replacement is a major factor in the repair programme.

The first step is the obvious but sometimes the most difficult – identifying the stone. If the building is earlier than the railway age, that is, around the middle of the nineteenth century, the likelihood is that it came from within 10 or 20 miles, which narrows the possibilities. However, there are exceptions, which should be borne in mind. When moved by horse and cart, stone was difficult and expensive to move, but the availability of river transport made a big difference. Roughly speaking, a horse can pull 1–1½ tonnes on land, given a reasonable road, but about 20 tonnes when pulling a barge. Sea transport was even easier. Hence, in the fifteenth century, Huddlestone stone from Yorkshire was taken by river and sea for the building of Eton College, and vast quantities of Purbeck were used in Lincoln cathedral in the thirteenth century. These are exceptions, however, and the local area is usually the one to concentrate on.

Local masons, particularly in an area with a long and continuing tradition, will very often have no difficulty in identifying the stone, and frequently the particular bed in the quarry. Where this cannot be done, the services of a geologist may be necessary but even the most detailed petrological analysis may give only the general type of stone. It is often a matter of trial and error to determine the original source.

If the quarry is still working, the bed should be identified where possible and tested to ensure that the stone is still fit for the purpose for which it is intended (see below).

Where the original quarry cannot be identified or used, a suitable replacement must be found. As noted above, it should be limestone, magnesian limestone, or sandstone, as appropriate. The colour should match as closely as possible, allowing that some variations are to be expected in a natural material. This must be checked on a sawn or worked face, and when the stone is wet as well as dry. The best way of judging the colour is to see a building in the area known to have been constructed in stone which came from the same bed of the quarry.

Allowance must be made for changes in colour when weathered; it is of little use to choose a stone which matches when newly sawn but weathers to a quite different colour. For example, Clipsham stone may be brown or blue when quarried (the blue is much harder to work), but both will normally weather to a uniform grey–brown shade. When newly quarried, the whiteness of Roche Abbey nearly resembles Huddlestone at a quick glance, but Roche weathers to a strong grey while Huddlestone tends to produce a lighter shade of whitish or creamy grey.

The importance of colour relates to its weathered state as new stone will almost always stand out, perhaps for as many as 5 or 10 years. This is something that has to be accepted as part of the price to be paid for making durable repairs in solid stone.

The testing of stone

The selected stone, whether from the original quarry or another one, must be tested for its resistance to the various forms of weathering to which it will be exposed. The local climate and level of pollution can have a marked effect on the performance of a given stone.

In the UK the standard laboratory test for durability is the salt crystallization test, carried out by immersing a number of 40 mm cubes in a 14% solution of sodium sulphate for 2 hours and drying at 105°C. This cycle is repeated 15 times and the loss of material recorded. The test is carried out using a sample of stone of known durability as a control. Where sandstone is to be used by the sea, or where salt contamination is likely to be significantly higher than normal, a saturated solution of sodium sulphate is used. Calcareous sandstones can be eliminated before the salt crystallization test by immersing them in sulphuric acid for 10 days.

The tests give the likely resistance to damage by soluble salts. They are sometimes taken to give an indication of the stone's resistance to frost but this is not necessarily so.

The salt crystallization test has been in use for some 60 years and is a useful tool to use when considering a stone, although its limitations must be realized. It provides what is in effect an accelerated weathering test, which is often much harsher than may be met in reality, but stone that passes this test may show different results in practice for a number of reasons.

First, a successful test applies only to the bed from which the samples were taken as different beds may give quite different results. Secondly, each bed will vary along the exposed quarry face, although the change is not always obvious. In limestones especially, there may well be marked variation not only within a single bed but also within a single block. Bill Holland, to whom this book is dedicated, provided, against instruction, samples taken for testing from only one block rather than from different parts of a quarry – some samples passed and others did not. This is not to say that the tests are unimportant or can be ignored, but rather that they should be considered carefully as they apply to an infinitely variable natural material. In the end, after the intelligent application of laboratory testing, the only certain test is to use the stone and see how it has behaved after 200 years.

Durability is not the only factor to be considered. The stone must be sufficiently workable to carry the detail and surface finish required at an economic rate, although durability must not be sacrificed to satisfy the balance sheet.

Selection of blocks

Once the choice of stone type and quarry has been made, selection of the individual blocks is best left to the quarryman, unless the mason has considerable familiarity with the stone. If purchasers select the blocks, then the quality is their responsibility. When dealing with a reputable quarry, it should be sufficient to agree on a sample, after which unacceptable variations are the responsibility of the quarry. It used to be the practice in at least one quarry to set aside doubtful blocks in the hope that architects and others would select them.

When buying stone in block for conversion in the masons' yard, blocks are often sawn top and bottom bed, or slabbed to convenient bed heights, by the quarry. Although naturally more expensive when bought this way, it ensures that the block will fit the masons' primary saw and, especially in a small yard without specialist sawyers, can prove economic in saving valuable time for the masons. A sawn face will also reveal something of the interior of the block.

The availability of stones is constantly changing, as new quarries are opened and old ones close. For full details of all stones currently being quarried in the British Isles, *The Natural Stone Directory* is an essential handbook. Stones no longer available are also listed, together with much other useful information.

TYPES OF WALLING AND SURFACE FINISH

Ashlar

This term is sometimes used by those outside the trade to describe any facing stone but its use should be confined to stones which meet the following criteria. Ashlar has carefully worked beds and joints, finely jointed [generally no more than 4.5 mm ($^3/_{16}''$)] and set in horizontal courses. The stones within each course should be of the same height, although successive courses may be of different heights. In elevation the stone should ideally be perfectly rectangular and the face, unless rubbed or left off the chisel, must be bounded by neat, well-chiselled margins worked straight and square to the beds. Ashlar

Figure 3.2 Ashlar and rusticated ashlar.

is described according to the surface finish, of which the following are the most common.

1. *Plain* or *rubbed ashlar* has a surface that has been rubbed, either by hand or mechanically, to remove all toolmarks (see Figure 3.2).
2. *Boastered ashlar* (Figure 3.3) is left with the marks of the boaster showing clearly, set at the usual angle. The toolmarks should be neat and all drafts set at the same angle, without being excessively regular. The drafts should overlap. It is also referred to as 'left off the chisel'. When replacing single stones in a wall of this type, the angle of the boaster should approximate to the original (left-handed masons please note). The term should not be confused with 'boasted for carving', an instruction to the mason to leave projections, etc. roughly blocked out for later attention by the carver.
3. *Punched ashlar* has the surface left off the punch inside the marginal drafts. The punch marks may be random or regular according to specification, but are usually either in regular lines (*furrowed*, see Figure 3.4, if straight, or *feathered*, if curved), or as small and very even indentations (*pecked* or *picked*, see Figure 3.5).
4. *Rock-faced ashlar*. Here the surface is left in its natural state, or with a little assistance from the pitching tool within the chiselled margins.

Figure 3.3 Boastered ashlar.

Figure 3.4 Furrowed.

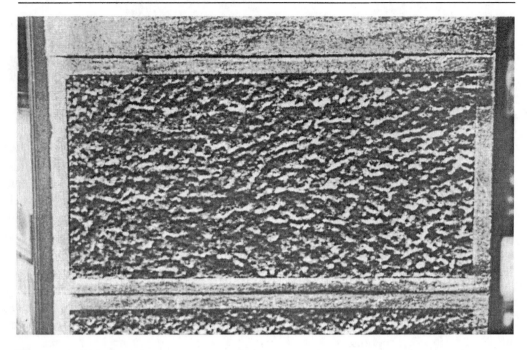

Figure 3.5 Picked panel.

Figure 3.6 Tooling or batting.

5. *Tooled* or *batted ashlar* (Figure 3.6) is finished with regularly spaced chisel marks, resembling small flutes, set vertically on a rubbed or sawn surface, and specified at so many batts per inch (usually six, eight or ten). It represents not so much a stage of work but a deliberately applied design, evolved in the eighteenth century and especially popular in the nineteenth. It should never be confused with or used as a substitute for boastered work.

6. *Rusticated ashlar* is that where the joints are sunk below the marginal drafts in a distinct step to a second draft (Figure 3.2). The surface may be finished in any fashion. It is usually used for basements and ground floors, the shadows thrown by the recessed joints giving an air of solidity. This term must never be used as a synonym for rock-faced work, which is totally different in terms of both appearance and cost.

7. *Reticulated ashlar* has the surface covered with small sinkings, which are supposed to give a network effect (Figure 3.7).

8. *Vermiculated ashlar* has a surface of small channels and ridges designed to give a worm-eaten appearance. It is chiefly used for quoins.

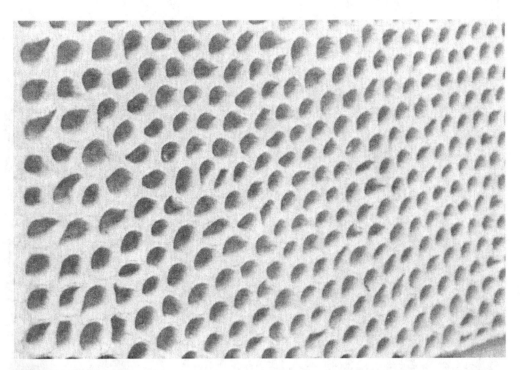

Figure 3.7 Reticulation.

Block-in-course

This is a rather old-fashioned but convenient term to describe the large blocks of masonry seen in dock and railway engineering. The blocks are squared and brought to fair joints, and the faces are usually either rock-faced or punched. Massive solidity rather than sophistication is the keynote of this class of work (Figure 3.8).

Rubble

This should not in any way be taken as a derogatory term. The majority of ancient buildings in this country are in coursed or random rubble, and many have stood for centuries without any regular maintenance. Rubble is much more cost effective than ashlar, which has always been very costly. Ashlar looks expensive, which was often the reason for its use. Rubble depends to a greater extent than ashlar on the hold of the mortar but this is not a reason for using cement mortars as a good lime mortar will remain effective for tens if not hundreds of years.

1. *Squared rubble.* The stones are squared up, more or less roughly according to the quality of the work, to about the same height within each course (Figure 3.9). Course heights are generally between 6" and 9" (150–225 mm), and the joints may be ½" (12 mm) or more. It is normal for joints to be worked to a taper, as this both increases the hold of the mortar and makes accuracy in working, and thus the cost, less important. Walling hammer and pitcher were the tools most commonly employed. The use of the saw on the beds and joints, the norm from the nineteenth century onwards, gives a much more regular effect, which looks out of place when repairing older buildings. The use of pitched-face stone with sawn beds and joints (Figure 3.10) looks nothing like the original squared rubble.

   In parts of Northamptonshire and Lincolnshire it is common to find walls of squared rubble, worked to fine joints, laid dry and hearted-up with lime mortar. This is of course quite different from drystone walls, where random or coursed rubble is laid dry throughout, often with a soil and small stone filling, and with slightly battered sides.

2. *Coursed rubble.* Here, stones are used more or less straight from the thinner beds in the quarry but are selected to give something like the same height within each course, although courses may taper over a distance. Joints tend to follow the profile of the stones, varying from almost nothing to 1" (25 mm). The stone

Figure 3.8 Block-in-course.

Figure 3.9 Squared rubble.

Figure 3.10 Pitched-face walling.

is usually from highly fissile beds between 3″ and 6″ thick (75–1590 mm) (Figure 3.11).

3. *Random rubble.* This is walling in which the thin-bedded stones have merely been broken to about the right depth and are laid as they come to hand, little or no attention being paid to coursing. Joints and thickness are as for coursed rubble (Figure 3.12).

Where the stones are so placed as to level up to a horizontal course at intervals, the work is known as *random rubble built to courses* (Figure 3.13).

Figure 3.11 Coursed rubble.

Figure 3.12 Random rubble.

Figure 3.13 Random rubble built to courses.

4. *Polygonal* or *rag walling*. In this work the stones are of any size
    or shape as they come from the quarry, laid so that they fit best
    with their neighbours after a minimum of hammer dressing. The
    effect is rather like crazy paving set vertically.

4

Setting-out:
The Fundamentals

Setting-out is the process on which all subsequent operations on the stone depend. It includes the full-size drawing of all moulding profiles, elevations and sections, the making of templets, and the calculations of the overall sawing size of all the stones.

The setter-out should be an experienced stone mason, a reasonable draughtsman and have a knowledge of geometric construction techniques. Some familiarity with basic algebraic and trigonometrical functions may be of use from time to time. Ideally the setter-out should be disciplined, tidy and efficient in his work. He must understand what templets will be required by the mason and what information must appear on the templet.

The practical directions given for setting-out for repairs may appear immensely time-consuming and elaborate, but this is necessary for repair work which aims to reproduce faithfully the lines of historic features. New work is much simpler; it is very much easier to build a new cathedral than to repair an old one.

Accuracy is paramount. If a stone is drawn 1 mm too small, the joint width will be increased by 25–50 per cent. An error of 1 mm in a metre means that a 5 m elevation will be out by 5 mm, clearly unacceptable whether or not it has to mate with existing detail. Furthermore, the finished templets should fit the drawing exactly. Near enough is not good enough.

Accuracy does not mean following rigid rules laid down for constructing mouldings or tracery; the setter-out on repair work must follow faithfully what is to be replaced. If the original setter-out made an error, then the same error must be identified and built into the new drawing. The modern 'understanding' of an ancient style is irrelevant. The master mason of the time may not have followed what is now seen as typical of the period and it is what is actually there which must be reproduced. The great mistake of the Victorian restorers was to reduce everything to a series of rigid conventions. Never assume that two mouldings on the same feature are the same, even though they may look the same.

We do not see the work of the original master mason directly but only through the work of the masons who dressed the stone. Here the setter-out must use his judgement, based on his training as a mason. If there is good evidence that the mason has been somewhat at fault, then the original intention must be followed. The modern banker masons will introduce their own minor errors and unintentional variations, which will give sufficient character to the work. This is another argument for replacement stone to be worked by hand, even if all the roughing-out is done by machine.

THE SETTING-OUT SHOP

It is appreciated that the following is a model, and it may not be either necessary or possible for small firms to provide such facilities. Much setting-out can be, and is, carried out with the minimum of space and equipment, but it seems sensible to set down the ideal system of setting-out to the highest standards, which can be varied to suit the circumstances.

The shop and the table

For work of any size and complexity, the setting-out shop should be a large, clean, dry room (Figure 4.1) capable of taking a drawing table at least 2400 × 3600 mm (8′ × 12′) with comfortable working space around it. The table must have straight edges, square corners and a smooth surface. This is most easily achieved by mounting three sheets of 18 mm marine ply on a stout frame. If selected with care and fitted by a joiner, ensuring that the edges are dead straight lines, this will provide a suitable working surface.

The table should be high enough to draw on comfortably while standing alongside, yet low enough to stretch across. The standard 750 mm (30″) may sometimes be too low but it is easier to raise it on wooden blocks if needed than to saw the legs off. At times it will be necessary for the setter-out to climb onto the table to work, in which case the drawing should always be protected with a sheet of clean paper. Drawings should be covered with a spare length of paper when not being worked on.

There should also be room for a templet-cutting table at least 1 m square, which should be kept as far away as possible from the drawing board and table as zinc dust is dirty.

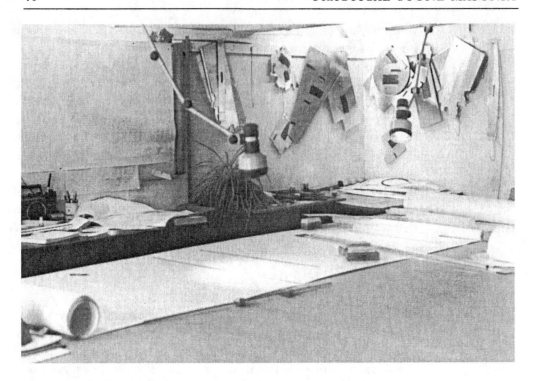

Figure 4.1 Setting-out shop.

Facilities in the shop for frequent hand-washing are essential as well as for cleaning technical pens.

Drawing board

A drawing board is needed for drawing moulding sections and scale elevations; A0 is a suitable size. It should be fitted with a good quality parallel motion or drafting machine.

Drawing materials

The drawing is done on good quality 155 gsm (grams per square metre) white cartridge paper, obtainable in 25 m rolls, 841 mm (33"), 1016 mm (40"), and 1524 mm (60") wide. The table can be covered with two overlapping sheets and, when the drawings are finished, they can be rolled to a convenient size for storage.

While cartridge paper is relatively cheap, it has disadvantages in that it is affected by changes in humidity and, in long-term storage as a part of an archive of repairs, it can be damaged by damp or rodents. The first point is easily overcome – when unrolled onto the table, it must be left to flatten and to stabilize at normal working temperature. Pin the paper down when stabilized and then, before any drawing is done, set up a control. In the centre of one long and one short side, draw a straight line in ink, carefully marked out at an exact length – at least 1m is desirable. Changes in humidity and temperature are most likely to occur overnight, when the heating is switched off, and drawing must never be resumed until the control lines have recovered their measured length. This is not merely a counsel of perfection – a 3600 mm length of paper can expand by over 3 mm, which makes a nonsense of previous drawings and measurements.

The reference to archival storage assumes that the building is of sufficient importance, or with a continuing repair programme, to warrant this care. Most repair works do not demand this.

On the drawing board, the use of tracing film is more appropriate. This is a plastic material available as either sheets or rolls. It comes in various specifications but 75 micron thickness, double matt, is suitable for general setting-out use. The matt drawing surface is extremely abrasive; hard pencils, and pens with tungsten points, may be preferred.

It is possible to make the drawings directly onto an emulsion-painted table, as in the past. The major disadvantage is that the drawings cannot be kept as a record and might have to be painted over before that part of the project is complete. The drawing is an essential reference for solving some of the problems which arise during fixing.

Drawing instruments and equipment

The following, although not exhaustive, is a good basic list based on experience of the most commonly used and useful items.

Pencils
Finely drawn lines are essential and a hard pencil is to be preferred, from 2H to 4H. A 0.3 mm 'micrograph' pencil eliminates the need for continual sharpening but this may be too thick for some construction drawings. A 2 mm clutch pencil makes a good alternative and leads of all grades can be obtained and they can be brought to needle sharpness.

Pens
Pens are needed to make a permanent, finished drawing in black Indian ink. Technical pens with a 0.25 mm point for cartridge paper and 0.18 mm for draughting film are the most useful, but both thicker and thinner points may occasionally be needed.

It is occasionally necessary to have two elevations superimposed, and it is useful to have other colours available to distinguish one drawing from the other. Red and green provide good contrast.

Compasses

A comprehensive set of high-quality spring bow dividers and compasses is essential for measuring and drawing curves of radii from 3 mm to 300 mm. The leads used with compasses should be of the same hardness as those in the drawing pencil. Adaptors allow technical pens to be attached to compasses.

For longer radii *beam compasses* can be purchased or made: the one illustrated (Figure 4.2) will strike arcs of up to 1 m (39″) radius. The use of a pair of trammel heads on a hardwood rod (Figure 4.3) will enable still larger radii to be drawn.

French curves

French curves are needed for drawing compound curves, that is, those with a constantly changing radius; a standard three piece set in plastic is sufficient.

Straight edges

Clear plastic straight edges are the best, ranging from 450 to 1500 m (18–60″) in length. They should be fitted with handles so that they can be lifted rather than pushed across the paper. The easiest source for the longer one is often the straight edge from a parallel motion.

Set squares

Adjustable and 60°/30° set squares, which should be as large as possible, are required. If inking edges are not provided, a few

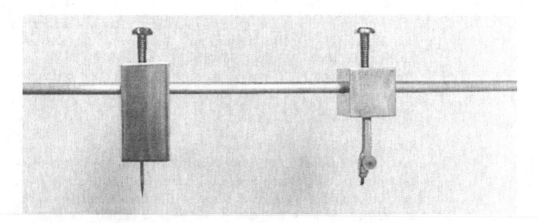

Figure 4.2 Beam compass.

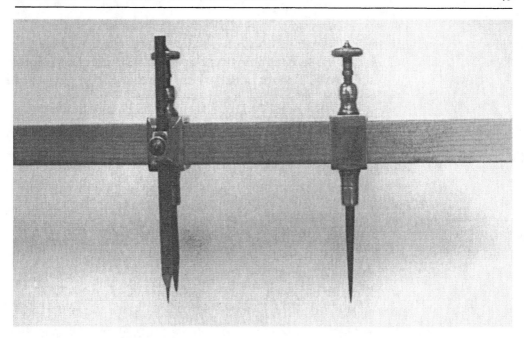

Figure 4.3 Trammel heads.

thicknesses of drafting tape will raise the edge sufficiently to prevent smudging. Again, handles should be fitted.

T-square
Mahogany T-squares are available up to 50" (1270 mm). Their successful use depends on the edges of the table being true and square. The T-square must be handled carefully and checked at intervals for squareness.

Measuring
Graduated plastic rules are available up to 1 m, but are unsatisfactory for longer measurements. For use on the table, a refill for a 3 m steel tape is ideal. The hook must be carefully removed and the tape must be of the type where the hook fits into a notch in the end of tape, that is, the tape must be full length and not use the thickness of the hook as part of the overall measurement.

Scale rule
The triangular type with up to 12 scales is the most convenient and economic. Both Imperial and metric versions are available.

Erasers
The white plastic type is used for pencil on both paper and film, a yellow chemical eraser will remove ink from drafting film. White correction fluid can be used for ink on cartridge but fine lines can

often be removed successfully by scraping gently with a scalpel; the paper must be rubbed smooth with the handle before redrawing, or the ink will run. A soft 'putty' rubber is useful for cleaning up large areas of drawings. An *eraser shield*, as used by typists, is essential when correcting parts of a completed drawing.

Brush
A soft hand brush for removing eraser and other dust from the drawing board or table is required, as brushing with the hand rubs in the dirt. A clean drawing is more conducive to accuracy than a grubby one.

Reel of black cotton
When setting-out long straight lines points are pricked off along the stretched cotton.

Drawing pins
They are useful for holding large sheets of paper securely – 25 mm flat-headed ones are best.

Paper-weights
Paper-weights are useful when referring to a previously rolled drawing. Softwood blocks that are well-sanded and weighted with scrap lead are ideal. These should be varnished all over to prevent the blocks picking up and transferring dirt.

Drafting tape
Drafting tape is useful for short-term holding of paper or film, but tends to become immovable after several days.

A portable drawing board
See 'Setting-out elevations' below for details of the best type.

Lighter fuel
Lighter fuel is very good for cleaning the drawing instruments, which must be done frequently.

Templet-cutting table

A table at least 1 m square is required with a top hard enough to resist wear but soft enough to minimize damage to scriber points. Formica or hardboard are both suitable surfaces.

Templet-cutting equipment

The following list covers the essential tools (see Figure 4.4).

Scriber
This should be of fire-sharpened steel, with as fine a point as possible.
A tungsten-tipped scriber is no good for zinc.

Sheet metal cutters (tin snips)
Two sizes are needed, 50 mm and 25 mm, with straight blades. A
small curved pair can be useful.

Steel straight edges
One should be at least 1 m long.

Files
A selection of fine-cut files is needed, including flat, half-round and
triangular. A set of needle files is useful for cleaning up small corners.

Dividers
Stout engineers' dividers are best, 150–200 mm long, with sharpened
scribing points and a locking bar to prevent movement. The legs
should not flex as pressure is applied when scribing a curve.

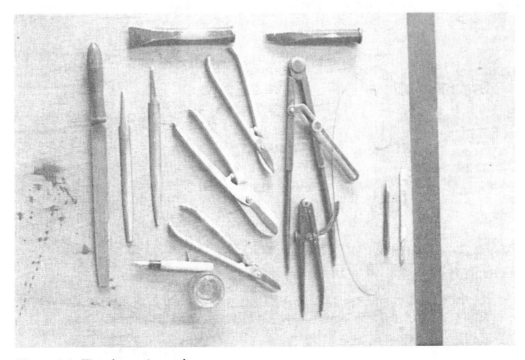

Figure 4.4 Templet cutting tools.

Trammel heads
A large pair of trammel heads with stout steel points is required for radii greater than can be scribed with dividers.

Fine sandpaper and wire wool
For finishing the edges of a templet and to clean the area on the face of a templet where written information is to be set down.

French curves
A set of curves should be cut in heavy gauge zinc using a plastic set as masters.

Copper sulphate
Information can be written on zinc templets using copper sulphate solution, which reacts with the zinc and turns black. It has a known long life and is to be preferred to a felt-tipped pen. A good pinch of crystals in a tablespoonful of water will give the proper medium to deep blue colour. The solution should be kept ready for use in a small screw-topped jar. The crystals are obtainable from a pharmacist, and 50 g will last a long time.

Pen
A cheap fountain pen, dipped not filled, serves very well for writing with copper sulphate.

Permanent marker
A wide, waterproof, felt-tipped pen for highlighting the copper sulphate text.

Scalpel
For cutting card. The Swann Morton surgeons' scalpel is recommended. A variety of sizes and blade shapes is available.

Scissors
Good quality scissors are needed for cutting card and paper.

THE PRINCIPLES OF SETTING-OUT

Replacement of moulded and dressed stone, from a single block with a simple chamfer to the most complex multiple mouldings, demands a planned and disciplined approach. The following example is used to illustrate the technique of setting-out a single moulding.

Setting-out a moulded string course

Figure 4.5 shows a typical string course section which is to be measured and reproduced as an example.

The decayed state of stone that is to be replaced means that some time must be spent identifying the best piece to measure from; survival is often best in angles away from the prevailing wind. Beware of taking details from a previous restoration, which may not have been an accurate copy of the original. Examples of the best parts of each element of the moulding may have to be taken from half a dozen stones and assembled onto one drawing.

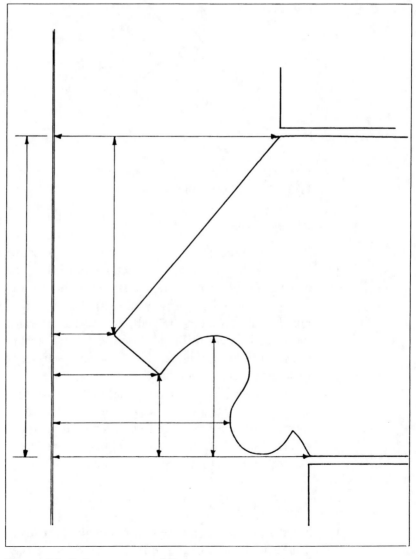

Figure 4.5 String course moulding.

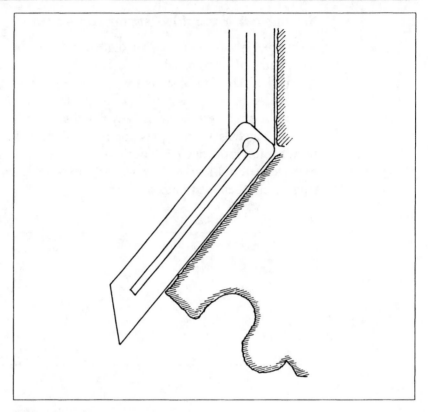

Figure 4.6 Using the sliding bevel.

Measurement

Basic measurements must be taken first as shown in Figure 4.5. Although they are not all directly useful, they are of assistance in making up the profile and act as a check when the whole moulding is drawn out. Clean off any moss or lichen with a stiff brush, and rake out mortar from the bed joints to ensure that the full height of the stone is being recorded. Use the sliding bevel to check the angle of the weathering (Figure 4.6). Make any necessary allowance for the weathered state of the ashlar.

A *heavy* plumb-bob (about 1 kg) and line will give a reference for measuring offsets, as will a large square in conjunction with a sinking square. It is more accurate to take small measurements with callipers and read them off against the steel tape rather than trying to measure directly.

Taking the profile

For the next stage, it is sometimes convenient to saw out the mortar from a joint, when the profile can be drawn directly onto card slid into the joint. Owing to the difficulty of getting a pencil to follow rough stone in small and confined mouldings, the outline will be always be approximate.

The joint is where the original templet was placed, so one might assume that the geometric form is accurate here. However, one must bear in mind the possibility that the stone was pared-in after fixing, an operation which affects the profile at the joint. On the other hand, toward the middle of the stone, deep scotias or undercuts may not always have been worked accurately, even though they may look right.

If, as is often the case, the joints are damaged, the profile gauge can be used. Owing to the limited size of most profile gauges, it is not always possible to reproduce every element in a moulding but, if they are used efficiently, they can provide enough information for an initial profile which can be used as a basis for building an accurate reproduction. Using the profile gauge alone is *never* sufficient, even for a simple, unweathered chamfer – it is useful *only* as a guide.

At this point the judgement of the setter-out comes into play as allowances have to be made for weathering. Surfaces rarely weather uniformly and harder parts of the stone stand proud; these may only be tiny peaks, but they represent a minimum for the size and form of the original stone. Never reduce the moulding to match the existing weathered profiles.

Each part of the moulding should be checked with reverses (that is, a negative of the profile), cut from thin card. The check measurements will ensure the correct relationship of one part of the moulding to another. If necessary, several reverses can be held together with drafting tape.

Drawing the section

On the drawing board, draw parallel lines representing the top and bottom beds, and draw in the wall lines above and below the moulding. Set the angle of the weathering as obtained with the bevel and draw the other elements in their correct measured positions. It will be necessary to make adjustments by straightening lines, and to find whether curved lines should be drawn with compasses or French curves. None of these adjustments should be made on the basis of geometrical construction or similarity to other mouldings, or to match 'typical' mouldings of the period. All that matters is what the moulding in hand was like originally. Never follow geometrical mould construction from a textbook and never assume that two apparently similar mouldings are, or were, identical. The recovery of each mould is a separate detective story.

Once the section of the stone has been drawn up (in pencil), a cardboard templet can be made. This is checked against the stone and corrections made until an exact copy of the original has been reproduced. Slide the profile into the joint and, by holding a thin, straight edge along the various elements of the moulding, the accuracy of the templet can be checked. Any variations must be entered on the drawing and a new templet made. It is quite likely that an experienced setter-out will make two or three card templets before being satisfied, and it is at this stage that the patience and accuracy of the setter-out is of the greatest importance – near enough is not good enough.

The other dimension needed is the depth of the stone into the wall. If possible, one stone should be chopped out as part of the setting-out process. This is always a good idea to give better access to the moulding. It lengthens the fixing process if some of the core has to be cut out to accommodate an over-long stone, and if the stone is shorter than the original, a large void may be created, which the fixers must fill if possible. In any case, the new stone should at least be deep enough so that it will not tip forward without relying on cramps to hold it in place, a point easily checked by balancing the templet on its wall line. As a general rule, new stone should be at least 150 mm 'on bed' (that is, into the wall).

Once completely satisfied, the drawing can be inked in and the final templet made. The lengths needed can be measured from the existing stones, and the cutting list made out. Experience emphasizes that it is extremely unwise to give sizes before the final templet and any related drawings have been completed.

For the correct bedding of string courses and other features, see below.

Missing mouldings

If a moulding is missing or so decayed as to be quite unrecognizable, there are two possible courses of action.

A new moulding may be designed to reproduce in rough outline the presumed original form, but consisting of a series of simple chamfers in place of rolls and hollows. This has the 'merit' of not faking what has been lost, but has little else to commend it. It is a course favoured by some architectural historians.

It is, in fact, very rarely that a competent setter-out cannot discover enough evidence to establish the size and form of a moulding. Surviving *original* mouldings elsewhere on the building, serving the same function *and built at the same time* can often be used to resolve any doubts. It will take time, but can usually be achieved with persistence.

Returns

If any right-angled returns are required, the size can be calculated by adding the projection of the moulding to the length on the wall line. If the return is not a right angle, a full-size plan of the stone must be drawn and a bed mould made to accompany the profile section of the stone.

Enrichment

Where mouldings carry some form of formalized enrichment, such as egg and dart, it is not usually necessary to provide a templet. Dependent on the type of enrichment, either a fully dimensioned scale drawing or a full-size drawing will serve for the mason or carver to mark out the stone. Templets of individual parts of the detail may be needed to ensure uniformity. The joint mould should carry the profile of the outer limit of the enrichment as well as the form of the basic moulding.

THE BEDDING OF STONE

Stone is rarely a consistent material and there are minor differences in the successive layers of sediments which made up the stone. It is along these bedding planes that any weakness will lie. The beds are very like the leaves of a book: a book will support much more weight when laid flat than when stood on end and, to a lesser extent, stone behaves in the same way.

For normal building purposes, stone is laid on its natural bed. If *face-bedded*, that is, with the beds parallel to the wall surface, the face of the stone is very likely to fall off. However, if the upper surface of a natural-bedded stone is exposed as in a coping, or the underside as in a cornice, there is a chance that the beds will separate or *delaminate*.

To guard against this, stone in these positions is laid edge-bedded, that is, with the beds on end and running back into the wall (like the leaves of a book as it stands on a shelf). Pressure from the stones on either side keeps the beds tight.

The following should be edge-bedded: cornices, copings, sills, string courses and stone ridges. For any of these features to be used at the corner of a building, the stone must be carefully selected for soundness and laid on its natural bed, as otherwise it would be face-bedded on the return. Voussoirs should be laid with the bedding planes at right angles to the line of thrust, that is, parallel to the joints.

DIMENSIONS

Stone sizes are *always* given in the same order: length of face × depth into the wall × bed height. If only two dimensions can be given they should still be in the standard order and annotated to prevent misunderstanding. This order is followed not just for the sake of consistency but so that, in a list, the bed height comes last where it is more easily identified. It is the bed height which is usually the most critical when sawing stone.

When the stone is to be fixed off its bed, it is the natural bed which remains the bed height when giving the size. A string course might be ordered as 150 × 225 × 600 mm. The stone is 150 mm high as fixed, runs 225 mm into the wall and the length must be sawn from a bed 600 mm high. A voussoir is listed as depth from intrados to extrados × thickness from front to back of the arch × the maximum distance between the joints.

TEMPLETS

Purpose and materials

The purpose of a templet is to provide sufficient information to the mason to enable him to work the stone. Much of this information is transferred to the stone by scribing round the templet. The material must therefore be strong enough for it to be drawn around with the scriber, durable enough for this to be repeated for the requisite number of occasions, and yet economical in manufacture.

A variety of materials have been used to make templets in the past, including thin boards in the mediaeval period and sheet steel in the nineteenth century. Nowadays the more common materials used are cardboard, plastic sheet and zinc sheet.

Cardboard can be successful but, if used repeatedly, the edges wear and damp stone can cause it to disintegrate. Card can be used to make simple templets which are to be used only once or twice but it must be of good quality. An ideal type is known to the printing trade, from whom it is easily obtained, as 'energy board'. It is smooth on both sides and cuts very cleanly. Resist using old cereal packets, corrugated cardboard boxes or roofing felt – the authors have encountered some dreadful attempts to make templets out of these materials. Hardboard is very difficult to cut accurately and should be avoided.

Semi-rigid orange plastic sheet is used quite successfully in many prominent restoration businesses and, without too much use, it will keep its shape. However, like card, it can be difficult to scribe around accurately, especially on the harder stones, and it has a tendency to curl.

Zinc sheet is the prime material for templets. It can withstand the weather, be used repeatedly with little damage to its edges, and can survive the rigours of the workshop. It can then be put aside and perhaps used again during a future restoration programme. Zinc has only one apparent disadvantage: it is relatively expensive both to buy and to cut, but as a percentage of a whole project the cost is minimal. Its advantages make it by far the best material to use.

Zinc is generally supplied in 8' × 3' (2438 × 914 mm) sheets as a zinc/titanium/copper alloy to BS 6561 Part A – the trade name is Metizinc. The thicknesses recommended for templet making are 8 gauge and 6 gauge, the latter being slightly thinner and more suited to smaller templets. Small quantities are usually delivered in rolls, which should be unrolled carefully and left to flatten naturally. The best (and perhaps only) place for this is under the setting-out table.

A selection of zinc templets is shown in Figures 4.7– 4.10, together with the drawing from which they were made and stages in working the stone.

Templet-cutting

Templet-cutting demands care and patience, as well as the strength of mind to discard a part-made templet if any part has been cut slightly too small.

It is now possible to cut plastic sheet templets automatically to the direction of the CAD program – see 'Computer-aided design' at the end of Chapter 5.

To make a templet by hand, a sheet of material is placed underneath the drawing; plastic is sufficiently transparent to be placed on top of the drawing. Using a sharp, fine scriber (for zinc) or the point of a pair of dividers (for card), make prick marks through the drawing onto the material underneath at strategic points – such as line junctions and changes of direction where moulding lines cross the edge of the templet, and centres of curves – so that on removal of the zinc or card the original lines can be redrawn simply by joining the dots. It is essential that the pricking through is done with a fine point and as accurately as possible.

To cut out a card or plastic templet, after redrawing in pencil, a steady hand and a surgeon's scalpel are needed to give a fine, accurate edge. Do not try to cut curves right through card in one pass. The edges of good-quality card can, and should, be cleaned with fine sandpaper.

For zinc templets, use a scriber to redraw the lines. Where lines represent the edge of the templet, the line should be scored four to six times with reasonable pressure. Curves should be scored with engineers' dividers or, if a curve has no centre, with a scriber against a zinc French curve.

Large radii can be difficult to score accurately. To avoid ruining a large templet, make a reverse of the curve on a separate piece of zinc, using the trammel heads, and cut and file exactly to shape. The reverse can then be placed on the templet and the curve scribed on. The reverse should be marked with its radius and kept for future use.

The tin snips are used to cut away the waste, not along the scored line, but by cutting through the waste with the middle of the blades to within 1 mm of the line at intervals (more frequently around curves). Cutting right up to the line will crease the templet, as will

Figure 4.7 Templets for finial.

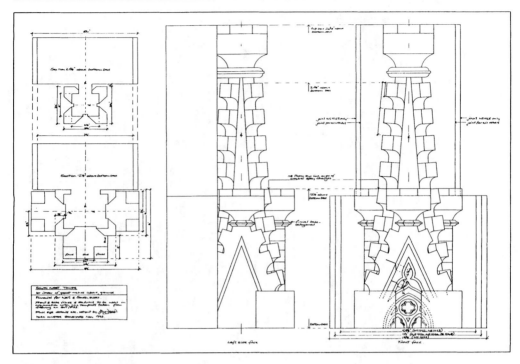

Figure 4.8 Drawing for finial.

Figure 4.9 Part-worked finial (1).

Figure 4.10　Part-worked finial (2).

closing the snips. The waste, with a little teasing up and down, will break away to give an accurate cut. The edges should be lightly filed, along rather than across the edge and supported by the edge of the templet table. The templet (having been dusted off) is then placed on top of the original drawing to check for accuracy. It should fit exactly, that is, the line must not be wholly revealed, nor should it be hidden. This gives a latitude of 0.25 mm, which, with practice, is readily achieved.

To finish off the edges, fold a small piece of fine sandpaper between the thumb and forefinger, and rub around all the edges. A smooth finish will result and the edge is also cleaned for marking if required.

A hole must be cut in the templet to allow it to be hung up in the workshop when not in use. With card and plastic, this can be done with the scalpel. Zinc is best cut with an old ½" chisel, with the templet resting on a firm surface, such as a block of stone. Tidy any rough edges to the hole by tapping with the head of the chisel.

The title, any reference numbers and directions to the mason should now be marked on. For card use the drawing pen, for plastic sheet use a felt-tipped pen, and for zinc use copper sulphate after lightly cleaning an area of the face of the templet with sandpaper. Using a cheap fountain pen dipped in copper sulphate solution allows easy and permanent marking. Shake off a little of the solution before writing, as too much copper sulphate does not dry properly. If a mistake is made, the area must be cleaned off again with sandpaper for a fresh start.

The writing can be coloured over with a wide, waterproof, felt-tipped pen. The advantage of this is that it prevents the cleaned zinc from re-oxidizing and thus allows the text to stand out.

It is usual to make clear to the mason which edges of the stone will be visible, and must therefore be worked clean, by putting a black band around those parts of the templet. This is done by filing a step about 4 mm wide in the other end of the pen, dipping this in the copper sulphate and drawing it around the edge. It takes a little practice to perfect the technique. On card and plastic the marking is done with a black felt-tipped pen. Figure 4.11 gives an example of a completed templet.

If any reverses will be needed, it is best if the setter-out makes these at the same time as the templet and issues them as a bundle. Check very carefully that the reverses fit the templet *exactly*; an ill-fitting reverse does not give the mason confidence in the setter-out.

Whatever the templets are made of, only the best material of its type should be used, carefully cut, finished and marked up. A shabby templet usually results in shabby stonework.

SETTING-OUT ELEVATIONS

As a rule, a simple moulding needs to be drawn in section only and only the joint mould is needed. More complex features such as

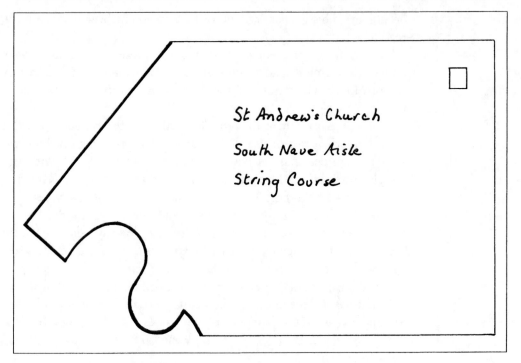

St Andrew's Church

South Nave Aisle

String Course

Figure 4.11 Completed templet.

pinnacles, pilasters and columns with entasis, and blank or open tracery must be drawn in elevation in order to obtain the face moulds. This can be intimidating owing to the size, which might run to 12–15 m (40–50') in total height, and to the number of mouldings, which can be complex and perhaps merge or cross one another. A disciplined approach is essential.

Following the list of tools needed, the worked example sets out the approach in detail and indicates some of the problems likely to be encountered. It is impossible to cover all eventualities but, once the basic principles are mastered, more difficult projects can be tackled from the setter-out's own experience.

Tools and equipment

A wide variety of tools will be needed for taking details from the existing stonework. They may not all be needed but, as it is both time-wasting and inconvenient to keep descending the scaffold to pick them up, especially if the site is at a distance from the shop, it is good practice to carry them at all times. A long canvas tool bag is easy to haul up on a rope or a purpose-made box, as shown in Figure 4.12, will protect the tools and keep them in orderly fashion.

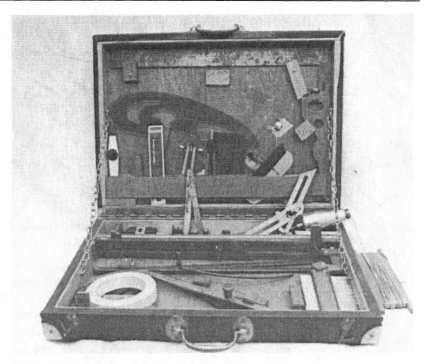

Figure 4.12 Box for setting-out tools.

Steel tape (3m)	Heavy (1 kg) plumb-bob and line
Straight edges	Set square
Dividers	Large and small bevels
Profile gauge	Small spirit level
Square	Pencils and sharpener
Chisels	Notebook
Punch	Universal saw
Hammer	Masonry nails
Large and small internal	
and external callipers	

If moulding profiles are being drawn on the scaffold, the following will also be needed:

Portable drawing board	Card
Compasses	Scalpel
Sheet of tracing film	Light steel straight edge
Adjustable set square	Drafting tape
French curves	Small sheet of formica on which to cut card

The best type of drawing board for this purpose is one with a rack and pinion parallel motion (wires get in the way), with a folding desk-top stand incorporated. The Tech-style board is excellent for the purpose; the A2 size copes with a good range of mould sizes and is small enough to carry conveniently around the scaffold. The stand allows it to be rested comfortably on the knees when sitting on the scaffold boards or, with a little ingenuity, can be clamped to the guard rail using putlog clips. The use of a box rather than a bag for the tools means that drawing instruments can be carried without risk of damage.

A waterproof sheet to cover the board, held in place with elasticated straps, is very useful. When not keeping the board dry, it keeps the person from direct contact with wet scaffold boards.

Measurement

There are several basic rules that must be kept in mind at all times:

- Always measure from a single fixed point or line rather than from A to B, and B to C.
- Always measure at least twice.
- Always take more measurements than you think you will need.
- Never assume that what looks like a right angle is exactly that, nor that the feature will be symmetrical just because common sense says that it ought to be.
- When recording a measurement always be *certain* that it is done in such a way that it will be clear in 3 days' time to which points the measurement relates.

The following worked example, shown as the finished drawing in Figure 4.14, is a gable as might be found above a Gothic niche or buttress top, with a gabled weathering behind it. It is made up of a gable mould (similar to a string course), ornamented with crockets and a finial, beneath which is a recessed ashlar panel. As is common with this design, the gable mould and crockets are separated by a vertical joint from the weathering behind.

Recording the gable

First choose a base line to which all vertical measurements must be related. In the example this is easy – the bottom bed of the gable. If the horizontal moulding running below the gable were being replaced, the same base line would still be best, being easier to measure from, with the joint and moulding drawn on below the base line. Make a rough sketch of the gable in the notebook and mark in the base line, clearly and unambiguously. A typical notebook sketch is shown in simplified form in Figure 4.13.

For clarity, it is often easier to identify with letters the various points which must now be measured and record the measurements in the form of a table.

Next, find the centre line. Suspend the plumb-bob so that the line is just touching the point of the gable and secure it to a masonry nail

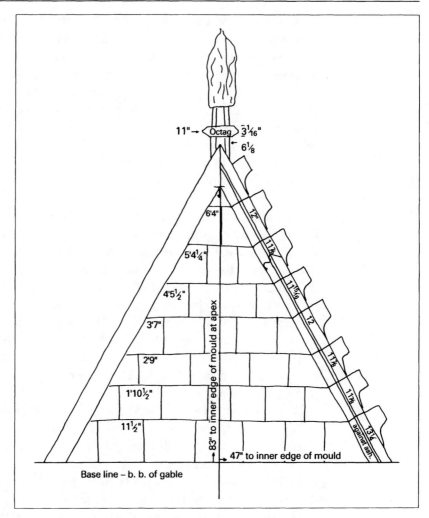

Figure 4.13 Working sketch of gable.

driven into a joint, or to the scaffolding if it is close enough; a short length of aluminium tube and a putlog clip can often be used to provide a suitable point of suspension.

Measure the distances from the centre line to a point on the moulding at each side. The outer nose of the splay will be in the same plane as the plumb-line and the best point to choose in this case. If the plumb-line is exactly in the centre of the base line, or at least within a millimetre or so, only one half of the gable need be set out; symmetrical features are always set out in this way. The mirror image on the other side of the centre line is worked by applying the templets 'lines down'. If the plumb line is off-centre, then both halves of the gable may need to be drawn; the amount of discrepancy which can be allowed comes with experience. The new stonework must fit in the place of the old.

However, if the building is leaning, the plumb-line cannot be used. The angles of the gable must be taken with a bevel and checked to make sure that they are the same. A decision must be taken as to whether the new work is to be replaced at the same angle of tilt, which is the normal course, or whether it is to be rebuilt upright. If replaced to a tilt which is due to the whole building sinking sideways, then the base line can be drawn horizontally on the board. If, on the other hand, the tilt is caused by one side of the feature having dropped, then the base line must be drawn at an angle and the elevation drawn in its distorted form.

Transfer the centre line to the ashlar by using a square (doing it by eye will be inaccurate), and measure the distance along the base line to the inner edge of the moulding. If there is a joint between ashlar and moulding, ignore it for the moment. Measure the vertical distance from the base line to the junction of the inner edges of the mouldings where they meet at the top, again ignoring any joint. It may be difficult to get the tape into the junction, in which case use dividers to mark a fixed distance down, say 150 mm, and measure from that point, not forgetting to add on the first distance.

Take the length of each stone in the moulding, at a point where the joints are best defined; also, measure the joint widths, even though these may have to be varied slightly as will be seen.

Where the the ashlar is worked on the same stone as the gable mould, the ashlar bed heights should be given by the lengths of the moulding, but it is as well to record all of them. The lengths of the ashlar will vary according to whether they are measured on the top or bottom beds. It is a good policy to form the habit of always taking the bottom bed measurement so as to avoid ambiguity.

The shaft of the finial base is likely to be either an octagon or a hexagon, or, rarely, a pentagon. In this example it is taken as an octagon. Take the overall width across as many faces as possible and the width of each side. The latter will almost certainly all be slightly different and the shaft must be reconstructed as any moulding would be. Measure the height to the base of the cap from the base line. As a check, take the length of the shaft on its longest sides but be aware that this measurement may be affected by the way in which the splays have been worked.

The profiles of the gable moulding and the moulding around the cap should be taken using the method given above under 'Setting-out a moulded string course'. A plan of the cap must also be taken, including the base mould of the finial shaft. There will probably be a slight splay on the shaft but it is unlikely to be possible to take the angle with a bevel. Instead, measure across the flats at the base and again at a known distance up – take it as high as possible. Also note the overall height and maximum width/diameter of the finial. The carver will be responsible for reproducing the details of the carving.

Take a simple outline of the crockets, bearing in mind that each will have been carved to a slightly different size. What is wanted is a standard form, large enough to allow for carving while not allowing for the finished crockets to be too large. If possible, discuss with the carver before finalizing the size. The setter-out is not responsible for attempting to draw the carved detail. It is useful to remember that the top of the outline crocket can often be drawn at right angles to the gable mould, however naturalistic the carving. Along the outer line of the splay, measure off from the base line the position of the top of each crocket. Note the thickness of the crockets, and the width and thickness of any carved band running between them.

Recording the weathering

In the simple example chosen, the weathering behind the gable has a vertical fillet below the splay on each stone, and runs back to the main wall from the carving and crockets.

Measure the overall angle of the weathering by setting up a straight edge on the main wall, set absolutely vertical, and take the angle with a long straight edge and the sliding bevel. It will not necessarily be the same as the angle of the gable. Similarly, take the angle of the splay on the individual courses, and measure the length of splay and the height of the fillet, as well as the course heights. Take the profile of the roll moulding on top of the weathering in the usual way. The height of the weathering is most easily obtained by measuring down from the gable cap.

Sufficient information should now have been gathered to begin drawing the elevation.

Drawing the elevation

Take a little time to plan what templets, and therefore drawings, will be needed so that the main elevation drawing is in the most convenient place on the table. In this example, only the face moulds and joint moulds are required. If complex returns are involved or if there were blank tracery beneath the gable, full bed moulds might be needed. If so, and if the table were not long enough, the plan could overlie the elevation; a side elevation can likewise be drawn over the main elevation. If there is room, set the base line high enough to leave room for the plan.

Only half the elevation needs to be drawn; the other half will be a mirror image and worked from the same templets applied 'lines down'.

Cover the table with cartridge and allow it to stabilize as described under 'Drawing materials' above. At this point remember that the setter-out who has not at some time been intimidated by the vast expanse of unmarked white paper has not been born. Don't panic: work in simple steps, and the job will take shape of its own accord.

Drawings and templets of the various mouldings must be made as the first step. Their dimensions will form part of the elevation drawing and must be established before work on that begins.

Draw in the base line in pencil and select a suitable point for the centre line. Draw the lower part of the centre line with the T-square, find the measured position of the centre line at the top of the table and draw in the upper part. Join the two parts of the line with stretched cotton, mark points along the cotton with a divider point and draw in the line with the straight edge. When satisfied that base and centre lines are in the right position, ink them in with a thin (0.18 mm) continuous line – a chain or dashed line is not suitable for measuring from. All other lines are drawn in pencil until the whole is finished; however certain one might be, errors might be revealed at a much later stage.

The centre line must of course be perpendicular to the base line. It is worth checking this at the start of each drawing as a check on the accuracy of the T-square and the table edges, using a 3–4–5 triangle. The measurement, from the junction of the two lines, must be accurately made using a beam compass set against the tape, rather than using the tape directly. Mark three units (e.g. 300 mm) along the base line and four units (400 mm) up the centre line. The distance between the two points must be exactly 500 mm.

Mark where the inner line of the moulding touches the base and centre lines, and draw in the line. At a suitable point where it will not interfere with other detail, perhaps half way up, place the templet of the gable on the line and draw round it. Mark on the base line the position of the nose line and draw this parallel to the inner line. The line should run exactly through the nose on the templet; if not, check all measurements until the reason for the error is found. It would be possible to draw in the nose line using just the position given by the templet, but the more checks that are introduced in the drawing, the less the chance of error. 'The setter-out is not paid to make mistakes.'

Similarly, mark in and draw the line of the inner edge of the fillet, and the outer edge of the splay. The four parallel lines are all that is needed to represent the gable mould.

Mark the position of the crockets and draw in the outline; it may be useful to make a templet for speed and consistency. Draw the carved band running between the crockets as a straight line, leaving sufficient stone for the carver to work with.

Although only half the gable is being drawn, it may be convenient to draw the apex stone to its full width. At the apex of the gable, mark in the width of the shaft below the cap and the width of the middle face of the octagon. Measure from the base line the height to the base of the cap, mark in the width and thickness of the cap and draw the moulding.

Using the horizontal centre line of the cap as a centre line, draw the top bed mould of the cap. This will consist of an outer line representing the overall size of the cap, with an inner line representing the seating for the finial. If there is a marked splay on the upper element of the cap moulding and the finial, the bottom bed of the finial will be slightly smaller. There is no need to draw this, as it will be taken care of when making the templet.

Draw the shaft of the finial and a rectangle representing the outline of the shape. If the carving is in two or more 'bunches' with shaft appearing between, draw this with separate rectangles for each piece of carving. This will help in roughing out the finial.

The ashlar enclosed by the gable can now be drawn, along with the joints on the gable mould, and the joint between cap and finial. Here, some variation can be made from the original. Joints in old buildings are often very tight indeed, perhaps no more than 1.5 mm ($^1/_{16}$"), which can cause undue pressure to fall on the arrises and allows for very little flexibility in the building. As a general rule, joints should not be less than 3 mm ($^1/_8$").

This completes the outline of the elevation drawing and the weathering behind the gable can now be drawn as the opposite hand from that chosen for the gable, using the same centre line. Mark the overall height of the weathering and, using the prepared templet, draw the moulding at the apex at the correct height; again, this may be drawn out in full rather than stopping at the centre line. It will overlie the drawing of the apex of the gable but will be easy to distinguish. Draw the course heights, with suitable joints, and the overall angle of the splay. Then draw in each stone, together with any return to the ashlar on the main wall.

The drawing is now finished and, when it has all been double-checked, number each stone on the elevation, enclosing the number in a frame for clarity. As only half the elevation has been drawn, each stone will have two numbers, one for lines up and the other for lines down. All plain ashlar must be numbered as well as the moulding.

The drawing can now be inked-in using a 0.25 mm pen. Rub out all pencil lines and clean the drawing using the putty rubber. Label it with sufficient information to enable the location to be clearly identified later and add the date. The completed drawing is shown in Figure 4.14.

If the elevation is too large for the table, complete the lower part

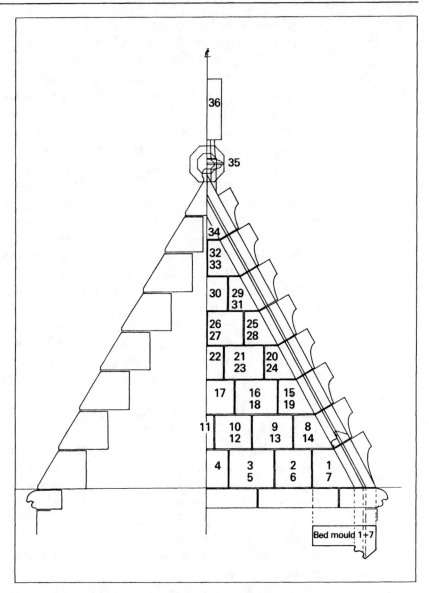

Figure 4.14 Completed full-size elevation of gable.

of the drawing in pencil and draw a line across the top at a convenient point; this may be at a bed joint or at some prominent feature. Transfer this line to the bottom of the next sheet, marking all points on the line very carefully and continue with the drawing. Take careful note of whether or not the last mortar joint on the first sheet was included on the new sheet.

The templets

The following templets will be required.

Face mould

A face mould is needed for each stone which carries the gable mould. The outline of the crocket and carving will be included without the black edge as they are left off the claw for the carvers. Face moulds are a direct copy of the drawing, showing the lines of the mouldings, relevant centres of circles and so on. The profile of the moulding is usually drawn on the templet.

It is often necessary to make only one face mould, equal to the largest bed height, and marked 'set to bottom bed'. The lower bed heights are marked on the edge of the templet with the numbers of the stones against each one.

Where, for economy, a templet does not run the full length of the ashlar part of the stone, cut a *large* nick in the shortened edge to show that it does not represent the edge of the stone.

Gable mould section

This will include the section through the band of carving and the plan of the crocket, or at least the beginning of it to show the width. Again, do not mark those edges in black.

Gable mould raking section

This is for the bottom bed of the stone at the base of the gable. Show the carved band only if it reaches the bottom bed.

Face mould for gable apex

This can be done as a half elevation but it is easier for the masons if the templet is of the complete elevation.

Top bed mould for gable apex

This follows the outer line of the moulding of the cap and may include part of the weathering apex mould as well as the line of the seating for the finial. Make small holes at the centre and at the angles of the finial seating, just large enough to allow the mason to mark through onto the stone.

Raking section of cap mould

The mason will work the cap as a plain octagon, and then apply the raking section. A true section is thus not required.

Base of finial

If this is also to be used for the seating on the cap, mark the templet 'leave line in on cap' and 'finial (lines down) take line out', if the splay makes this necessary. Mark the front so that the carver will know which part of the carving will be at the front.

Finial shaft
An L-shaped reverse to be applied to the bottom bed in order to give the angle for the shaft.

Finial
A templet is rarely needed. When it is, show the shaft exactly as it should appear, and the carving as one or more rectangles.

Weathering section
As suggested for the gable face mould, only one templet is needed, marked up appropriately with the smaller bed heights.

Bed mould for weathering
This will be needed only when the weathering is returned into the ashlar. Mark one end 'weathering section' and the other end 'vertical ashlar'.

Each templet must be marked not only with its function but with the number of the stone it describes. Where one templet serves for two or more stones, each number must be given, and whether each one is lines up or lines down. The templet is normally marked up on one side only.

Scale drawings

At this point make scale drawings on film of the whole gable and both sides of the weathering, showing each stone marked with its number. These drawings will be needed by the fixers, and are also very useful in showing the progress of working the stones. Drawings on film can be reproduced as dye-line prints or on a photocopier.

Schedule of stone sizes

Take each numbered stone in turn and measure carefully the overall size of the rectangular block of stone which will contain the finished piece, allowing for the angled joints and for any projection of the top of the crocket above the rest of the stone. The plain ashlar will help to tie the gable into the weathering and must be deeper into the wall than the gable proper. List every stone by number and size in the correct order of length of face × depth into the wall × bed height. In this example, the stone is all laid on its natural bed as it appears on the drawing, except for the apex moulding on the weathering, which is edge bedded.

In large workshops each stone should have its own progress card on which any further instructions to the mason can be noted. These should be made out at this time and, if done at the same time as each templet is made, can be used to build up the schedule.

Some time may elapse between the drawing up of the schedule and the working of the stone. Tie all the templets into a bundle, using the holes provided for hanging up, and hang them to one side. Issuing them to the shop before they are needed encourages their loss or damage. Roll up the drawings in one bundle and mark the outside clearly with the job reference – they will be needed to solve disputes during fixing.

As stones are worked, the templets must be retrieved by the setter-out, and when all is finished they can be bundled together and kept as a record. Tie them with wire rather than string and attach an indelible label. Progress cards should likewise be kept.

It is impossible to cover every kind of work which might be met but the above review of setting-out an elevation can, with experience, be applied to almost any kind of work, using the methods given in Chapter 5 entitled 'Setting-out: the application of geometrical techniques'. The following summary of work to a gabled return is as far as general advice can go in this book.

SETTING-OUT A GABLE RETURN

A buttress is frequently surmounted not by a simple gable as described above, but by a pinnacle, with gables on three or four sides. The method of drawing and making the templets is not very different, but a few points can usefully be made.

The principles of measuring and drawing given above can be followed until the elevation of the gable has been drawn. Then, instead of a weathering, gables on the return faces must be set out. If the same design is repeated on the returns, the jointing will probably be identical on all faces. This makes the job very much easier and the only additional setting-out needed is the junction of the faces; this is what is assumed in the following. Remember, do not assume anything in practice. Check every measurement and every moulding. Even if they look the same as on the face they may not be, in which case new templets will be needed. As an example of how mouldings which appear identical can vary, Figure 4.15 shows sections of the right- and left-hand jambs of an actual doorway. No further comment is needed.

When looked at end-on, from the front of the buttress, the outer line on the return face will be the outer nose of the splay and fillet on the gable mould of the return. Measure the distance of this from the centre line on the front elevation and, on the base line, erect a

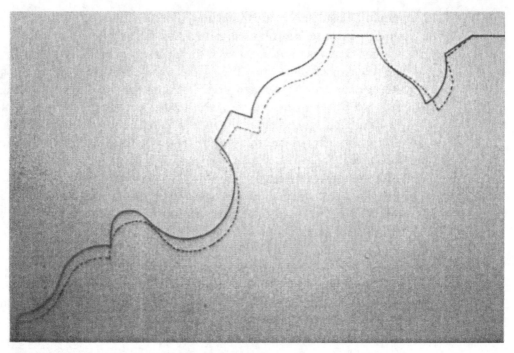

Figure 4.15 Discrepancies in a jamb mould.

vertical at this point. Using the templet of the gable mould, draw in the inner and outer line of the crockets, and the end view of each crocket. Also add the side view of the cap and finial.

Between the faces there will be an ashlar quoin, splayed on both faces, which should be drawn in. If the splay on both faces is not identical, see below. Put in the joints on the end view of the gable and across the ashlar quoin.

What is now on the table is the right-hand half of both the front face and the back face, and the end view of the right-hand return. It is also the right-hand half of both the left-hand return and the right-hand return, and the end view of the front face and the back face. The undrawn mirror image represents the left-hand half of these views. If this sounds confusing, it will be less so in practice but the setter-out must be able to see the drawing as whichever of these views he needs at any given time.

If the sides are not the same as the face, they must be drawn out; at least they should be the same as each other. Draw out the left-hand half against the right-hand half of the front face, which is already on the table (see Figure 4.16). Care must be taken with any ashlars which cross the centre line from either half. Make notes on the drawing to differentiate between the joints for each half. This is where different coloured inks are useful. If the back is different again – it may be plain ashlar – half of this is put on the same drawing.

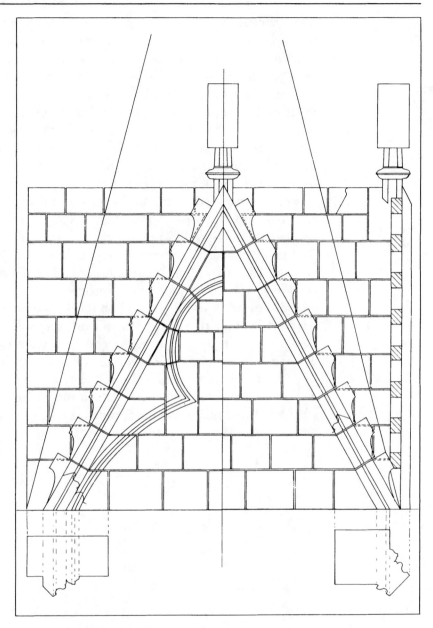

Figure 4.16 Full-size gable return elevation.

Making the face moulds is exactly as described above but bed moulds will also be needed. These are obtained by squaring down points from the face, either to below the base line or to a relatively uncluttered area of the drawing, or onto a blank sheet pinned onto the table for the purpose. If one gable mould and its attached ashlar is drawn out, the position of the other gable, or of the ashlar quoin if the stone does not contain parts of both gables, is obtained by measuring its position from the elevation and transferring the measurement to the bed mould. If the faces are not identical, the measurement must be obtained from the other half of the drawing.

Similarly, if the ashlar quoin is not the same on all views, take this from whichever view is appropriate. It may be useful to draw in on the bed mould the centre line of the return face (as a line parallel to the main base line, and thus at right angles to the centre line of the front face) and measure from this to ensure that the elements are in the correct position relative to the front elevation. Remember that the gable seen on the drawing in end view is shown in front view on the opposite side of the elevation drawing.

If parts of two gables are on the same stone, the beds will not all be in one plane. The gable mould joints will be at an angle, the ashlar between the gables will have a horizontal joint running from the top of this angle and, if any ashlar beneath the gable is included, its horizontal joint will run from the lower end of the angle. This will call for great care in making the templets.

The student of setting-out will be relieved to hear that all this is much easier to sort out in practice than it sounds. The setter-out must have, or rapidly acquire, the ability to see a two-dimensional drawing in three dimensions, and to rotate this in his mind to see just how it will be worked and what templets are required. A very useful aid is a block of plasticine, which can be roughly carved into a model of particularly awkward stones.

5

Setting-out:
The Application of
Geometrical
Techniques

This chapter provides examples of plane and solid geometrical construction from simple polygons to circle-on-circle arches and domes. Some of the examples resemble the methods shown in the books by Purchase and by Warland, but differ in significant points. The methods must not be confused and any attempt to combine them will result in disaster.

As mentioned in the previous chapter; rigid rules are irrelevant when reproducing historic work. If a hexagon is found not to be a regular hexagon, then it must be drawn as it is. If a vault seems not to have been set-out according to the method given below, then the method must be amended accordingly.

ARCHES

A universally applicable point which must be kept in mind is that the joints in any arch must radiate to the centre from which the curve in which the joint lies was struck.

The flat arch

Joints radiate from one point on the perpendicular centre line (Figure 5.1).

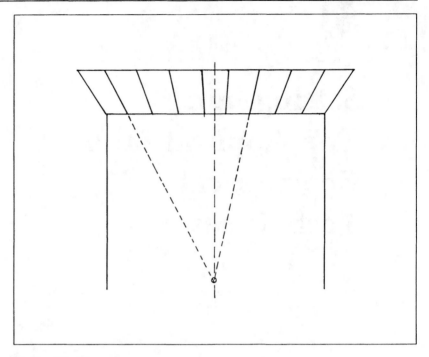

Figure 5.1 Flat arch.

The flat arch with quadrant corners

The keystone rests between skewbacks using joints radiating from one point on the perpendicular centre line (Figure 5.2).

The semicircular arch

AB is the span and CD the rise (Figure 5.3). Joints radiate from the centre C.

The segmental arch

Where the desired span AB and rise ED are known, the centre C can be found thus (Figure 5.4). Draw the chord AD, the bisector of this line will meet the centre line at C. With radius CA the curve may be drawn.

The three-centred arch

The span AB and rise ED are given (Figure 5.5). With centre E and radius EA, draw the quadrant AF. Draw the chord AD. With D as centre and radius DF, cut the chord AD in G. Bisect AG and produce this line to meet the produced centre line DE at C which is the centre for the middle portion of the curve. The centre for the outer portion

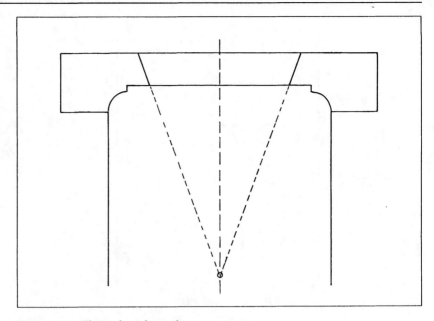

Figure 5.2 Flat arch with quadrant quarters..

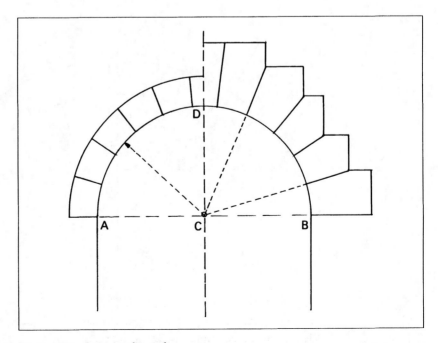

Figure 5.3 Semicircular arch.

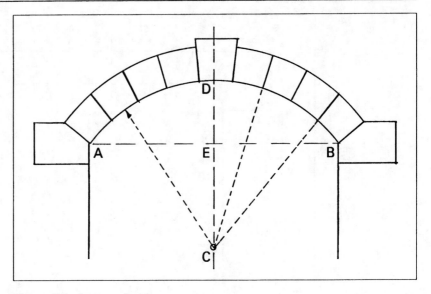

Figure 5.4 Segmental arch.

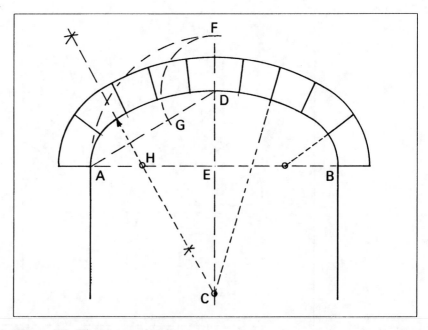

Figure 5.5 Three-centred arch.

of the curve is the point at which the bisector cuts the line AB as at H.

The four-centred arch (Tudor arch) (1)

Divide the springing line AD into four equal parts, marking B and C at the first and third quarters, respectively (Figure 5.6). With B as centre, radius BC, describe an arc below the springing line. Cut this arc at E with another arc of the same radius with C as centre. Join BE and produce this line to meet DF at G. B is the centre for the quicker curve at the lower part of the arch, and G is the centre for the remaining part. The joints for each part radiate from the respective springing points.

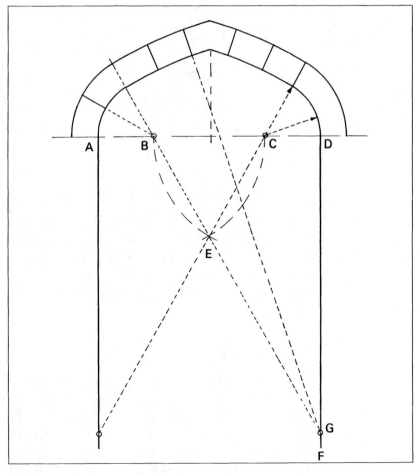

Figure 5.6 Four-centred arch (1).

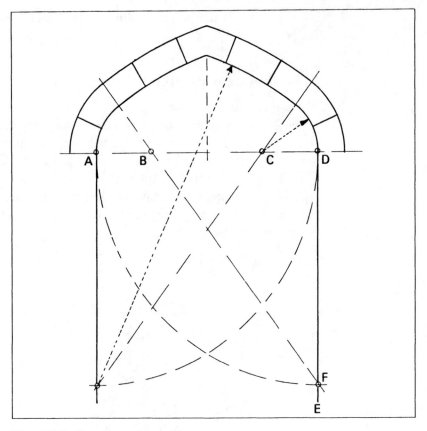

Figure 5.7 Four-centred arch (2).

The four-centred arch (Tudor arch) (2)

Divide the springing line AD into four equal parts, marking B and C at the first and third quarters, respectively (Figure 5.7). With centre D, radius DA, strike an arc cutting DE in F. B will be the centre for the quicker part of the arch, and F the centre for the remaining part. The joints for each part radiate from the respective springing points.

The semi-elliptical arch

To draw the arch joints, mark points on the soffit where desired joint lines are required. With C as centre and half the major axis AE as radius, describe an arc cutting AB at points F and F (the foci) (Figure 5.8). From F and F draw lines to meet the soffit at G (one of the joints). Bisect the angle FGF and produce this line above the soffit. This gives one of the joint lines. This procedure should be repeated for the remaining joints.

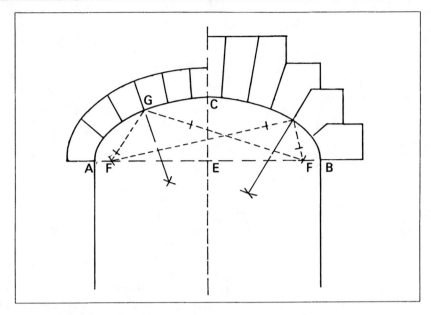

Figure 5.8 Elliptical arch.

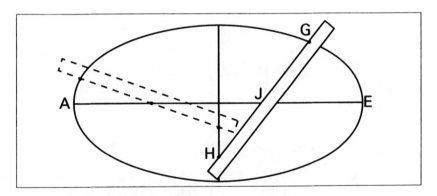

Figure 5.9 Ellipse construction.

Ellipse construction using a trammel

Draw the major and minor axes. Using a strip of paper, card or more rigid material if working on a large scale, mark on one edge the distance of half the major axis AE as GH (Figure 5.9). From G mark a point J equal to half the minor axis. By keeping point H on the minor axis and point J on the major axis, the curve of the ellipse will be traced by point G.

The equilateral arch

The springing points on the soffit are the two centres from which the joints radiate (Figure 5.10).

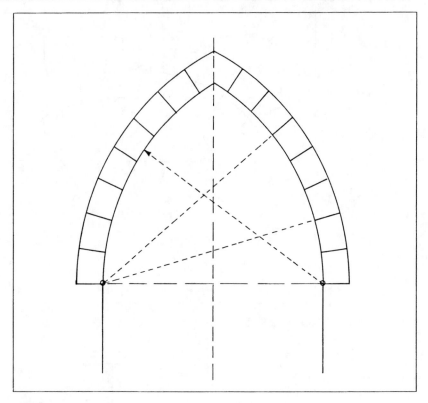

Figure 5.10 Equilateral arch.

The lancet arch

The centres are set on the springing line but outside the springing points of the soffit (Figure 5.11).

The drop arch

The centres are at springing level but inside the two springing points (Figure 5.12).

The lancet Moorish arch

The centres are above the springing line AB and outside the line of the soffit (Figure 5.13).

The rampant arch

An arch made up of two different radii with a centre at two levels (Figure 5.14).

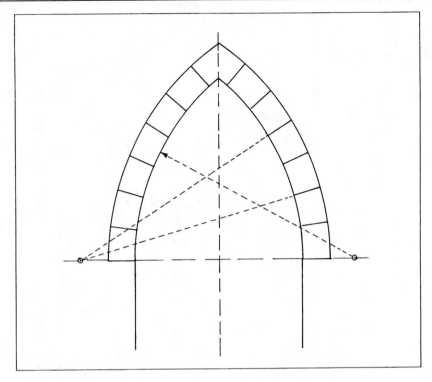

Figure 5.11 Lancet arch.

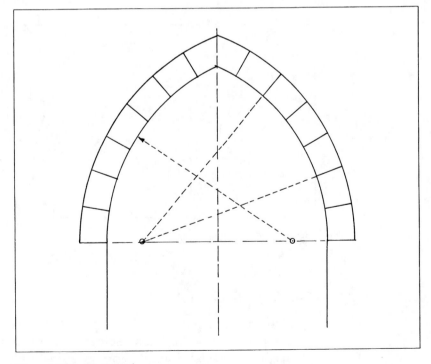

Figure 5.12 Drop arch.

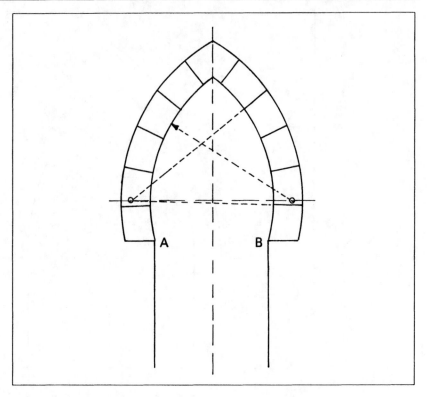

Figure 5.13 Lancet Moorish arch.

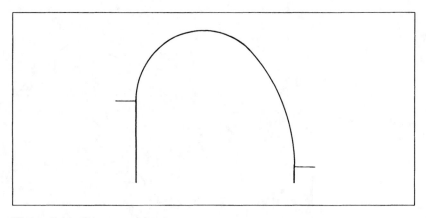

Figure 5.14 Rampant arch.

The hyperbolic arch

1. Draw the springing line AB, and produce it beyond each of these points (Figure 5.15). Draw the centre line CD, where D is the height of the arch from the springing line.
2. To the left of A erect a perpendicular equal to CD and divide

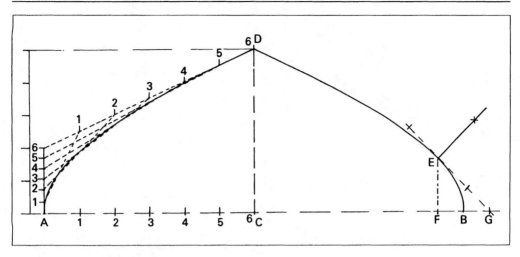

Figure 5.15 Hyperbolic arch.

      this line into five equal parts. From A erect a perpendicular equal in height to the first two divisions of the line just drawn to the left of A.

3. Divide the perpendicular drawn from A into equal parts, in this case six. Divide the line AC into a similar number of equal parts.

4. From point 6 on the perpendicular drawn from A, draw a line to D. Along this line mark points 1–6, which are perpendicularly above points 1–6 on the line AC.

5. Join 1 to 1, 2 to 2, etc. A fair curve drawn through the points of intersection of these lines will produce half the arch. In practice when setting-out full size, more than six points would be required.

6. To produce a joint line anywhere on the curve – in this example at E. Drop a perpendicular from E to F on the springing line AB, mark point G where BG is equal to BF. Join GE, which is a tangent to the curve. From E erect a line perpendicular to EG – this is the radiating joint line.

The parabolic arch

The method of producing the curve is similar to the description given for the hyperbolic arch (Figure 5.15), except that the perpendicular to the springing line drawn from A should be half the length of CD. To produce the joint line at point E on the curve (see Figure 5.16):

1. Join DB and bisect it in F. From F produce a line parallel to AB cutting the curve of the arch in G.

2. From E draw a parallel line to DB cutting FG in H. On the extended line FG, make GJ equal to HG.

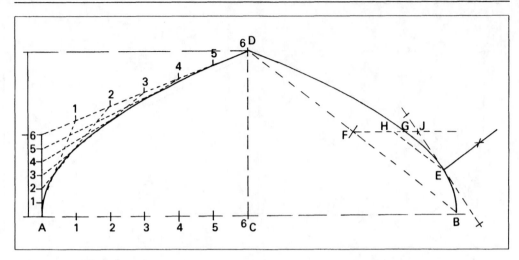

Figure 5.16 Parabolic arch.

3. Draw a line from J through E. This produces a tangent at point E. Erect a perpendicular to this tangent at E, which is the required joint line.

Skew arch

This example shows a semicircular arch through a wall, offset from front to rear by 12° (Figure 5.17).

1. Draw a plan of the opening within the thickness of the wall. Let the opening on one side (the front) be AB and the other (rear) be CD. The centre points on AB and CD are E and F, respectively.
2. Above the plan, draw a springing line and mark points A, C, E, F, B and D transferred from the plan.
3. With centre E and radius EA, draw a semicircle to represent the soffit line of the front side of the arch. Similarly, with centre F and radius FC, draw a semicircle to represent the soffit line of the rear side of the arch.
4. Draw outer semicircles to represent the outer joint line of the voussoirs.
5. Choose points on the arc AB from where joints are to radiate and draw them, as at GJ. To transfer the joint line GJ to the rear elevation, either drop a perpendicular from G to the line AB in plan, make CH equal to AG and raise a perpendicular from H in plan to the arc CD in elevation. Draw HI radiating from centre F or draw a horizontal line from G to cut the arch CD – this will give the same point H. In practice, it is best to do this both ways to check the accuracy of the drawing.

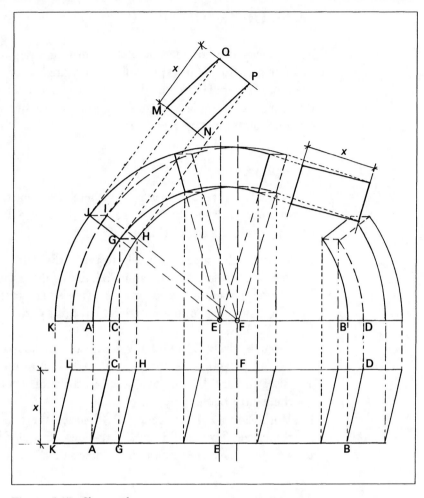

Figure 5.17 Skew arch.

6. The full-face mould of the left-hand springer can now be identified enclosed by the points JIHCK, showing the relative positions of the superimposed front and rear faces. The bottom bed mould can be seen in plan AKLC.

7. To produce an intermediate joint mould as at JGHI: at a convenient place on the drawing, draw a line parallel to JG and erect perpendiculars on JE from points J and G to cut the parallel line in M and N. Draw another line parallel to MN at a distance x from MN (x being the width of the wall). From points I and H erect lines perpendicular to IF to cut this line in Q and P. MNPQ is the top joint mould for the springer and the lower joint of the stone above.

Other joint moulds are similarly found as illustrated.

CONSTRUCTION OF POLYGONS

Any plane figure bounded by more than four straight lines is known as a polygon (from Greek, meaning many angles). If all the sides and therefore the angles are equal, it is known as a regular polygon, and, if unequal, an irregular polygon. A pentagon has five sides, a hexagon six sides and an octagon eight sides.

The pentagon

To construct a regular pentagon where the length of one side is known (the same method can be used for any polygon where the length of side is known) (Figures 5.18):

1. Produce the given side AB towards the left. With centre B, describe a semicircle of radius BA to cut the produced line in C.
2. Divide the semicircle AC into as many equal parts as the polygon is to have sides, in this case five. Do this by trial using compasses or dividers.
3. From B, draw B2. This gives the second side of the pentagon. For all polygons, always use the second point on the semicircle.
4. Bisect B2 and BA and let these bisectors intersect in D, which is the centre of the polygon.
5. With radius DA and centre D, describe the circle. Mark off on the circumference the remaining sides 2E and EF, equal to AB. Here we have the completed pentagon AB2EF.

The octagon

To construct a regular octagon with the distance between opposite sides being known (Figure 5.19):

1. Draw a square ABCD, each side of which is equal to the full distance across the octagon's opposite sides.
2. Draw the diagonals AC and BD.
3. With centre A and radius AB mark off the point E on the diagonal AC. Repeat this process using B, C and D as centres to find points F, G and H.
4. From E produce perpendiculars to the lines BC and CD. Similarly produce perpendiculars from points F, G and H to their corresponding sides.
5. The points at which these perpendiculars cut the lines AB, BC, CD and DA are the corners of the octagon.

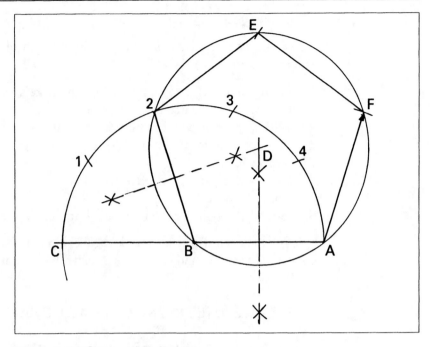

Figure 5.18 Constructing a pentagon.

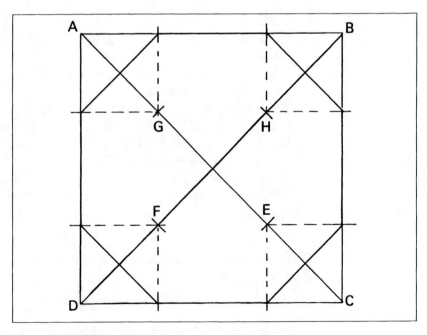

Figure 5.19 Constructing an octagon.

The hexagon

To construct a regular hexagon when the length of one side AB is known (Figure 5.20):

1. With radius AB, and centres A and B strike arcs intersecting at C. This is the centre of the hexagon.
2. With C as centre and radius CA, describe a circle.
3. Produce the lines AC and BC to cut the circle in D and E, respectively.
4. Draw a line parallel to AB through centre C to cut the circle at points F and G.
5. Join all the points on the circle to produce the hexagon.

It is worth remembering that a regular hexagon is made up of six equilateral triangles and can be constructed by a number of methods.

OTHER GEOMETRICAL CONSTRUCTIONS

Inscribing any number of equal circles within a given circle

This description is for six circles (Figure 5.21):

1. Divide the circumference into as many equal parts as there are to be circles, numbered here 1 to 6, and draw in the radii O1, O2, etc.
2. Bisect, for example, the angle 4O3, the bisector meeting the circumference in point A.
3. Through A draw a line perpendicular to OA meeting in the produced lines O4 and O3 in B and C, respectively.
4. Bisect the angle OBC. This line will cut OA in D which is the centre for one of the inscribed circles.
5. For the remaining centres, with centre O and radius OD, mark off points on the bisectors of each of the other segments 3O2, 2O1, etc.

Constructing any number of equal circles around a given circle

This description is for five circles (Figure 5.22):

1. Divide the circumference of the given circle into twice as many parts as there are to be circles, and draw the radials from centre O to these points and produce them outside the circumference.

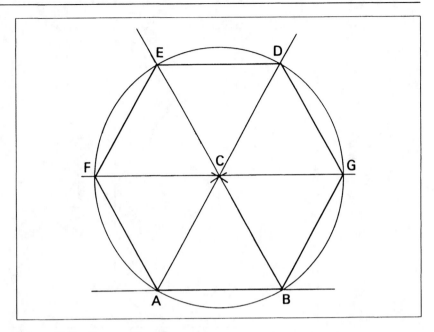

Figure 5.20 Constructing a hexagon.

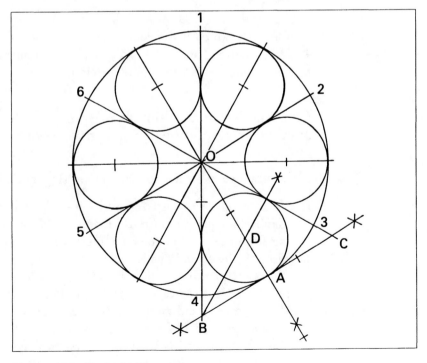

Figure 5.21 Circles inside a circle.

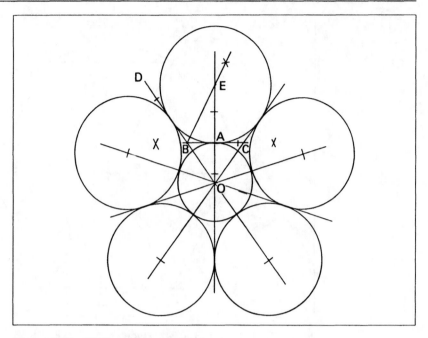

Figure 5.22 Circles touching a circle.

2. Through point A, draw a line perpendicular to the radial forming the tangent BC.
3. Bisect the angle DBA – the bisector cutting the extended radial OA in E, which is the centre for one of the circles.
4. With centre O and radius OE, cut the remaining alternate radials to provide centres for the other circles.

Constructing an Archimedean spiral of any number of revolutions with a given overall radius

In this example two revolutions are used (Figure 5.23):

1. With the given radius CA describe a circle and divide it into any number of equal parts (in this example eight with radials projecting from centre C to the circumference).
2. Bisect CA in B, and divide CB and BA each into eight equal parts (the same number as for the circumference). Every alternate point on AB is represented as 2, 4 and 6.
3. With centre C and radius C1 (CA less one division) describe an arc cutting the radial C1.
4. With centre C and radius C2 (CA less two divisions) describe an arc cutting the radial C2.
5. Continue this procedure. Arcs drawn from the points on BC will form the second (inner) revolution.

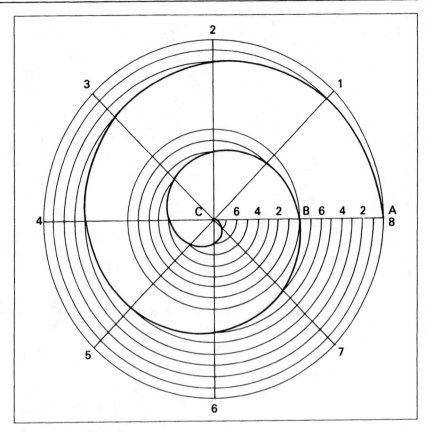

Figure 5.23 Archimedean spiral.

6. Points at which the arcs intersect the radials are points on the spiral.

FINDING THE RADIUS OF A CURVE

Figure 5.24 shows that, by using a formula developed from Pythagoras' theorem, the radii of regular curves can be obtained without difficulty.

Only the final part of the formula is relevant to the setter-out:

$$R = \frac{a^2 + b^2}{2a}$$

Finding the radius of a regular curve

All that is required is a straight edge and a tape measure. Hold a straight edge of precise length under the soffit of an arch and very carefully measure the maximum rise a (Figure 5.25). Very great care is needed in measuring. A small error in the length of the straight

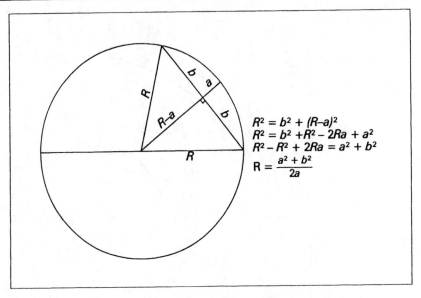

$$R^2 = b^2 + (R-a)^2$$
$$R^2 = b^2 + R^2 - 2Ra + a^2$$
$$R^2 - R^2 + 2Ra = a^2 + b^2$$
$$R = \frac{a^2 + b^2}{2a}$$

Figure 5.24 The use of Pythagoras' theorem to find the radius of a curve.

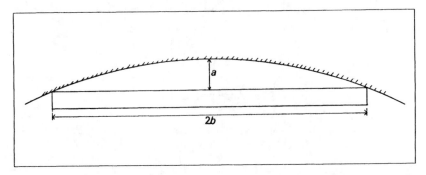

Figure 5.25 Measuring the rise and span of a curve using a straight edge.

edge, or in taking the rise, will lead to major inaccuracy in the calculated radius. If the rise is small, it is usually best to use callipers to take the measurement, or use a sinking square, remembering to subtract the width of the straight edge. Use a steel straight edge with sharp corners.

Once the measurements are made, the radius is simply found by using the above formula, where b represents half the chord (that is, half the length of the straight edge). Any element of an arch or tracery stone can be measured in this way, but always remember to use as long a straight edge as possible and to take measurements of the rise at a number of points. Average out any discrepancies and make a reverse to the calculated radius to check the work. Always make the reverse as long as possible – never check the radius against a single voussoir as it will invariably be too small.

If the space between the line of the curve and the straight edge looks asymmetrical, then the curve might be made up of more than one centre or be parabolic, hyperbolic or just distorted, perhaps by settlement or by poor previous restoration.

DRAWING CURVES OF LARGE RADIUS

When curves of large radii are to be drawn, it is often very impractical to strike an arc from a centre. If this is attempted, inaccuracies arise from flexibility in materials being used to strike the curve.

Using a development of Pythagoras' theorem (above and Figure 5.24), points on a curve can be plotted and, when joined together, will produce the desired curve. Using this method, a computer can produce information for a completed curve but for practical purposes a calculator will suffice. Figure 5.26 shows the application of the method.

Draw a straight line representing a chord, sufficiently long to give the length of arc required. The line should also be of a length suitable for division into whole numbers of unit measurement for ease of calculation. Draw in the centre line and mark unit divisions along the chord. The divisions should be as small as practicable, but will depend on the length of arc and the radius of the curve. The number of points needed will come with experience.

Using the formula

$$a = R - \sqrt{(R^2 - b^2)}$$

the height of the curve above the centre point of the chord will be a, where b is half the length of the chord and R is the known radius (see Figure 5.26).

Each point at each side of the centre line is denoted by y_1, y_2, etc. The heights y_1, y_2, etc., will be points on the curve and are found by using the formula

$$y = \sqrt{(R^2 - x^2)} - (R - a)$$

where x is the distance of the point from the centre line. Plot the points y_1, y_2, etc., and join them to form a smooth curve.

There are two other formulae which can be useful when setting-out:

1. The length of an arc of a circle of set radius can be described as

$$\frac{2\pi R\theta}{360}$$

where π is the constant 3.1417, R the radius of the curve and θ

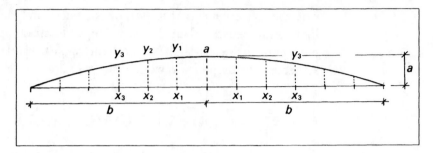

Figure 5.26 Plotting the co-ordinates of a curve.

the angle in degrees between the two radii which define the arc. This formula might be used when checking the length of a developed curve.

2. The sum of the internal angles of a polygon equals $180N-360$, where N equals the number of sides.

It must be stressed, however, that measurements of the values of angles and use of their sines, cosines and tangents should be used sparingly, and only for checking measurements already taken and set down.

RAKING SECTIONS

Raking sections are required where the joint on a moulding is not 90° to the face. This simply involves 'stretching' the moulding in one direction or another and, once this principle is understood, following the method is quite simple.

Producing a raking section of a string course where the joint is angled from top to bottom bed

1. Draw the front face of the string to show the angled joint which runs from A to B (Figure 5.27).
2. In line with the run of the string course, draw the true moulding section of the string as at C, and draw a perpendicular line DF between the top and bottom beds at the extreme front of the moulding.
3. From D produce a line to E parallel to AB. This is the line which will cause the 'stretching' of the section between the top and bottom beds.
4. From E and D produce lines perpendicular to the line DE. Now the raking can commence.

5. From points on the true moulding section, produce horizontal lines to touch the line DE, and continue these lines onwards but perpendicular to DE.
6. From the same points on the true moulding from which the horizontal lines were drawn, drop perpendiculars to the line of the bottom bed. Using compasses and centre D, draw arcs from the bottom of these perpendiculars to meet the bottom bed of what will be the raking section.
7. From the point of contact of these arcs with the line of the bottom bed of the raking section, produce perpendiculars which will be parallel to the line DE.
8. The point of contact between each corresponding line parallel and perpendicular to DE will be a point on the raking section.
9. The points of contact, when joined together, will produce the section required.

Curves which are regular on the true section will need to be produced using French curves on the raking section. The illustration shows the production of a raking section drawn to scale. In practice, when setting-out full size, many more points on the true moulding section should be transferred across to produce the raking section.

Producing a raking section of a string course where the joint is angled from the back to the front of the stone

The procedure is similar to the description shown in Figure 5.27 except that the requirement this time is to 'stretch' the true moulding section in the other direction.

In this case (Figure 5.28), the stone is drawn in plan indicating the angle of the joint AB. The true section is drawn, as is the angle of the joint DE. From this point onwards, proceed as in Figure 5.27.

Obtaining the raking section of the cyma recta moulding on a pediment

1. From points on the true moulding section draw lines parallel to the inclination of the pediment (Figure 5.29).
2. At a convenient distance above the true section, draw a horizontal line cutting a perpendicular drawn from the lowest point of the true section in A.
3. From the points on the true section chosen in step 1, erect perpendiculars to meet the horizontal line drawn from A.
4. With A as centre, strike arcs from these perpendiculars to meet a line drawn from A parallel to the inclination of the pediment.

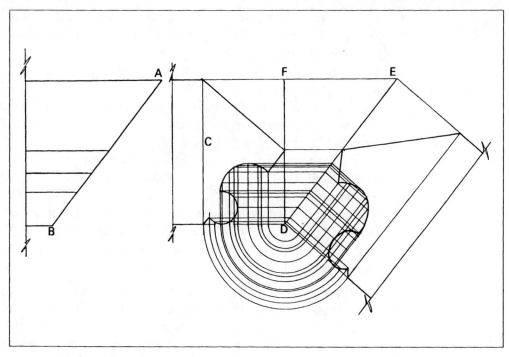

Figure 5.27 Raking section (1).

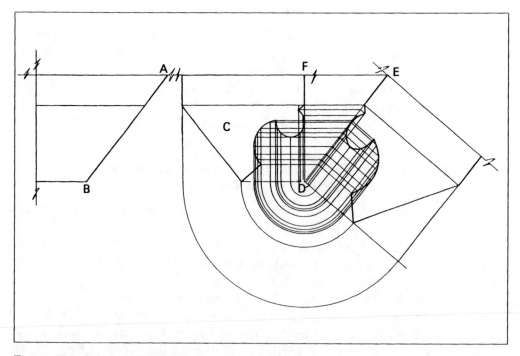

Figure 5.28 Raking section (2).

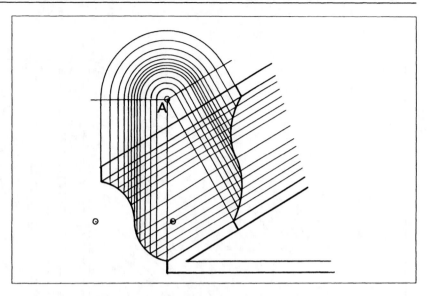

Figure 5.29 Raking section on a pediment.

5. At right angles to the inclination of the pediment, produce lines from the points where the arcs meet the inclined line drawn from A.
6. The points at which each of these lines meet the corresponding lines drawn in step 1 gives the points on the raking section.

Obtaining the raking section for the joint mould at the apex of a pointed arch

1. Above the springing line AB is drawn the left elevation of the arch (Figure 5.30). B is the mid-point of the span of the arch above which is drawn the centre line, which becomes the joint line on the elevation. Below the elevation, draw the true section of the arch moulding.
2. From points on the true section, draw lines parallel to AB to touch the centre line below B. With B as centre, strike quadrants from these lines up to the springing line produced beyond B. Perpendiculars to the springing line should now be erected from these quadrants.
3. From the same points on the true section, erect perpendiculars to the springing line. Using centre C (the centre for the left side of the arch) strike arcs from these perpendiculars to the centre line drawn from B.
4. Horizontal lines to the right of the centre line should be drawn from points where these arcs touch the centre line.
5. The raking secton can now be drawn through the points of intersection of corresponding horizontal and perpendicular lines.

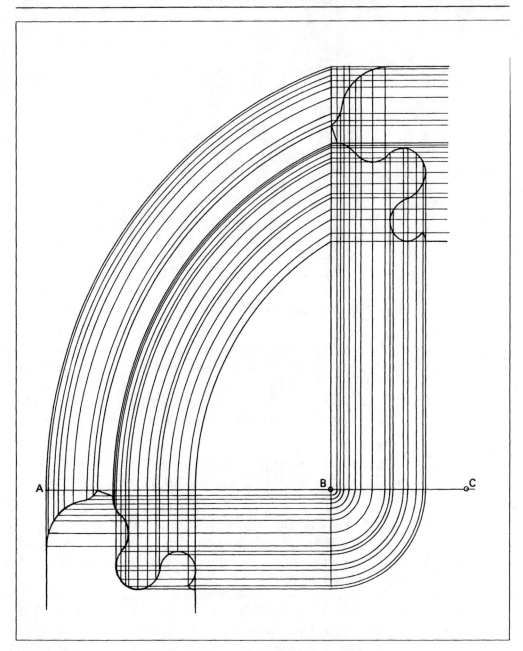

Figure 5.30 Finding the raking section of a curved moulding.

Note: if the radius of the arch is inconveniently large, set the line AC to run through the final joint before the apex. B will be the point at which that line crosses the centre line. The same method is used to obtain the raking section of any curved moulding.

SETTING-OUT THE ENTASIS OF A COLUMN (THE CONCHOID OF NICOMEDES)

The 'swelling' of columns used in building is designed to avoid the hollow appearance the eye would perceive if the lines were straight.

1. Draw a base line and produce a perpendicular from a point A to B (the full height of the column). This will be the centre line for the column (see Figure 5.31).
2. Draw the predetermined diameters of the bottom and top beds using centres A and B, respectively.
3. With the bottom bed radius and using centre C (one side of the column at the top bed), strike point D on the centre line below the top bed.
4. Divide AD into any number of equal parts.
5. Draw a line from C and continue through D.
6. At a convenient distance from the centre line, produce a perpendicular from the base line to cut the extended line CD at E.
7. Divide this perpendicular from the base line to point E into a similar number of equal parts as AD.
8. Join the corresponding points set out in steps 4 and 7, and continue these lines through the centre line AB.
9. Using the bottom bed radius and centres at the intersecting lines on AD, strike points on the extended lines drawn in step 8.
10. The curvature of these points when joined together will form the entasis on one side of the column.
11. For the opposite side of the column, draw horizontal lines through the centre line from the previously defined points on the entasis and transpose each respective distance across.

Each of the lines intersecting the two perpendiculars would meet at one point on an extended base line but, for large columns, to use such a point to strike from might not be practicable because of its distance away. The use of drawing the perpendicular to point E avoids this.

In this example, the line AD has been divided into eight parts. A greater number of equal parts will give more points on the entasis enabling a more accurate line to be drawn. Purchase's *Practical*

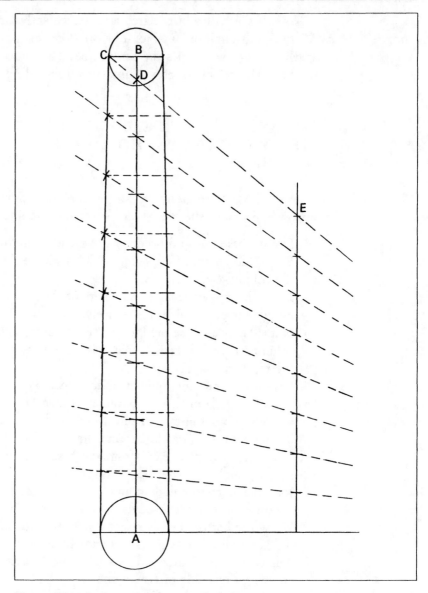

Figure 5.31 Setting out the entasis of a column.

Masonry describes the trammel method of drawing the entasis. A brief description of this is given in Figure 5.32.

THE IONIC VOLUTE

To construct an Ionic volute of given height (Figure 5.33):

1. Divide the height into 16 equal parts numbering divisions from top to bottom.

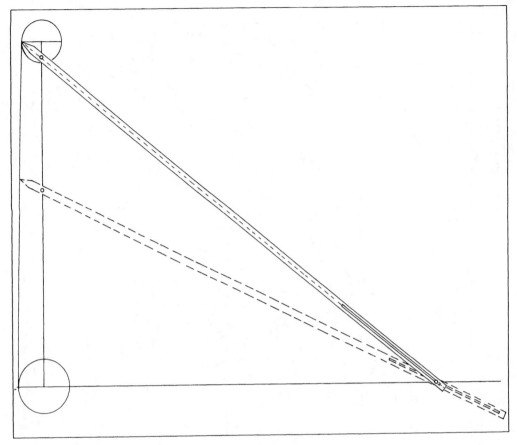

Figure 5.32 Finding the entasis using the trammel method.

2. From points 8 and 10 draw horizontal lines 8A and 10B each equal to eight divisions on the calibrated vertical axis.
3. Construct a circle, the circumference of which will pass through points A and B. This will be the eye of the volute.
4. Form a square ADBC within the circle, and cut this square into four equal quarters by drawing the lines 1,3 and 2,4 and produce yet another square 1,2,3,4.
5. Divide the diagonals 1,3 and 2,4 each into six equal parts, giving centres for the construction of the outer curve of the volute. These centres are numbered 1–12.
6. From the centre 4, draw a line through 1 to E, which is on a horizontal line drawn from 0 on the vertical axis. With centre 1 and radius 1E, draw the quadrant EF, F being on a horizontal line from 1 produced through 2.
7. With centre 2 and radius 2F draw the quadrant FG, G being on a vertical line from 2 produced through 3.
8. Repeat with centre 3 and radius 3G to find point H.
9. The next quadrant in fact is slightly more than a quadrant. With

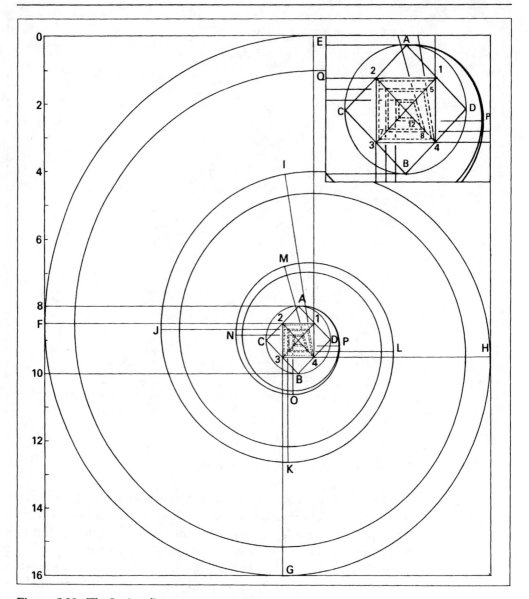

Figure 5.33 The Ionic volute.

centre 4 and radius 4H, draw the arc HI, I being on the line
produced from 4 through 5.

10. Continue this process with centre 5 for IJ, 6 for JK, etc., until
the last arc PA of the outer curve is drawn using centre 12.

11. To construct the inner curve, on the line E–1–4, make EQ equal
to one graduation on the vertical axis.

12. The centres for successive quadrants are found along the diagonals 1,3 and 2,4. For the inner curve in the quadrant EF, the
centre is a point one quarter of the distance from 1 to 5.

13. Similarly, for the inner curve in the quadrant FG, the centre is a point one quarter of the distance from 2 to 6.
14. Continue, to complete the volute.

CIRCLE-ON-CIRCLE

Setting-out a semicircular arch in a curved wall

The inner and outer elevations of an arch in a curved wall will not be the same. If the outer arch is semicircular the inner will be elliptical with the major axis set vertically.

In this example, the semicircle is taken to be on the outside of the wall, that is, the side having the larger radius.

The arch will be symmetrical so only one half need be drawn. To produce the voussoirs, three templets are required: the bed mould, inside face mould and outside face mould. For any moulding on the stone, a joint mould will be required, but for clarity no moulding is included in this example.

1. First draw a plan of that part of the wall within which the arch is to be set (Figure 5.34a). The centre for the curvature of the wall is at O, and the position of the springing point of the arch on the ouside of the wall is at A.
2. Above the plan, develop the outside (convex) line BA from O to A as in Figure 5.34b, and with O as centre, draw the quadrant AC representing the soffit of the arch.
3. Divide the quadrant AC into any number of equal parts. Seven are used in this example, although in practice many more would be required. Drop perpendiculars from these points to the springing line. Transfer the distances of these perpendiculars from centre O onto the segment line from B to A in Figure 5.34a. The distances are not measured onto AB as a straight line measurement but in small steps measured around the curve. Draw lines from these points on AB radiating towards centre O. Now the inside (concave) elevation can be drawn.
4. The line DE should now be developed along the springing line to the right of the centre line. The radiating lines from the points on the line AB cross the line DE. The distances of these points on the line DE should be transferred to the springing line from O to E, and perpendiculars erected.
5. Horizontal lines should now be drawn from points 1 to 6 on the quadrant AC across to the corresponding perpendiculars 1 to 6 erected from the line OE. These points of intersection, when

joined together, will form the elevation of the arch soffit on the inside (concave) face of the cylindrical wall.

6. Any joint lines can now be put on the outside elevation (Figure 5.34b) radiating from the centre O, and the desired design of voussoir should be drawn on this elevation. In this example, joint lines are drawn from the ordinates 2, 4 and 6 on the line AC. It follows that the joints will come off the inside elevation curve EC at the corresponding points, 2, 4 and 6.

7. For the outermost points of the radiating joints to be transferred on to the interior elevation (Figure 5.34c), perpendiculars must be dropped from these points (Figure 5.34b) to the springing line OA. Distances from these points from O should be transferred to BA (Figure 5.34a) as described above. Lines radiating from these points to O give the positions on ED that are similarly

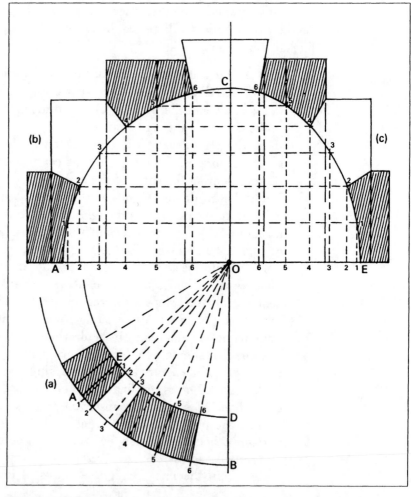

Figure 5.34 Setting-out an arch in a curved wall.

transferred to OE (Figure 5.34c). Perpendiculars are erected to intersect the radiating joint lines.

8. Through this method of transferring ordinates from Figure 5.34b to Figure 5.34a to Figure 5.34c, the three essential templets can be produced – outside face, plan and inside face, respectively. In the figures, two voussoirs have their mould outlines hatched.

Setting-out a dome

1. Draw a horizontal springing line AO (Figure 5.35a) and erect a section through the elevation of the dome. In this instance the inside of the dome is a quadrant of a circle BC and centre O. The outside surface is a segment of a circle drawn to diminish the thickness (and therefore the weight) of the stone as it

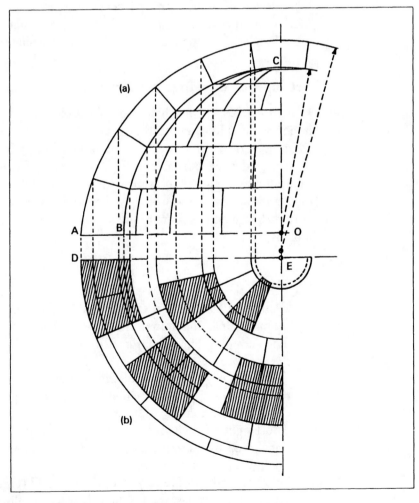

Figure 5.35 Setting-out a dome.

reaches the top. Joint lines radiating from centre O must now be drawn.

2. Figure 5.35b shows a quarter plan of the dome. By dropping perpendiculars from the inside and outside of each joint in Figure 5.35a to a line parallel to AO, namely DE, the top and bottom plan of each course can be drawn using centre E.

3. Joints in plan can now be drawn in whatever the desired arrangement. In this example, the joints are arranged so that each stone in a particular course is the same. Hatched areas are plans giving the required top and bottom beds of each stone.

The same method is used to set-out a half-dome or niche-head.

NODDING OGEE ARCH

This design of arch, found particularly in the Decorated period of Gothic architecture, requires a face mould, a developed side face mould and a developed section for any intermediate joint.

Setting-out drawings required

In Figure 5.36a, the left half of the front elevation of a nodding ogee hood mould is drawn with the accompanying true moulding section, which is also the bottom bed mould. The line JJ is a joint running normal to the run of moulding in elevation, but horizontally back to the wall line. Figure 5.36b shows the side elevation of the projection of the arch from the wall line, and the joint section raked from the bottom bed mould. Figure 5.36c shows the two developed side face moulds.

Method

1. Front face moulds are taken directly from the front elevation (Figure 5.36a) and stones are shaped accordingly.

2. The springing line is continued to the right of Figure 5.36a and the side profile erected.

3. The outer edge of the moulding in Figure 5.36a is marked with points as at 1, 2, 3, etc., which are equidistant points along the curve in elevation.

4. The height of each of these points above the springing line is transferred across to Figure 5.36b and marked accordingly on the side profile, as at 1, 2, etc.

5. Below the side profile is set a developed grid (Figure 5.36c). The vertical graduations are the actual distances along the curve in

Figure 5.36a set out in a straight line. If the outer curve of the elevation were a piece of string, then the right-hand graduated line in Figure 5.36c is that string straightened out.

6. Horizontal lines are drawn from each equidistant point on the right side of Figure 5.36c. From points 1, 2, 3, etc., on the side profile (Figure 5.36b), lines are dropped down to Figure 5.36c to meet the horizontal lines 1, 2, 3, etc. By joining the points formed by the intersecting lines 1,1, 2,2, etc., the developed side profiles are obtained.

7. These side profile templets can be applied to the outside faces of the stones, which have been worked to the front face moulds.

8. When working the side profile, the distance back from the

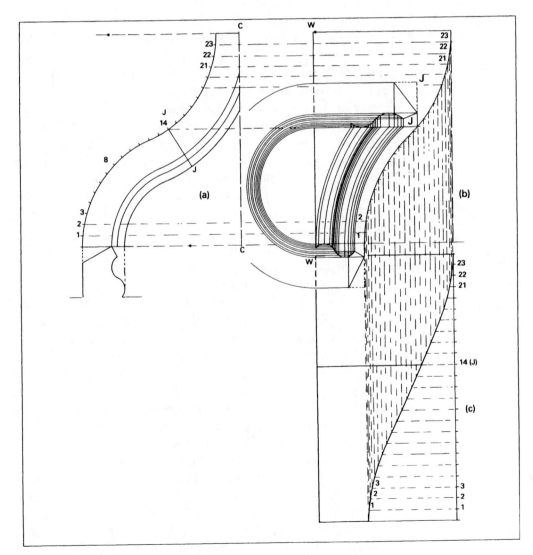

Figure 5.36 Setting-out a nodding ogee.

extreme front of the stone to the profile, say at point 8 in Figure 5.36a, is same for that of the outer and inner curves along a normal line to the curve.

9. Once the front and side faces of the stones have been worked, then the bottom bed moulding section and the raking (joint) section can be applied and the mouldings worked.

10. Figure 5.36b shows the required method to obtain the joint (or raking section) with the 'stretching' point in line with point J on the outside curve of the front elevation. (For raking sections, see above.)

TRACERY

Most people would regard the setting-out of tracery as very difficult. In fact, it is treated as a straightforward elevation drawing, with each separate part measured, recorded and transferred to the drawing table. It is no more difficult than any other elevation, although the work may be lengthy and call for painstaking attention to detail, following the very simple rules set out below.

Tracery is set-out using a pattern of intersecting centre lines of various mouldings. Tracery with one elementary moulding section will have a pattern in elevation involving one centre line intersecting at different points. Any measurement for replacement or restoration of tracery should be based on these centre lines and the width of section drawn either side of the line. Most tracery designs are foliated, involving cusps and eyes, and so have a secondary centre-line system, as the foils are made up of mouldings which run into and are part of the main moulding section.

As shown in Figure 5.37, more complex tracery will have major and minor sections intersecting, each section having a centre-line system, and the foils making up a third centre-line system.

Do not attempt to draw in the elevations of the mouldings until the centre-line pattern has been established, although, as always, the moulding sections must be taken as the first stage of work if only to establish the relative positions of the centre lines. Draw the moulding sections in their correct position beneath the springing line and use these as starting points for the centre-line system.

In most textbooks, the positions of the centres of curves that make up tracery have been emphasized and laid out according to rigid rules. To the restorer, these rules are irrelevant – the centres of curved elements are wherever the original builders or the settlement of the building have set them, and should be found by measurements of different arcs and the points at which they intersect. As always, never

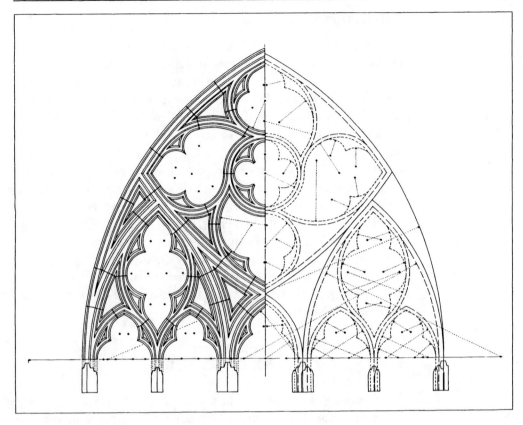

Figure 5.37   Setting-out of tracery.

follow someone else's view of how the design should have been generated.

Measurement of tracery is relatively simple. Using the springing line and the perpendicular centre line as axes, strategic points of intersection can be marked in relation to both axes. The curvature of particular elements can be measured and checked as individual items and the design drawn out by adding one part to another until the whole is complete. The relative positions of joints are drawn after the elevation is completed.

Joints in most cases are drawn normal to the curve, changing direction where necessary midway between the two centre lines, where one secondary centre line starts to deviate from the primary moulding.

As with any elevation, if the existing work is distorted by settlement, a decision must be made at the outset as to whether it is to be replaced 'as is' or 'as was'. If distortions are to be reproduced, it may be necessary to draw both halves of the tracery, instead of using the templets for one half as lines up and for the other as lines down.

Half-section repair of tracery

It is sometimes possible to replace only the outer face of tracery, thus preserving the inner, usually undamaged, half (see Chapter 10 on fixing). In this case it may be possible to draw the tracery directly.

When the outer half has been cut away, set up a board (a sheet of plywood is the easiest) on the outside of the window, securely fixed and bearing on the part to be replaced. The board should be painted white or have a sheet of paper pinned to it. From the inside, carefully draw around the stone, after carefully cleaning off any mortar used to seal the glass. This gives an outline, which should be cleaned up as necessary – it is unlikely that the stone will be entirely pristine and smooth. The centres of the curves can be established quite simply and the nose lines, etc., drawn in, and the templets made.

This method is suitable for use when small parts of tracery are to be replaced, but for half-section replacement of the full elevation of a large window, it is probably better to measure and draw as described in the previous section.

SETTING-OUT A RIBBED VAULT

The following example is chosen to draw attention to a very important factor: the curvature of vaulted ribs may not be the same over their whole length, so that any replacement of stone ribs should be set out with care and with constant reference to the original. (See also Chapter 10 for general notes on the construction of vaults.)

Figure 5.38a shows one quarter of a vaulted ceiling which is square on plan. In the top left-hand corner is the springing point, and clockwise from the top are the wall rib, intermediate rib, diagonal rib, intermediate rib and wall rib. These ribs meet two ridge ribs where the circles represent bosses. The ribs are outlined and have a dotted centre line, which would be the centre line of any moulding. For clarity, no moulding is shown here.

In this example, the ribs spring from the top of a capital with an abacus forming the segment of a circle. Therefore the noses of all ribs on the centre lines begin in a similar formation – around the curved dotted line in the top left of Figure 5.38a.

Having drawn out all the ribs and centre lines in plan, the true elevation of the ribs can now be constructed.

The wall rib

The curvature of this rib has a constant radius for the whole of its length. The centre C is positioned on the extended centre line of the

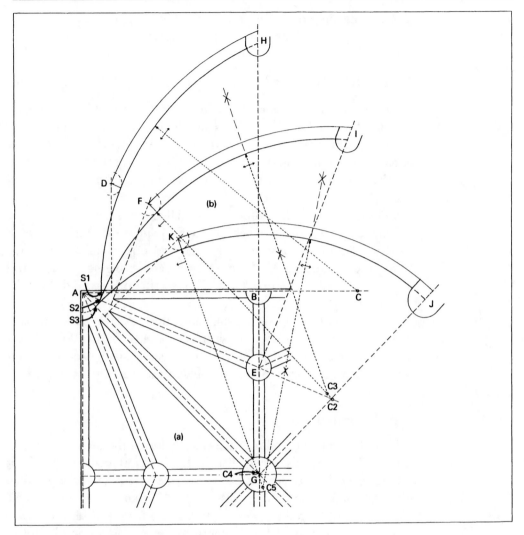

Figure 5.38 Setting-out a ribbed vault.

wall rib, AB on the plan. The springing point of the soffit of the rib is at the coincidence of the line AB and the dotted segment, at S1.

The height H of the vault is marked along the extended centre line of the ridge rib, so the height is BH (Figure 5.38b). Only one point on the extended line AB will provide a centre for an arc which will pass through both S1 and H. It can be found thus: the bisector of the chord S1H will meet the extended line AB in C, which will be the centre from which the soffit line of the rib can now be struck. The position of the soffit of the web is marked and that curve also struck.

To find the point of separation of the ribs on the elevation, a line perpendicular to AB is erected such that, if continued below AB, it would meet the point of separation of the wall rib and intermediate rib, cutting the arc of the web in D. The height D above the line AB is the point at which the ribs will separate.

The intermediate rib

From point E erect a line perpendicular to the centre line of this rib and mark point I, so that EI is equal to BH. Erect a perpendicular on AE such that, if continued below AE, it would meet the intersection of the intermediate rib and the diagonal rib, and mark F so that the distance of F from AE is equal to the distance of D from AB.

Refer back to the elevation of the wall rib, and set the compasses to the depth of the rib between soffit and web. With centre F describe an arc as illustrated. By trial and error, find a centre C2 along the centre line AE from which an arc springing from S2 will touch the arc drawn around point F. Describe this arc and draw the line FC2.

For the continuation of the soffit line, draw a chord between I and the point at which the arc drawn from S2 cuts the line FC2, bisect it, and the point at which the bisector cuts FC2 is the centre C3 for the arc that completes the soffit line and the web line of the rib.

The diagonal rib

This follows the method for the construction of the intermediate rib. Erect a perpendicular on AG such that, if continued below AG, it would meet the intersection of the intermediate rib and the diagonal rib, and mark K so that the distance of K from AG is equal to the distance of D from AB and F from AE (the height of separation).

Draw an arc around K, the depth of the rib, as previously drawn around F. Find a centre, C4, along the line of AG to produce an arc springing from S3 to touch the arc drawn around K. Draw the arc and the line KC4.

For the continuation of the soffit line, draw a chord between J and the point at which the arc drawn from S2 meets KC4, bisect it, and the point at which the bisector meets the extended line KC4 is the centre C5 for the arc which completes the soffit line and web line of the rib.

Summary

As mentioned above, this example is only a guide to setting-out a vault. It is by no means a description of how all vaults should or could have been set out. The intention is to make the reader aware of the discipline involved when confronted by vault restoration.

In this example, the ridge is assumed to be horizontal. If it is not, then simply adjust the heights of H, I or J accordingly.

RAMP AND TWIST

This is a simple but effective method of setting-out a stone that is not only curved in plan but also rising at a regular inclination.

Owing to the geometric nature of this type of work, an initial decision must be made prior to setting-out as to whether the joints at the ends of the stone are be at right-angles to the inclined plane or not. This is only possible on the concave or convex sides – not both. In this example, the convex side will have the right-angled joint.

1. In Figure 5.39a, a plan of the top surface of the stone is drawn ABCD with concave and convex surfaces centred on E, through which a perpendicular boning line is drawn.
2. To develop the convex face, divide the line AB in Figure 5.39a into as many equal parts as is practical (in this case 16). Reproduce the length of AB as a straight line (Figure 5.39b).
3. The vertical rise of the top surface of the stone is indicated by x (Figure 5.39b). Draw the top surface of the stone over the distance from AB and rising by x.
4. This top surface should now have right-angled joint lines drawn at each end to a length equal to the chosen height of the stone, completing the convex developed surface.
5. From the bottom of the joint lines at each end, draw perpendiculars down to the line AB extended beyond B. Transfer these points F and G on AB to the arc AB in Figure 5.39a.
6. In Figure 5.39a, draw radials from points F and G towards the centre E, cutting the concave arc DC (extended) in H and I.
7. In Figure 5.39a, divide DC (the concave side of the stone) into a similar number of equal parts as for the convex side. Do this by radiating any point on AB back to E and marking the points on DC.
8. To draw the concave developed surface: as in Figure 5.39c, draw the developed straight line DC and mark off the positions of H and I.
9. The rise for the inclination of this face is the same as for the convex face, namely x, though over the shorter distance DC.
10. The depth of stone remains the same, so lines representing the top and bottom beds can be drawn. Perpendiculars raised from DC and HI will give the top and bottom joint limits respectively.

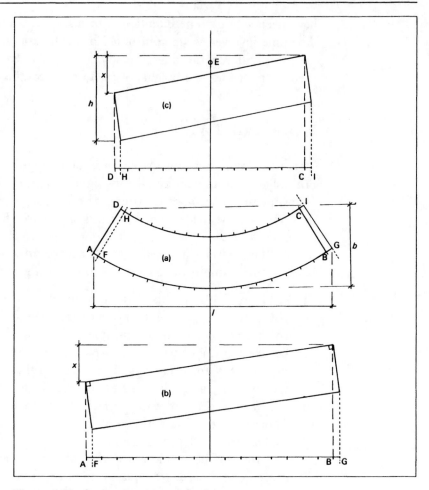

Figure 5.39 Setting-out ramp and twist.

The joints on this developed face are not at right angles to the inclination.

11. The boning line must be marked on all templets and be lined up when the templets are applied to the stone.

12. The overall dimensions of the stone can be found by using the true bed section (AGID, Figure 5.39a) for length and breadth (*l* and *b*) and measuring the full height *h* (Figure 5.39c). The full bed section must be worked first and then the developed faces marked on.

If right-angled joints are required on the inside face and not on the outside, then this face should be developed first, and the positions of joints transferred through the plan to the convex face.

If right-angled joints are not required at either side, a developed section should be produced through the length of the plan half-way between the arcs AB and DC. This section should be given right-angled joints to the inclination. Then the relative positions of the joints are transferred back through the plan to the two outside arcs, using radiating lines (as in steps 5 and 6). Development of the outside faces can then continue.

COMPUTER-AIDED DESIGN

The potential of computer-aided design (CAD) in relation to full-size setting-out has grown enormously. Originally developed to produce relatively simple scale drawings, and with limited functions, CAD's complexity and sophistication has grown out of all recognition, and is continuing to develop. The following is an outline of the way CAD can be used in the setting-out process.

Systems

CAD systems consist of a computer (the hardware) and a program (the software) linked to a plotter, which produces the drawing to any required scale. Both hardware and software are changing extremely quickly and this is not the place to discuss the continuing developments in this field. Information is stored either on a floppy disc or on the main computer memory (hard disc). A roller ball (mouse) is used to move a pointer around the screen and to input instructions; instructions are also given from the keyboard.

Software

There are a number of programs currently on the market. Among others, Intergraph MicroStation has been used very successfully for setting-out both in the UK and in the United States. For setting-out, the main requirements are not necessarily a vast range of technical features but rather the speed of operation, which depends partly on the hardware, and accuracy. The ability to show three-dimensional views of a drawing, either as a solid object or as a wire-cage diagram, which can be rotated, is a useful feature. All programs will now show smooth curves and accurate junctions.

Using CAD

In general, all work is carried out at small scale on the screen, the final size being dependent on the plotting instructions. Thus, once an elevation has been drawn, it can be produced both at full size and to scale, a significant time-saving feature. Where only half an elevation is drawn, the image can be mirrored to provide the full elevation. Also, where return elevations are involved, all views can be laid out side by side without any redrawing by the setter-out.

Working on a small screen may seem very inaccurate, but in fact the image on the screen is only a representation of digital information held in the memory, which is extremely accurate – far more accurate than the limitations of the plotter. In addition, the operator can zoom in or out, to get a complete overview of the whole drawing or to fill the screen with the smallest detail, which can then be amended as required.

In simple terms, drawing is done by marking points on the screen, using the mouse, and instructing the computer to join the dots either by straight lines or curves of specified radius. Success still depends on the setter-out choosing the points and setting the radii according to the measurements taken.

Where a mould section has been drawn by hand, a hand-plotter can be used to send the co-ordinates to the computer, which will then store the outline in its memory, to be called up and fed into the elevation or other drawing. In the same way, trial templets can be cut and altered, and then plotted without further hand drawing. Profiles can be stored in the permanent memory (the hard disc), and called up at a later date for use in other work.

There is a danger in this last point. When setting-out in the traditional way, similar moulds may be remembered and brought out to form a basis for new work. On the computer, it is very much easier to find a roughly similar moulding and there may be a temptation to use it as it is, as being 'near enough'. The process of finding, retrieval and use of a stored profile takes only seconds, instead of perhaps several hours to measure and check the current profile. This can be a great saving in time and money, but the temptation must be resisted. However the setting-out is being done, the setter-out must remember that near enough is not good enough. Historic buildings deserve only the best efforts and the most accurate reproduction.

This brings up an important point. CAD can make the drawing easy but it does not replace the need for painstaking measurement on site, and the careful checking and rechecking of moulding profiles. Accurate reconstruction of the original form is still vital if the building is to be properly cared for.

One distinct and very practical advantage of CAD is the ability to draw curves of large radius. With the manual system, anything more than 4–5' calls for two people to handle the large trammel rod, and a curve of 20' radius, which is not uncommon in Gothic architecture, has to be worked out from co-ordinates, or the drawing pinned down to the floor of a very large room. On the computer, the given radius is fed in and the machine does the rest. This is especially useful for large landscape features such as curved retaining walls, where a 200′ radius might be needed.

Plotting

The greatest potential limitation of the CAD system is the plotter. This is simply a pen which draws out the information sent by the computer either on paper or film. Plotters may be of two types: a flat-bed plotter, which is a large table over which the pen is moved on an arm; and a pinch-wheel plotter, where the paper is drawn backwards and forwards under a fixed arm. The latter type has become the norm. Whatever plotter is used, the pens must be as fine as those used for manual setting-out.

Plotters work to impressive-sounding limits: 0.1% sounds very good, until one realizes that this is 1 mm in a metre. A 5 m long drawing may thus be incorrect by 5 mm. In practice, the inaccuracy lies more with the medium than the plotter, and the use of film is essential for the best work. At these sizes, even film is affected to a small extent by temperature, but this will usually not be significant and the discrepancies should be within acceptable limits. This must be carefully checked when either considering or maintaining a CAD system.

The width of the drawing is usually limited to about 36″ (914 mm), which means that a complete drawing may have to be composed of several sheets laid side-by-side, but this is common with large drawings on cartridge and so should be no great disadvantage. To achieve larger-area output in a single pass of the printer, the cost becomes prohibitive.

Once the plotting is complete, there should be a large table available on which to lay out the drawings, as well as the usual templet-cutting facilities.

Templets

Once the drawing has been plotted, templet making follows the usual course, with whatever material is best suited to the work in hand. However, the computer can be linked to a machine which cuts plastic templets directly. Apart from the limitations of plastic templets already mentioned, the accuracy of the cutting must be carefully checked against the drawing and the templet recut if necessary. Again, the potential savings in time and skill must not be allowed to override the requirements of historical accuracy.

It is also simple to transfer information from the computer, either by floppy disc or by wire, straight to a numerically controlled (NC) machine which will cut the stone without the intermediate use of templets. For drawings of simple mouldings and profiles, the co-ordinates can be transferred directly to the NC machine with the use of a computerized drawing head.

Summary

CAD is not cheap to set up when compared with a manual system. For a large, highly mechanized business this outlay will probably be economic, but small masonry firms, which still form the bulk of the trade, are more likely to rely on traditional setting-out. A CAD system represents substantial capital which must be used to the full, whereas a setting-out shop can be left idle if no major setting-out is required. However, CAD has a significant contribution to make to the masonry trade and its potential should not be overlooked.

6

Masons' Hand Tools

TOOLS FOR WORKING STONE

'The bad workman blames his tools'. Accidents will happen when the mason is let down by tools which are unsuitable, not sharp enough or of poor quality. The answer is to obtain better tools and look after them carefully. Good or specialist tools are expensive, but collecting and maintaining a good tool kit is essential for the craftsman. Many tools can be made relatively easily and some suggestions are made at the end of this chapter. The best sources of masons' tools are retired masons, if they can be persuaded to let them go.

Tools, working practice and names of tools all vary a little from one part of the country to another. All masons have their individual preferences, both for tools and methods of working. This chapter gives a general view based on the working experiences of the authors. Most tools are still sold in Imperial widths and weights, which have become traditional names rather than sizes.

The *mallet* (Figure 6.1a) is traditionally made of a wood which is dense but not too hard; beech and hickory are excellent, but oak is a little too hard and lacks a certain amount of 'spring'. Scottish beech is said to be better than English, being slower growing and more durable. Fruit woods, especially apple and pear, can be good for small mallets. Plastic mallets are gaining in favour with many masons but their circular shape is not ideal. Most wooden mallets sold commercially are even worse in shape, being not only circular but too shallow (Figure 6.1b), and the only way to obtain a good one, other than second-hand, is to have one specially made.

Ideally a mallet is not circular in plan but elliptical. This gives a better blow, swinging easily without the tendency to turn in the hand, which circular ones have. If of wood, the grain must run along the length and not vertically, as in the case of most bought ones. The point of impact (the beat) must be on the end grain, which is harder

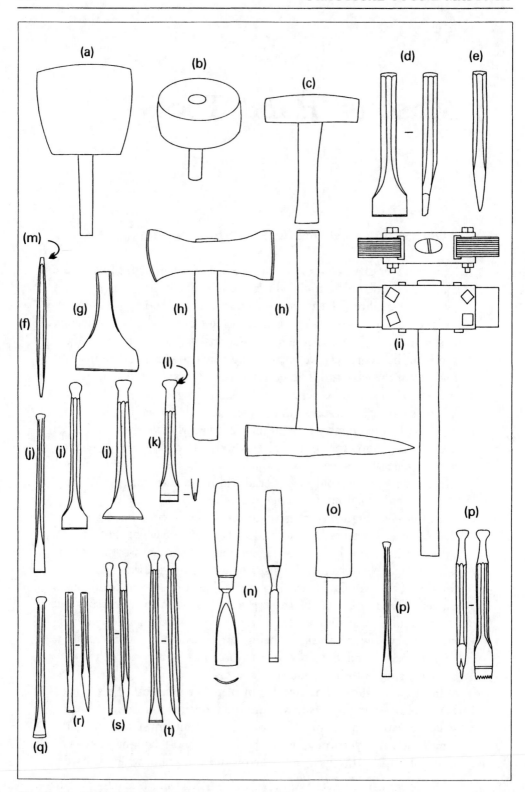

Figure 6.1 Masons' hand tools.

and less likely to wear. If the grain is vertical, the wood will tend to break up.

One area in which the plastic mallet scores over the wooden one is when used on a scaffold. If a wooden mallet gets wet, it will rarely recover.

The size, weight and material of the mallet is very much a matter of personal choice. As a rough guide, a heavy one might be 160 × 145 × 120 mm high (6¼" × 5¾" × 4¾"), weighing around 1.8 kg (4 lb). The falling weight of the mallet does most of the work, rather than it being impelled by the hand and wrist. The handle must not be too long – it is very easy to damage a stone by catching it with the end of the handle. The mallet should rest on the hand and the handle project through the fist by just enough to make it feel secure.

As the mallet rests on the hand rather than being gripped tightly by the shaft, the top of the fist can at first be rubbed raw. A circle of leather under the head of the mallet will help to reduce the friction until the hand is hardened and the mallet worn smooth.

Masons work with a slow, steady stroke for most of their work, at a rate of something like one stroke a second. Working for an hour with a 3 lb mallet is equal to lifting more than 3 tonnes, so anything that reduces the effort is welcome. The mallet is held loosely, as to grip the shaft tightly would soon tire the hand – a slightly loose, almost floppy grip is most comfortable, with the fingers exercising just enough control to make it manageable. If the arm is held with the elbow out, the strain on the muscles is unnecessarily high. The elbow must be held close to the body and the forearm swung vertically. This may feel awkward at first, but any tendency to let the elbow move out is easily checked by holding a chisel between the upper arm and the body – if the chisel falls, the arm is being held too far out.

The *hammer* (Figure 6.1c) has a variety of uses. It is used in place of the mallet for working granite, for driving the punch and the pitcher in roughing out on limestones and sandstones, for lettering, and for a good deal of carving work. Not surprisingly, hammers come in a variety of shapes and sizes.

The masons' hammer is long-headed, weighing 2–6 lb (0.9–2.7 kg) depending on the type of stone worked and the preference of the mason. A length of 150 mm and a weight of 3 lb (1.4 kg) is a good average size. The striking faces are relatively small and should be set at a very slight angle, inwards towards the shaft. The faces must be kept bright and clean. Even if in regular use, the face will pick up specks of rust from chisels, small particles of metal, and stone dust. Clean it periodically by rubbing stone dust on the banker softening and wiping clean. A dirty hammer will slip much more easily and hit the hand holding the tool. The same applies to tool heads – keep them bright.

The masons' hammer has a short shaft and is held with the hand towards the head, perhaps an inch or so below. It is usually necessary to shorten the shaft on a new hammer, which is best done by taking off the head and recutting the top so as to preserve the swell at the base of the shaft. Again, like the mallet, the hammer is held loosely with the elbow close to the body.

Lettering/carving hammers are shorter in the head, a little like small club hammers, weighing between 1 and 2 lb (0.5–1 kg). Very often, in delicate work, the chisel is struck with light taps on the side of the hammer.

The *pitching tool* (Figure 6.1d), also called a *pitcher*, is used with the hammer for removing surplus stone in large pieces. The back of the blade continues the line of the thick shaft, while the upper side tapers down to a 6 mm thick edge, about 50 mm (2″) wide. The edge is not quite square but has a slight bevel against the flat back. This angle must be kept reasonably sharp rather than being allowed to wear to a round, but sharpening should be on the thick edge rather than the back of the tool. Using the pitcher is one of the few occasions when the hammer is used with a sideways swing, as hard as possible. It tends to be more successful on hard stone – soft stone crushes a little under the edge, which softens the blow somewhat.

The *punch* (Figure 6.1e) is used for roughing-out or removing large amounts of stone comparatively quickly. The end is drawn out either to a point for working harder stones, or to a short cutting edge 3–5 mm wide, for softer stones. It is generally used with a hammer but may be mallet-headed for soft-stone work. It is usually a rather robust tool, the smaller and finer ones used for rouging out carving or other small detail being known as *points* (Figure 6.1f). The length is usually around 175–200 mm but longer ones are useful for deep sinkings. Like all tools used with the hammer or mallet, the punch is lifted from the stone between blows. The tool remains in contact with the stone while being repeatedly tapped with the hammer only for light work in awkward corners or fine detail.

Useful for splitting (coping) stone is the *nicker* (Figure 6.1g), a chisel-like tool not unlike the bricklayer's bolster but with a blade which is rather thicker, tapering to a blunt V, and a short shaft. It is held at right angles to the surface, struck hard with a heavy hammer and moved along to form a continuous line around the stone. Stones up to about 300 mm square can be split by this method to give a reasonably clean break. Sandstone flags or slabs can be cut very cleanly this way, but it is advisable first to score a line all round the stone. After going all round with the nicker (the slab should be held on edge with the cut line vertical), tapping with the hammer up the back of the slab will give a clean break.

Axes (Figure 6.1h) are still used to some extent in this country, generally on softer stones, although their use is more widespread on the continent. In the hands of an expert, they can be used for both roughing-out and for finishing. A toothed edge is commonly used in roughing-out. The *patent axe* (Figure 6.1i), with a number of interchangeable steel blades locked into a head, is used for finishing on granite and similar stones.

Chisels (Figure 6.1j) may be made entirely of steel, and known as fire-sharpened from the manner of forging and sharpening. A great many chisels of all kinds are tipped with tungsten carbide (Figure 6.1k), a powdered metal that has a great resistance to wear. They are especially useful on sandstones but are also useful in working hard limestone. They do have disadvantages: the tip has little strength and is reliant on the support of the steel into which it is set. When less than the full width of the blade is used or when there is a sideways pressure on the tip, it may crack or break off; repairs can only be made by the specialist supplier. They are also generally not capable of taking such a fine edge as a good steel chisel, which can be a disadvantage in working details. The good craftsman will have a range of both steel and tipped tools in his kit, using each as the occasion demands.

Chisels are known by the width of the blade, usually measured in eighths from ⅛"–1", thereafter in ¼" steps. Above 2", a chisel is known as a *boaster*. Many amateurs refer to 'straight' or 'plain' chisels. In the trade, the term 'chisel' means a chisel which is straight in both elevation and end view. The length of shank varies according to manufacturer and individual taste. Typically they are about 175–200 mm long, but a selection of longer ones is useful for deep sinkings and awkward detail.

Chisels of all kinds are of two basic types intended for use *either* with a mallet *or* with a hammer. The mallet-headed chisel has a narrow neck and a wide, rounded head (Figure 6.1l) designed to give a good contact with the mallet and to avoid damaging it. The head is ideally wider than the shank and has a very shallow dome. Hammer-headed chisels have a parallel shaft with a very slightly tapered end (Figure 6.1m). The smaller the cutting edge, the greater the taper, both to preserve the balance of the chisel and to give a concentrated blow, as they are often used with very light taps of a hammer or dummy.

For working the softer limestones *wood chisels* (Figure 6.1n) are often used; they keep their edge well and give a fine cut with less effort than a mason's chisel. The broad finishing chisel equivalent to the boaster is known as a *driver*. They are not used with a mallet, as the wood to wood contact produces too soft a blow. Instead a small circular hammer known as a *dummy* is used (Figure 6.1o). This may be made of iron, brass or zinc, weighing 2–4 lb (0.9–1.8 kg); 2½ lb (1.1 kg) is a reasonable weight. The dummy is also useful for very light, delicate finishing work or in awkward corners, with either hammer- or mallet-headed chisels.

For roughing-out after the punch, a *claw chisel* is used (also known as a *waster*). This is either a chisel with deep notches formed in the edge before hardening, or a *patent claw*, which is a shaft holding a replaceable toothed blade (Figure 6.1p). For softer stones four or five teeth to the inch are used, and seven or eight for hard stones and marble. The usual size of the patent claw is 1″, but both smaller and larger sizes are available. The use of a toothed blade means there is less likelihood of the stone plucking out when large amounts are being removed.

The patent claw is very convenient, as wear on a toothed chisel can be quite rapid, whereas changing the blade is quick and easy. However, the thickness of the holder can be a nuisance at times, and a claw chisel may have an advantage. Tungsten claws are available and, while usually thicker than a steel claw, are extremely useful, especially on the harder stones.

For working concave curves the *gouge* is used. Like the chisel, these tools are identified by the width, but they also vary in the radius of the curve – they may be quick or slow. The woodworking gouge (Figure 6.1n) can also be used for soft stones. For some profiles a *bullnose chisel* is preferred. This is an ordinary chisel with the edge ground to a curve (Figure 6.1q). They are particularly useful for finishing double concave surfaces.

For small undercut work, a chisel with the shank reduced in width behind the cutting edge, known as a *quirk*, is useful (Figure 6.1r). It is also used for cutting narrow grooves where the clearance is needed immediately behind the edge.

Fillet chisel is the name sometimes given to small chisels with the edge cut at an angle to make access to small detail easier (Figure 6.1s).

Curved or *bent* chisels are useful for working some awkward mouldings (Figure 6.1t). Whatever the shape or size of the blade, the shaft is bent by the requisite amount at the point where the blade runs into the shaft.

On soft stones, *saws* can be used for cutting out large parts of unwanted stone. Ordinary hand saws sold for woodworking can be used with great success, but for sandstones and some of the harder limestones, saws with tungsten-tipped teeth are much better. Tenon saws can be used to saw directly into fillets, but the handle may get in the way. A patent saw with an adjustable handle, which can be swung upwards, is preferable (Figure 6.2a).

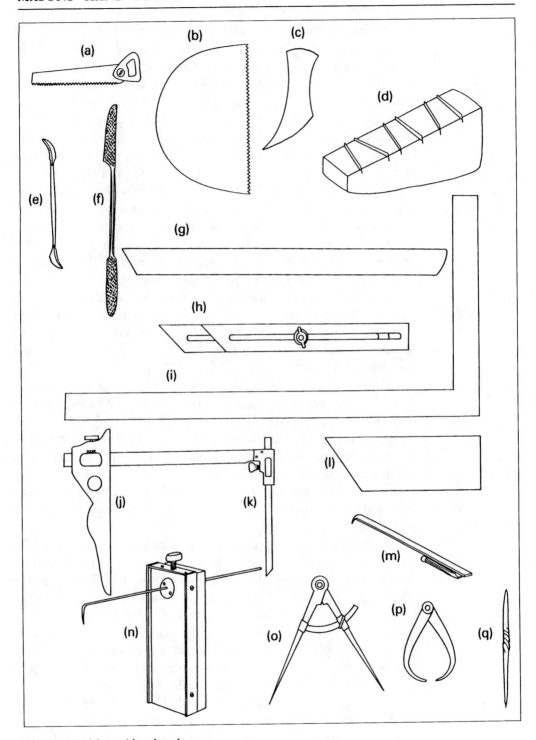

Figure 6.2 Masons' hand tools.

A variety of tools is available for finishing. It should always be remembered that working the stone is done by chisels, and the finishing tools are used for the final smoothing or cleaning only. The *drag* (Figure 6.2b) is a thin steel plate with a curved upper edge, for the comfort of the user, and teeth cut in the lower edge, which may be straight or convex. There is no set on the teeth. It is used for final finishing to remove toolmarks, where this finish is called for on soft or medium stones. The teeth are usually fine but, in some soft-stone areas, coarse drags are used for working down to a flat surface in place of the boaster. Each successive stroke of the drag should cross the previous one roughly at right angles or an undulating surface will result. The method of holding and using the drag is best taught by example. Small, thin, fine-toothed drags cut to a selection of curves are known as *cock's combs*, and are used for cleaning small details and intersections of mouldings on both hard and soft stones (Figure 6.2c).

The *French scraper* (Figure 6.2d) is also used for cleaning flat or convex surfaces on soft stone. It consists of a block of wood with saw-toothed blades set at different angles, which allow it to be pushed in straight lines along the surface. It is less versatile than the drag but cleans a flat surface very efficiently.

Similar in effect to the cock's comb is the *mitre tool* (Figure 6.2e). This is a steel bar forged to a thin plate at each end and furnished with teeth. Its length makes it useful for cleaning in awkward corners. They are not readily available from masonry suppliers but a reasonable substitute for use on soft limestone is available from modelling suppliers as a plaster working tool.

Rasps, both flat and half round, are used for cleaning small areas. *Rifflers* are small, shaped rasps on a stem, used for small and difficult parts (Figure 6.2f).

For marking out the stone during working and for checking, several special tools are used. Most important is the *straight edge* (Figure 6.2g), which may be of either wood or steel. Wood has the advantage that it is less likely to result in accidental damage to the stone but a steel one is more likely to remain true. Steel edges are usually around 25 × 1.5 mm section for short ones and up to 35 × 3 mm for long ones. Wooden ones are about 75 × 6 mm thick, tapering at the edge to 3 mm. All straight edges should be checked at intervals for accuracy. A selection of lengths is useful.

The *sliding bevel* or shiftstock (Figure 6.2h) is used for marking and checking angles of chamfers. The carpenters' bevel, in which the blade moves around a fixed point on the stock, is not really suitable, as it is often necessary to work with a short length of stock. The true sliding bevel, with a slotted stock, is not easy to obtain now and may need to manufactured specially; details are given below. They are normally of steel but brass may be used for small sizes. It is useful to have two sizes, one with a 300 mm stock and another of 150 mm.

A good *square* is a basic necessity (Figure 6.2i). They are made of steel, normally from a single piece of plate. If it can be found, one with a built-up stock (like a joiner's try-square but with the thickening in steel rather than wood) is more accurate in use but they are not commonly available. Two sizes are usually sufficient: 300 × 450 mm, and 450 × 600 mm.

The *sinking square* (Figure 6.2j) is essential to any mason's tool kit, used for checking sinkings, depths and for square. It is not to be confused with the joiner's adjustable square, which is a poor substitute. The essence of the sinking square is a narrow blade sliding in a long shallow stock. One end of the blade is bevelled at 45° for ease of use when working sinkings. Traditionally made of hard brass or gun-metal and for a long time unobtainable, they are now made in stainless steel. It is converted to a *double sinking square* (Figure 6.2k) by replacing the blade with one which has a stock for a second blade to slide parallel to the stock of the first. It is used for checking sinkings parallel to and at a distance from a datum face.

The *mitre square* (Figure 6.2l) is a length of thin steel plate about 75 × 225 mm with a 45° bevel at one end. It is sometimes used for locating the straight edge when marking mitres on mouldings with an external return. Though useful at times, it is an optional rather than essential part of the kit, as an ordinary square and a straight edge are normally used instead.

When marking out the position of sinkings, etc., on curved work, a *trammel* is needed (Figure 6.2m). It can be simply a flat bar with a scribing point turned down at one end. A chisel is held tightly underneath the trammel, so that the head presses on the curved face of the stone with the scriber in the required position on the surface, which is at right angles to the one being followed. Pulling the assembly along the stone, keeping the trammel as a radius to the curve, will mark out the line. The making of large and small trammels, which can be locked in position, is covered below. The *box trammel* (Figure 6.2n) is a variant that can be useful when marking lines which are some way below the upper surface and where the upper surface has been largely cut away, giving very little guide to the standard trammel.

A pair of steel *wing-compasses* (Figure 6.2o) is used for marking out arcs and circles, and for transferring dimensions from the templet.

A useful, if not essential, tool is a small pair of *callipers* (Figure 6.2p) for checking diameters, and the width of rolls and internal sinkings. Small, simple ones are very easily made (see 'Making and repairing of tools' below).

A small *depth gauge* is handy for checking sinkings in small details where the sinking square is too large. This can be made or purchased from an engineering tool supplier, although the accuracy of manufacture of the latter is greater than is needed. A spare blade with a projecting scriber point is very useful for marking out on small-scale blank tracery and similar work.

The most satisfactory means of scribing round the templet or marking lines from the straight edge is a purpose-made *scriber* (Figure 6.2q), which is more accurate than the corner of a chisel and causes minimum damage to the templet or the straight edge. It is easily made from an old three-cornered file, as described at the end of this chapter. Tungsten-tipped scribers can be used for scribing on harder stones.

Clearing dust and chips from the surface during working should not be done by blowing; a small, soft *hand brush* is a necessary part of the kit. A small paint brush or similar is useful for small sinkings and mouldings.

An *angle grinder* or small *disc cutter* is used increasingly for

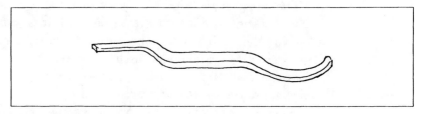

Figure 6.3 Pointing key.

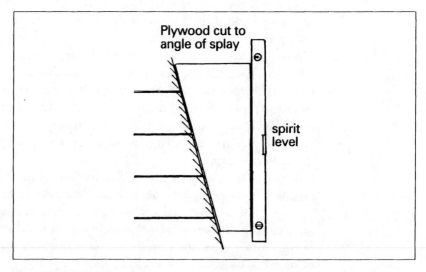

Figure 6.4 Splay board.

roughing-out. Used sensibly, they can save a great deal of time (see 'Machinery' in Chapter 7).

FIXING TOOLS

It is impossible to give a list of all the tools which may be needed by the fixer but the following will cover most eventualities. Many of the tools needed by the fixer are the same as those used on the banker, but wear and tear on tools tends to be much heavier on the scaffold and many masons prefer to keep a separate set of tools for fixing.

Trowels should be cast with blade and tang in one piece, not riveted. At least two sizes are essential: one with a 225–250 mm blade for spreading mortar, and one with a 100 mm blade for small work and for pointing (but see also below). Both bedding and pointing trowels are better with the end ground to a rounded profile on a grinding wheel. The blades should be strong enough for incidental use in lifting stones during fixing; as a guide, it should not be possible to bend the blade with the fingers. Those with a wide heel are usually the strongest. Both sides of the blade should kept spotlessly clean by washing after use. Any build up of mortar should be chipped off and the blade polished with sand.

Trowels are made with one edge hardened for brick cutting. Although cutting with a trowel is foreign to the mason, it may be useful for the left-handed mason to buy a left-handed trowel.

Pointing keys are sometimes more effective for pointing work than trowels, as the mortar can better be tamped into the back of the joint. The blade of the key must be a little narrower than the joint to be pointed, so more than one size is necessary. A suitable type is shown in Figure 6.3, with one end about 3 mm wide and the other nearer 6 mm. These keys will have to be made and, if chisel steel is used, the key should be strong enough to lift stones without bending. Plasterers' finger trowels, if strong enough, may be suitable for pointing rubble walls with wide joints.

A good-quality *spirit level* 1 m long is useful for general fixing work. A small *boat level*, about 225 mm long is often needed for smaller work and moulded stone where the long level cannot be used. When fixing splayed work, a triangle of 18 mm plywood cut to the correct angle will allow the level to be used for checking (Figure 6.4).

When fixing tall structures such as pinnacle shafts or a complete ashlar wall, the spirit level is not sufficient, and the old-fashioned *plumb-bob* comes into its own. It can be used in conjunction with a board, but this soon becomes too long and heavy to be practicable. Instead, the distance of the line from the wall can be checked at top and bottom with a fair degree of accuracy. The bob must be heavy enough to stretch the line tightly and to resist being blown by the wind. A weight of about 1 kg has been found in practice to be about right. Contrary to traditional usage, concentration of the weight of the bob at the upper end will tend to produce oscillation.

The fixer should have a selection of *heavy punches* for cutting out decayed stone. Longer ones than those used on the banker are best, and it is useful to have at least one much longer – up to 450 mm.

A *pitching tool* can be used for splitting stones as an aid to cutting-out, although a *nicker* may be better for the purpose. Both tools will be needed.

The *hammer* is the same as that used on the banker. A mallet and a selection of *chisels* will be necessary for making adjustments or rectifying faults before or after fixing. The fixer's mallet should either be of a material which can withstand getting wet, or should be old and worn enough for damage not to be of too great significance.

An ordinary *builders' line and pins* is used for fixing a run of ashlar or mouldings. A 3 m steel tape will be enough for setting-out and checking most work.

The fixer is often called on to set railings or other metalwork into stone using lead. The method is given in Chapter 10 on fixing, but to drive it solidly home a *leading iron* is essential; this is a bar of steel or brass with one end cut to a long taper.

MAKING AND REPAIRING TOOLS

The tools described below have all been made by one or both of the authors, and the sizes given are those which have been found to be useful.

In the description of materials, brass is frequently specified as it is much easier to work with than steel and will not rust. It can usually be obtained as off-cuts of thin plate from sheet metal firms, or from old-fashioned ironmongers. An even better material, which has been used by the authors for most of the thicker plate, the rod and the square sections, is manganese bronze, which can be obtained as off-cuts from glazing firms fitting high-quality leaded lights such as in church work. It is incorrodible and, while harder to saw than brass, is much more satisfactory in use; its trade name is Delta metal.

Taps for threading drilled holes are available from good tool shops at modest cost and are easy to use with a little practice. They come in three types – taper, second and plug – and are normally used in that sequence. If the second tap is started with care, the taper tap can usually be dispensed with and the plug tap is only needed when tapping a blind hole which must be threaded right to the bottom.

A tap wrench is essential; trying to turn the tap with pliers will lead to breakage.

Scriber

This is easily made from an old round or three-cornered file. Heat to a dull red and allow to cool; this will leave the metal soft. Grind one end to a point, which should have as long a taper as is consistent with strength and finish in a smooth cone, as sharp angles will damage the templet. Temper the scriber as described under 'Fire-sharpening and reforging of chisels' (see p. 139). The scriber must be harder than a chisel as the fine point will otherwise wear down quickly. A very fine point that has been made too hard will break off.

Small sliding bevel

Large sliding bevels can sometimes be found but there is no alternative to making small ones (Figure 6.5a). The stock is made from two pieces of 1 mm brass, 25 mm wide and 150 mm long. A slot wide enough to clear an M6 screw has to be drilled and filed out down the centre, starting about 9 mm from one end and 30 mm from the other. The two slots must line up closely, so it is best to clamp

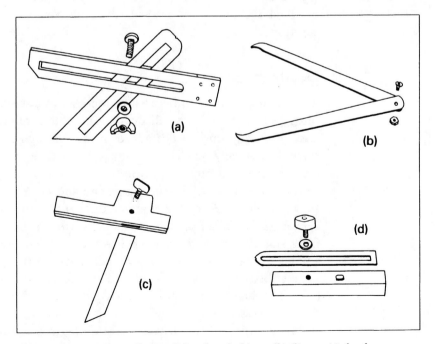

Figure 6.5 Making tools: (a) sliding bevel; (b) small calipers; (c) depth gauge; (d) small trammel.

the strips together in a vice and cut them as one. To complete the stock, another piece of 1 mm brass, the same width and about 20 mm long, is clamped between the two slotted strips at one end and four holes of 3 mm diameter drilled through the three pieces; the holes should be lightly countersunk. Rivets can be made by sawing off a section of the plain end of brass wood screws – No. 6 should be suitable, but make sure they are a fairly tight fit in the holes. Make the rivets about 2 mm longer than the thickness of the three plates, that is, about 5 mm, and by tapping lightly first at one end and then at the other they will mushroom out at the ends and expand in the middle to grip tightly. Hammer the rivets fully but without excessive force, which can stretch the plates. To be doubly sure, all three plates can be cleaned and fluxed before assembly, and solder run in after riveting.

The slide is made from 1 mm brass, 25 mm wide but only 140 mm long. At one end cut a 450 bevel and round the other end to a 12 mm radius. The slot, the width as in the stock, should stop about 9 mm from each end. The locking screw is made from a 6 mm steel coach bolt, which has the thread running right up to the square section beneath the domed head. It will be necessary to file down the square section until it closely fits the slot in the stock, that is, the same as the bolt diameter. Making the slot wide enough to fit the standard square on a coach bolt makes for undue sloppiness in the fit of the bolt and the slide. Use a standard 6 mm wing nut with plain and spring washers.

Depth gauge

The sinking square can be used for checking most sinkings but it is often useful to have a small depth gauge for confined spaces. It is possible to buy small depth gauges made for engineering work, but these are usually made to tolerances in excess of the mason's requirements and can be expensive.

Take two pieces of 2 mm brass plate and cut them to the shape shown in Figure 6.5c, with the length about 90 mm and the height 25 mm. Take one of the pieces and, down the centre of the upstand, file a slot 12 mm wide, making it as square as possible to the base, although extreme accuracy is not vital. Rivet the two plates together as described in the making of the sliding bevel. Drill and tap an M4 hole right through the plates on the centre line of the slot; this allows the locking screw to be used on either side as convenient. The clamping screw is a cheesehead brass M4 machine screw with a small piece of thin brass soldered into the slot. The blade is made from a standard hacksaw blade with the teeth ground off, and cut to the length and shape required. Reducing the width of the saw blade, but leaving a small projection on one end makes a small trammel for scribing moulding lines on small sinkings. When using this gauge to check the squareness of a sinking, it is advisable to set the blade accurately against a square unless the slot and the blade have been made with very great precision.

Small trammel

For marking out small details, a very small trammel is needed (Figure 6.5d). The base is made from a 12 mm square brass bar about 90 mm long, with the hole for an M4 locking screw at one third of the distance from the end and a locating peg in the centre. The locating peg, which keeps the the sliding part in line with the base, is made by screwing an M4 machine screw tightly into a tapped hole and filing the head to match the width of the slot. A little solder run under the head will secure it permanently. The sliding part is of 1 mm brass plate cut to match the width and length of the bar, the slot cut by drilling and filing. The slot need be long enough only to allow the slide to be pulled right back, that is about two-thirds of the length; it should be a fairly tight fit on the locating peg. The locking screw is made by soldering a wing nut to an M4 machine screw with the head cut off. A plain and a spring washer are desirable.

Large trammel

The trammel as described in the section on banker tools (p. 127) is perfectly adequate for most work, but one which can be locked to a set length can sometimes be convenient. Details are shown in the sketch (Figure 6.6). A semi-hardwood such as ramin is suitable, 15 mm square, the fixed part is about 200 mm long and the sliding part about 400 mm. The loops are made from 1 mm thick brass, 20 mm wide, secured with countersunk 6 mm No. 6 brass wood screws. They can be bent to shape over a square metal bar – the fit on the sliding part should be reasonably close but allowing free movement. The locking screw is made from an M4 machine screw with the head cut off and soldered into a wing nut. The end of the screw should be rounded to grip the wood without damage. An M4 nut is soldered onto the loop over a 6 mm clearance hole. The end of the sliding part is rebated to take a 1 mm brass plate secured with 6 mm countersunk screws. The notch in the end should be just large enough to take the tip of a scriber without any play.

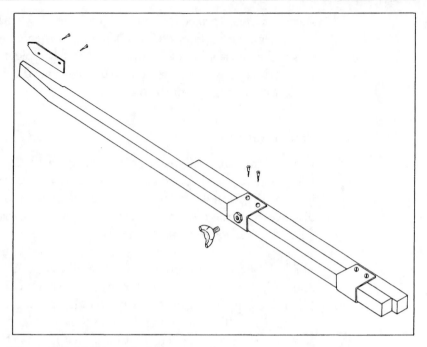

Figure 6.6 Making tools: large trammel.

Box trammel

Although not often needed, it is useful to know how to make and use one of these (Figure 6.7). In essence it is a block of hardwood about 75 × 25 × 150 mm. Near the top of one face, a hole is drilled through on the centre line to take a brass or steel trammel rod 225 mm long and 6 mm in diameter as a sliding fit. A brass plate screwed to the top is drilled through as far as this hole and the plate tapped to take an M4 locking screw made as described above.

The rod has a hole drilled through about 6 mm from one end, to take a thin steel rod, about 3 mm diameter. The rod must be well hardened and tempered as it acts as a long scriber; the length of the rod might be 150 mm. It is held by an M3 locking screw in a hole drilled and tapped into the end of the trammel rod.

Brass plates screwed to the sides of the block and projecting perhaps 3 mm will make it much easier to follow a convex surface when marking out curved work. A further refinement is to have the trammel rod passing through brass plates sunk into each face of the block, which makes it easier to have the rod sliding smoothly but without play.

Dummy

Iron or gun-metal dummies can be bought without much difficulty,

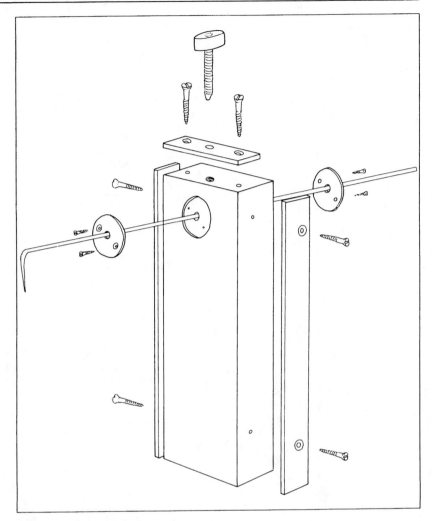

Figure 6.7 Making tools: box trammel.

but for occasional use and for use with wood chisels, a lead dummy is very easily made. Take a small glass jar – an ordinary jam jar will do, but a small pickle or coffee jar is better – and wrap it tightly with adhesive tape. Put a length of broomstick into the jar and wire it to the neck to prevent movement both sideways and upwards, as it will try to float on the liquid lead; it should project about 100 mm from the jar. Fill a bucket with *dry* sand and bury the jar up to the rim. This is essential as it will crack when filled with lead, and the steam from wet sand will cause lead to spit everywhere.

Melt sufficient scrap lead in a lead ladle. Note: the fumes from lead can be dangerous to health and the melting must take place outside on a dry day. A helmet with a plastic visor is essential and leather gloves are recommended. Adding about 25 per cent of scrap zinc (*not* templets) is advisable as it gives a harder dummy. The two metals do

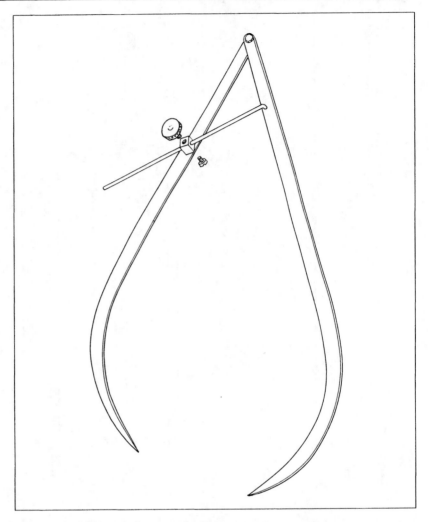

Figure 6.8 Making tools: external calipers.

not readily combine, but stirring immediately before pouring gives a usable mixture. Pour the lead/zinc into the jar, keeping well back while doing so, until it is full to the narrowing at the neck. The lead will set almost immediately. As soon as it has done so, pick up the casting by the handle with a gloved hand, jar and all, and drop it onto a wet cloth. Lay another wet cloth over it and splash water on from a safe distance. This will create a certain amount of steam but is safer than dropping it into a bucket of water. Rapid cooling is necessary to prevent the handle from burning and coming loose. Alternatively, it can be allowed to cool slowly and the burned handle later knocked out and replaced, but this is rarely satisfactory. Knock away the glass, trim any rough parts from the dummy and cut the handle to a suitable length. Owing to the inward curve at the base of jam jars it may be best to saw off the upper part. The lower part, uppermost when casting, may need sawing or rasping away to give a reasonable surface to rest on the hand. If constant use wears away or stretches the lead to the point where it is unusable, simply melt down and recast.

Callipers

Small callipers

These are easily made from old hacksaw blades. Cut a standard size hacksaw blade in two with a grinding wheel and grind off the teeth. Make the two pieces identical in length and grind the cut end of each to the form shown in the sketch (Figure 6.5b). An M4 machine screw run up tight and sawn off almost flush with the nut makes the hinge. Hammer the end of the screw lightly to prevent it unscrewing. Such callipers will measure internally up to about 200 mm and externally to about 75 mm.

Large callipers

Above this size, steel bar is needed, preferably no less than 3 mm × 12 mm. A thicker section is better for external callipers where the legs have to be forged to a curve. The larger sizes should preferably have a lockable stay to keep them in the set position. This can be made from a length of 3 or 4 mm welding rod, turned through a hole in one leg and peened over. The other end runs through a small brass block held to the leg with a brass screw set so that the block is firmly held but free to turn. A little solder run into the screw threads will hold it in position. The locking screw is made from a cut-down M4 screw with a wing nut soldered to it. If the block is set further from the hinge than the fixed end of the rod, the stay can be left straight without stiffness in use. Even without excessive forging, which can be difficult for the mason turned smith, the home-made 375 mm long callipers shown in Figure 6.8 will measure 450 mm externally. The stay is 175 mm long set about 80 mm from the hinge, with the locking block 125 mm from the hinge on the other leg. The hinge is the usual M4 brass machine screw peened over the nut.

The internal callipers shown in Figure 6.9 are 450 mm in length and will measure up to 750 mm. The method of manufacture is similar.

Sharpening chisels

Steel chisels

Plain steel chisels, known as fire-sharpened, will retain a sharp edge

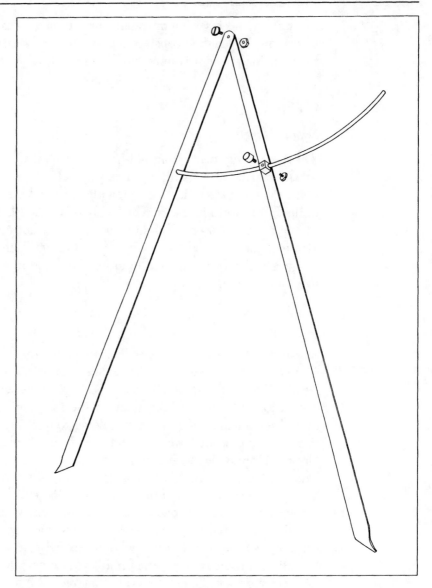

Figure 6.9 Making tools: internal calipers.

if rubbed up occasionally on a sharpening stone; a piece of fine-grained York stone about 150 × 75 mm is ideal. The stone should always be wetted first. If the chisel has become very dull, it should be sharpened by rubbing along the length of the stone with the edge at right angles to the movement; press fairly hard with the cutting edge just in contact with the stone. This grinds away a little of the steel immediately behind the edge to maintain a good cutting angle. Both sides of the chisel must be sharpened equally.

For a light sharpening, rub the chisel with the edge parallel to the movement, in a shallow figure of eight, concentrating on the edge. A few sweeps on each side of the blade will be sufficient.

A grinding wheel can be used if the blade seems very dull, but care must be taken not to grind away the hardened cutting edge. Always use a black carborundum wheel and keep the tool wet to prevent heat build up, which will destroy the temper. Sharpening on a green silicon carbide wheel will clog the wheel.

Tungsten-tipped chisels

These chisels can be sharpened only on a grinding wheel, which must be the green silicon carbide type, and must never be cooled either during or after sharpening or the tungsten will crack. Sharpen evenly and do not undercut or the tip will be weakened. When the cutting edge is in contact with the wheel, a line of yellow light will appear. If it is necessary to grind back the steel shank, do this on a black wheel.

Use and care of grinding wheels

Grinding wheels must be kept clean and true with the use of a wheel-dresser, which has a row of hardened steel discs which cut away the surface of the wheel to give a clean, flat surface. This, and the changing of wheels, must be done only by someone trained and approved for these tasks.

Always wear goggles when using a grinding wheel, and use only the edge of the wheel and never the side, unless the wheel is specifically designed for that purpose.

Fire-sharpening and reforging of chisels

The technique of sharpening chisels in the fire is based on simple principles but only experience will produce a usable chisel. A coke fire is needed, either in a purpose-made portable forge or, if the masons' shop has one, an ordinary fireplace. The essential element is a blast of air to raise the temperature of the fire. This can be provided by bellows or by connecting a length of steel pipe to the works' compressed-air supply. The fire must not be too hot – the coke should be glowing red but with a touch of blackness on the top. A white-hot fire will produce interesting but damaging results. An anvil is also necessary.

When the fire is at the right heat, push the chisel into the coke for about half its length; do not put it too close to the air supply. Inspect it at intervals and, when a good red colour is achieved (by the end in the fire and not over the whole length), hold it firmly on the anvil and draw out the end to the required form. As soon as the chisel begins to lose the red heat, replace in the fire and begin again. Never work steel which is too cold or cracks will result.

Once the shape is as desired, subject to grinding, lay the chisel aside to cool in the air. This leaves the metal in a soft, or annealed, state. The owner's banker mark is most easily put on at this point, using an old but sharp chisel.

When cool, use the black grinding wheel to finish the cutting edge to the precise form required. Being soft and malleable the chisel must be hardened and tempered before use.

Replace in the fire and heat as before until it barely reaches a dull red. It is particularly important at this stage not to overheat, or the result will be a 'sparkler', the newly formed edge giving off bright sparks as it burns away. Remove from the fire and quench the end 25 mm or so in cold water. Withdraw immediately and polish the end with emery paper to a bright finish – remember that the chisel is still very hot. Heat from the unquenched part of the chisel will travel down to the tip, changing the colour as it does so, from bright to straw, to pale blue, to deep blue. The colour gives an indication of the final hardness of the tip, which increases as the colour deepens. Only experience will show what is best for the stone being worked, but a mid to deep blue is a fair average hardness. At this point, quench the tip in about 10 mm of water and leave the chisel standing upright in the water. This 'fixes' the hardness of the tip, while allowing the rest of the chisel to cool slowly.

It is best to practise the technique on old chisels which will not be missed if damaged beyond repair. 'Sparklers' are not uncommon at first, and too hard a tip will result in breakage at the first use; too soft a tip will bend.

Making new chisels and other steel tools

This is very much the same as sharpening, except that making from new calls for the acquisition of appropriate steel. The all-important factor is the carbon content, which affects the hardness which can be achieved – too much carbon is as bad as too little as the strength is reduced. Chisels may have between 0.7 and 1 per cent carbon, or perhaps a little more. As a very rough guide wrought iron has about 0.05 per cent, mild steel (steel plate, much constructional steel) has around 0.2–0.3 per cent, railway lines 0.55 per cent, files about 1.2 per cent and cast iron upwards of 2.5 per cent. Files, if large enough, can be used to make chisels but reinforcing rod cannot.

Steel can be bought as hexagon bar from merchants and, so long as it is chosen with care, can be very satisfactory. Almost any mild steel can be used for making items such as callipers.

Drags and cock's combs

These may be made from old saws, but they may well need annealing before they can be cut to shape, even with a angle grinder. If existing teeth are to be used, the set should be removed while in the annealed state. Harden before use by heating to blue heat and quenching.

Checking and adjusting the spirit level

Modern levels are very reliable but they should still be checked at intervals. The most reliable way to do this is to drive two nails into a solidly fixed timber – a stout shelf will do – so that the ends of the level just rest on them. Adjust them until they appear perfectly level, and reverse the level. If the same reading is obtained, the level is true, if not, it must be adjusted. Repeat for the other edge of the level.

To check for plumb, use two nails in a vertical surface and set them accurately with a plumb-bob. Check both edges and both ends of the level.

Some levels have screws to provide for adjustment, while others can only be reset by returning them to the manufacturer. Some boat levels have the vials set in plaster, which can be dug out with a sharp point and the vials rebedded in plaster of Paris.

When using the level, it is always good practice to try it both ways.

Maintenance of wooden mallets

The mallet should always be kept dry, as dampness will soften the wood. A little linseed oil rubbed in occasionally will help to keep the body of the mallet free from cracks but it should be kept off the beat. Some masons favour standing the mallet upside down in 5 mm of linseed for a few days but it is uncertain how beneficial this practice is; it may be of value when a mallet has been kept in a very warm, dry atmosphere for a long period without use.

If a mallet is found to be too light, the weight can be increased by loading with lead. Drill a 25 mm diameter hole midway between the handle and the beat at each end of the mallet, and perhaps 25 mm deep. Be very careful to avoid coming too close to the beat, which will wear down over time. Pour in molten lead to the top of the hole, cooling it rapidly with a wet rag. Keep the water off the beat.

General maintenance of tools

Keep all tools clean, sharp and ready for use. At all times keep hammer and chisel heads clean and bright to reduce the risk of the hammer slipping. Hammer heads must be kept tight on the shaft for safety; use proper steel hammer wedges. In dry weather the head may still feel loose. Stand the hammer with the head in 10 mm of water overnight and the problem should disappear, but remember to clean any rust off the face before use.

7

The Banker Shop, Lifting Tackle and Machinery

THE BANKER SHOP

The banker and general arrangements

The banker, on which the stone is worked, is traditionally a large block of stone. It should be as heavy as possible, the better to resist any tendency to move as the stone is worked. Also, a large, heavy banker is less likely to move when heavy stones are being turned over – a block 900 × 600 × 300 mm is a size which will allow for the working of almost any size of stone. It should be supported on low, wide piers of either stone or concrete blocks placed at the ends and running the full width of the banker. When large stones are being moved or turned, they may have to rest on or against the edge of the banker, which must show no tendency to move or tilt. The supports should be stable without the use of mortar, as it is useful to be able to vary the height of the banker occasionally to cope with very large or very small stones. This should not often be necessary and, for general work, the height of the banker is generally best if a little below hip level. When large stones are being worked, it is useful to have a variety of small wooden platforms (known as boxes) for the mason to stand on. Working stone which is set too high can be very tiring. The floor, of course, must be strong enough to support the banker, weighing up to half a tonne, and the stone being worked, perhaps another half tonne.

Smaller and lighter bankers can be used for smaller work. Carvers often use a wooden banker, with a top about 600 mm square, which allows for a holding screw to pass through a slot in the top. Wooden bankers must be solidly made with screws not nails and, if the legs are splayed a little, stability is improved.

Steel plate bankers on an adjustable column are available as imports and can be useful where the stones worked range from very small to very large.

Stone is very easily damaged by pressure on the arrises and, for this reason, the banker must be covered with a layer of *softening*. A piece of old carpet (preferably woven rather than foam-backed) is one of the best materials for the purpose. It is hard wearing but resilient enough to protect the stone without allowing it to rock. Before the stone is put on the banker, the softening must be checked to make sure that no small pieces of stone, which will damage the stone or make it unstable, are either on or under it.

A shelf close at hand is very useful for storing tools which are not immediately in use; they are better not left on the banker alongside the stone. For one thing, there may not be room and they may also be overlooked when turning the stone, with the consequent risk of damage. Vibration of the banker may also cause tools to work their way off the banker onto the floor. The shelf must not be used to store templets, which must *always* be hung on a nail in the wall when not in use. Templets lying around on shelves or tool boxes, or on the banker being covered with stone chips, are a sign of a sloppy workshop.

This is not to suggest that masons' shops can ever be tidy and presentable. Stone dust hangs in the air, spalls and dust cover the floor, shelves, tools and masons, and every corner is likely to be full of boxes, wedges, blocks of stone for adjusting the height of bankers, and other potentially useful items. It is not uncommon for the mason to be standing on several inches of spalls. A spotless workshop is one where no serious work is being done, but some points must be attended to. The floor around the banker should be swept at least once a day for comfort as well as safety, templets should always be hung out of harm's way, and all tools and lifting tackle stored on a shelf or hook.

Lighting

Lighting is of prime importance. Fluorescent lighting is cheap but totally unsuitable for working stone. Overhead shadowless lighting is inappropriate for this work. Daylight is best, coming in through large north-facing windows but this is rarely easy to achieve. Skylights are little better than fluorescent lights. A combination of daylight, from any direction but overhead, and ordinary tungsten light is the best compromise. The light fittings must not be immediately over the banker and each one should be independently switched and preferably adjustable for position.

Dust

Masons generally feel that limestone dust is no more than a nuisance, while sandstone dust is highly dangerous. The latter view is quite true: deadly lung diseases such as silicosis used to be common among sandstone masons and are still a serious risk. Limestone dust can be merely a nuisance but most limestones contain some silica, which is released during working, and this can have an effect on the mason's health. Unless working in the open air, some form of dust extraction is now a legal requirement. Even with extractors in operation, it is still advisable to wear masks (see Chapter 2 on health and safety).

Pneumatic equipment

The use of hand-held compressed-air hammers is widespread, and provision for their use should be made at every banker by means of a quick release socket. Air is supplied from a compressor to a filter and delivered to the hammer through a flexible hose. The most convenient position for the filter and supply point is on the wall at the back or side of the banker. The size (output) of the compressor will depend on the number of tools likely to be in use. An on/off valve, which is adjustable for air flow, should be incorporated in the flexible line at a point which is convenient to hand but not so close to the hammer as to risk contact with the stone as the hose trails over it.

The compressor should preferably be sited outside the workshop to minimize noise levels, which will already be high from the use of the hammers.

Movement of stone

In all but the largest workshops, the simplest and safest means is with a four-wheeled, pneumatic-tyred trolley, capable of carrying at least half a tonne, with the wheels as near to the corners as possible to reduce the risk of tipping. A rectangular rather than a T-handle, attached to the steerable front axle, most easily allows for two people to pull it when fully loaded. For safety, the wheels should be as near to the corners of the trolly as possible, as an overhang of the platform increases the risk of the loaded trolley tipping. The platform should be of softwood which stands a little proud of the steel frame. Both sawn stone and worked stone should have softening underneath it. Always make sure that whatever surface the stone is being placed on is swept clean of all stone chippings.

LIFTING TACKLE

Owing to its weight and unyielding nature, all movement of stone is potentially dangerous to the fingers and toes of the mason. Hoisting stone on a tackle is doubly dangerous. Observing a few simple rules will greatly reduce the risks. Never use any lifting tackle that is not clearly marked with its safe working load (SWL). Always check that the SWL of the tackle is more than the calculated weight of the load. Never use tackle that is damaged in any way or otherwise suspect. Never stand beneath a stone when in the air, and remember that a falling stone may be deflected or roll sideways on landing. Keep well clear. A stone falling from a height of 2 m will hit the ground in ⅕th of a second – there is no time to run. The authors were present when a 5 tonne block slipped from 3 tonne dogs while being unloaded from a lorry. There was no perceptible interval – one moment it was in the air, the next on the ground. This sort of thing should not happen but it can if everyone involved is not always alert.

Where stones of any size are being worked, lifting tackle is essential for transferring the stone from trolley to banker. A simple *chain hoist*, manually operated, with a capacity of half a tonne is sufficient for most purposes. Ideally the hoist should run on a steel beam, with a hand-operated chain traverse gear for moving it along the beam on its trolley. The push–pull type of trolley is adequate, but considerable effort is needed to move large stones and this can set the stone swinging on the hoist. All parts of the lifting tackle *must* be installed and checked by a specialist contractor who is competent to issue the necessary safety certificate.

Attachment to the hoist

Dogs

There are several ways in which the stone may be attached to a hoist. The simplest way, often employed for bringing stones into the shop, is to use *chain dogs* (Figure 7.1). A shallow cone-shaped hole is cut in each end of the stone with a punch. The hole may perhaps be 10 mm deep for smaller stones and correspondingly deeper for large stones. The dogs are hooks with a ring in one end, through which a chain is passed; the two ends of the chain are put onto the lifting hook and the lifting action causes the hooks to bite into the stone as the stone rises.

The angle of lifting chains

The length of the chain is important. The angle at the top of the

Figure 7.1 Chain dogs.

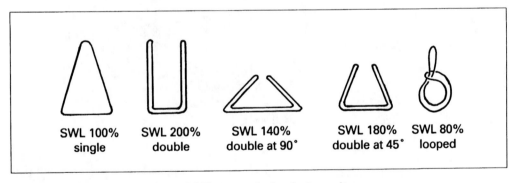

Figure 7.2 The effect on SWL of different methods of using a sling.

triangle formed by the chain should be as near 45° as possible; as a steeper angle reduces the bite of the dogs, and a wider angle will reduce the safe capacity of the tackle. The effect on the SWL of chains and slings resulting from altering their angles is shown in Figure 7.2.

If the chain is too short or too long, it must not be joined to another or shortened, but replaced with one of the right length and appropriate SWL. The yard should carry several chains of each weight in different lengths. The capacity of the dogs must be clearly

Figure 7.3 Three-legged lewis.

stamped on each one, they must be used only in their certified pairs, and the chain should also be independently tested and marked.

Lewises

Dogs are very quick and convenient to use, but are not appropriate for stones worked on more than one face. They are of little use in fixing, as they make it impossible to butt the stone up to its neighbour.

The alternative is the *lewis*. The three-legged version, in use in one form or another for 2000–3000 years, is still occasionally encountered and the principles of its use should be understood (Figure 7.3). The device consists of three steel bars drilled at the top to take a pin. The middle leg is parallel and the outer legs are each tapered on one edge. The rectangular slot to receive them must be undercut at each end to allow the lewis to grip at the bottom and *not* at the top, which would cause bursting of the stone. The lewis hole must be deep enough to take the full depth of the lewis to just below the pin, and no wider than is necessary. When the two outer legs are dropped in and the centre leg pushed between them the lewis should be a tight fit. Packing pieces may, if necessary, be pushed between the legs to achieve this fit, but they must *only* be of steel strip as wide as the legs and long enough to reach the full height. When the pin and shackle are connected, the lifting tackle may be hooked on. Although the cutting of the lewis hole takes time and care, used with a properly cut hole the three-legged lewis provides a very secure attachment for even very heavy stones.

The *two-legged lewis* may occasionally be found in a corner of the masons' shop. This has one tapered leg and one parallel. As the grip is on only one side of the hole, it is not a particularly secure means of attachment except for very light stones and is best not used at all, but consigned to a museum.

In almost universal use today is the *split-pin lewis* (Figure 7.4), which requires only the drilling of a hole of appropriate diameter, usually 25 mm for a half tonne lift. The lewis is simply dropped in and hooked onto the tackle. The curved arms provide a scissor action, which relies on the friction between the lewis and the stone. For this reason it is best to clean as much dust as possible from the sides of the hole. It is a generally safe method of attachment but, especially when handling stones of light weight, it is *essential* that manoeuvring of the stone is not carried out by gripping the arms of the lewis, which can cause the bite of the lewis to be reduced, allowing the stone to fall. This is not just a theoretical possibility – it has been seen in practice.

An electric or pneumatic drill is required for lewising; it must be capable of drilling a 25 mm diameter hole with reasonable ease. In soft stone a solid drill bit can be used but for harder stones a core drill may be preferable.

The *chain* or *C-lewis* is sometimes used. It consists of two curved steel bars connected by links to a single ring, and used in a hole which is similar to that used for the three-legged lewis but with less undercut. When the lift is applied, the flat backs of the C-bars are pressed together, forcing the lower ends to bite into the bottom of the hole. Again, the width should be just sufficient to take the lewis without giving room for it to rock sideways. It is less reliable than the three-legged lewis. Both this and the split-pin lewis depend on the curved portion of the bars having the strength to resist straightening under load.

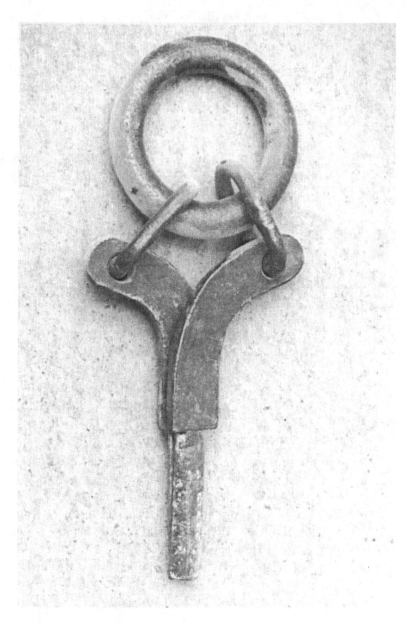

Figure 7.4 Split-pin lewis.

The *two-pin lewis* has two separate pins, each with a loose ring in the top through which a chain is passed. The pins are dropped into drilled holes towards the ends of the stone; the horizontal pull on the connecting chain causes the pins to bite against the sides of the holes. It is more suitable for use in the harder stones and granites which are better able to resist the bite, which comes at the top of the hole.

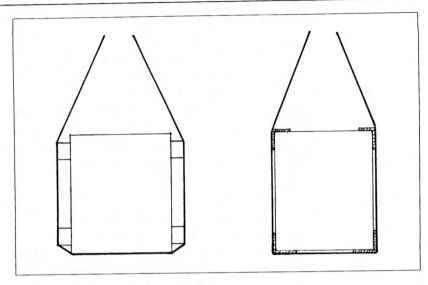

Figure 7.5 Ways of slinging worked stone.

Moving stone in the yard

It is convenient here to consider the movement of stone around the yard between the various machines. Large rough blocks may be lifted with chain dogs of a suitably large size, otherwise similar to the dogs used for moving small blocks. Chain or webbing *slings* and *strops* may also be used for moving large blocks. Chain slings will damage sawn edges, which must be protected by wood blocks to keep the chain away from the corners. The use of chains is best confined to rough blocks, as accidental damage is easily caused. Webbing slings are kinder to the stone, but it is still advisable to protect sawn arrises (Figure 7.5). They are also much lighter and therefore easier to use. Stone, especially when rough, can cause damage to the sling and protective sleeves should be used whenever damage is likely. Slings require that the stone is stacked on skids (short lengths of timber) with sufficient room to pass the sling beneath the stone.

Slings of any kind must never be shortened by tying knots; a range of lengths for each SWL should be carried. Chain slings may be shortened only by the use of purpose-made shortening clutches and by no other means. The alterations in the SWL produced by the way the sling or strop is used have already been mentioned (Figure 7.2). These illustrations and the effect on SWL should be memorized.

The weight of stone

It is important to be able to make a quick calculation of the weight of a stone before lifting. Most stone masons in Britain and France still use the Imperial cubic foot, or its metric near equivalent of a

300 mm cube, and known as a cube. Most limestone and sandstone can be reckoned to weigh 150 lb per cubic foot (70 kg per 300 mm cube, which is easier for mental calculation than the more accurate 68 kg). Measure the breadth, width and height of the stone, rounded *upwards* to the nearest quarter or half foot, and multiply them together. Multiply the answer by 150 or 70 as appropriate to give a rough estimate of the weight. With practice this is very quick, and will tend to overestimate the weight. On average, stone weighs less than 150 lb/70 kg per cube, and rounding up the measurements gives an additional safety factor.

It is useful to remember, on the same basis as the above calculations, that there are about 14 cubes to the ton (14/tonne). A metric tonne is 98 per cent of an Imperial ton.

Common sense is required. If the stone is known to weigh over 150 lb (70 kg) per cube foot and no rounding up of measurements was necessary, then the calculation has to be carried out more carefully than if the stone is known to be under 150 lb (70 kg) and all the measurements had been rounded up. Likewise if the rough, rounded up calculation showed that the stone was just too heavy for the available tackle, it would be sensible to calculate carefully before holding up the work and going to the expense of getting larger tackle.

MACHINERY

This book deals primarily with the traditional craft of the mason – the disciplined skill of shaping stone with mallet and chisel which everyone entering the craft must learn to do well. However, we have to combine the ancient craft of the stone mason with the view that 'time is money'. To work only by hand nowadays would mean either masons being poorly paid for their time, or having a generous sponsor to subsidize the work. Power tools have to be used if one is to compete for work. However, they should be used in such a way that the resulting work is acceptable in its context.

It is the poor appearance of some finished stone on restoration work, often produced not only without chisels but also without skilled stone masons, which supports that part of the conservation lobby which argues that stone should always be repaired and conserved rather than be replaced.

Machines have their place and, if used efficiently and with care, are of great benefit in making stonework viable. Over-use, however, can not only damage the reputation of some stone masons but of the industry as a whole.

The following generalized descriptions give an idea of the capabilities of the machines in use.

Figure 7.6 Primary saw.

Figure 7.7 Profile saw.

The primary saw

A rough, quarried block of stone once had to be split into suitably sized smaller blocks using plug and feathers, and squared-up by hand. The primary saw, usually a large circular saw with a diamond-tipped blade, now slabs the block into the required range of bed heights, and either the same saw or a smaller one converts the slabs into blocks of the right dimensions for working, sawn six sides and squared (at least in theory) ready for the mason to apply his templet. Most quarries and large masonry works have primary saws, which will cut to a depth of at least 30" (760 mm) (Figure 7.6). Frame saws, often with multiple blades, are also much used for converting block stone to slabs.

Profile saws

Perhaps the greatest advance in the masonry trade in recent years has been the development of the profiling saw. Automated systems can produce repetitive work by making numerous cuts under the control of a sensor, which follows the profile of a templet (Figures 7.7 and 7.8). These cuts can be so closely spaced as to approximate to the finished surface, or set wider just to remove the major part of the excess stone in advance of hand working.

The more modern profile saws can also take information in digitized form from computerized setting-out, either directly or by using an intermediate floppy disc (see 'Computer-aided design' in Chapter 5). Profile saws can also be configured as lathes for turning columns and balusters (Figure 7.9), and can turn out relatively straightforward circular-circular work.

In restoration work, stones produced on a profile saw should be finished by hand working to match the existing; this should never be a matter of merely running lightly over the faces with a pneumatic chisel, but involve removal of the sawn surface to a depth of at least 3 mm (⅛"). Machine-finished work, especially when rubbed, gives a totally dead appearance, which is particularly evident when put into a mediaeval building. The whole charm and character can be completely lost by the use of such unsuitable and unsubtle practices.

Pneumatic tools

Perhaps the most prolific mechanized masonry tools are pneumatic-powered chisels (see Figure 8.3). These have been of great benefit to the industry. However, overuse of these tools, especially with too much power and poorly sharpened tools, can lead to damage of the underlying stone. In the long-term, this does not appear to be too

Figure 7.8 Profile saw.

Figure 7.9 Profile saw configured for lathe operation.

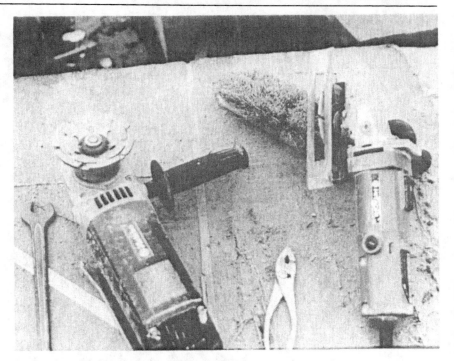

Figure 7.10 Angle grinders with depth gauge and milling head.

Figure 7.11 Cutting a drip groove with an angle grinder.

serious, although some early loss of faces can result (see 'The weathering and decay of stone' in Chapter 3).

Damage can also be caused to hearing, and shrinkage of blood vessels in the hands caused by the vibration can lead to the condition colloquially known as 'white finger' (see also Chapter 2 on health and safety at work).

As with other machines, pneumatics should be used in conjunction with other tools and not by themselves. There is both the room and the need for every type of mechanical aid to working stone, but they should be used with discrimination.

Angle grinders

Angle grinders, with their various blades, are now widely used as an aid to working stone. Within the industry, there is a lobby of traditionalists and idealists who shun the use of these tools but this view is unrealistic. Most small businesses have to use them to compete in the market. They are noisy, dirty and, above all, dangerous, and most masons would much prefer to use mallet and chisel the whole time. However, they have their place in the industry (see Figures 7.10 and 7.11).

Used with care, a skilled mason can remove almost all the waste stone with an angle grinder or even complete the stone, but the same arguments apply as to other machinery: that is, finished work for restoration must be sympathetic to the original work around it and should be fully finished off by hand.

8

Working Stone

In 1926 Warland suggested that the working of stone by hand was, for all except the more complex shapes, to a large extent superseded by machinery. Today, with the ever-increasing use of computer-controlled saws and profilers, the same is still being said, but the skilled banker masons remain the essential heart of the trade. For restoration work they very often have no substitute. Hand working is also an essential training in the understanding of stone.

Nowadays stone is almost invariably presented to the mason sawn six sides with each face at right angles to the others. Even so, variations do occur because saws do not always cut accurately and the stone may have to be squared up by the mason. Also, working stone from the rough block may sometimes be necessary when working on isolated sites. The ability to do this is essential for the skilled mason, and the discipline involved is the basis for all other working of stone.

All the steps described should be carried out as accurately as possible. To the uninitiated, it seems impossible to work stone accurately using only a mallet and chisel but the ability to do so is one of the hallmarks of the skilled mason. To work a draft 'straight' means just that: if daylight shows anywhere under the straight edge, the draft is not straight. This is not a matter of accuracy for the sake of it – many drafts are cut as the basis of further work, and if they are not straight the whole job will soon become a nightmare of planes and angles which cannot be related to the end result. The only way out will be to recut every draft – if there is enough stone left on the block to do so. An inaccuracy of 1 mm in 300 mm can be regarded as excessive.

It is not just a matter of further working. A moulding which is round can be tediously difficult to fix, and whether round or hollow, there is nothing worse than a run of moulding in which the stones cannot be made to form a straight line. By the same token, 'square' means square. If the joints and beds are not square to the face, then

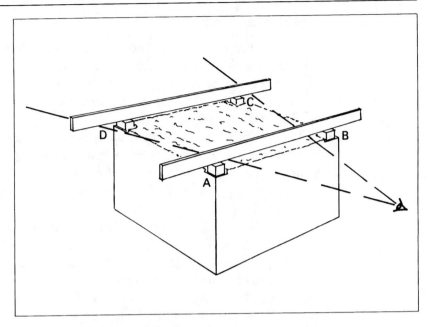

Figure 8.1 The use of boning blocks.

either the weight all falls on the front edge, which causes damage, or the joints cannot be closed up to the specified width and the job is spoiled. Quoins in which the adjoining faces are not square can be quite impossible to fix with any degree of success, whether moulded or not. There is no excuse for these faults; they are caused by lack of care or skill on the part of the banker mason.

Remember that the masons' craft cannot be learned from a book. This chapter presents an introductory explanation of basic techniques for those new to the trade. Practical guidance, tuition and example from a skilled mason are essential, accompanied by many hours of practice. Two or three years of constant banker work, 8 hours a day, 5 days a week, will make a person with some aptitude into a fair mason. Five or six years will make the mason reasonably good and in a position to take in the greater intricacies of the trade.

Tool sizes are given in Imperial measure, as most tools are still sold under that system and the sizes have become traditional names.

WORKING A PLANE SURFACE

For this, it will be assumed that the operation begins on a rough block.

Boning the drafts

First, identify two opposite sides of the block that are reasonably parallel; one side will have the first face worked on it and the other is for the stone to rest on. It is much easier to work if the face is horizontal and it is essential that the stone does not move while being worked. Use wedges to stabilize it.

At each end of one side of the upper surface (A and B, Figure 8.1), using a mallet and a ½" or 1" chisel, cut in a sinking to a depth which is below the lowest part of the surface. At the third corner (C), cut another sinking, which, by eye, is approximately on a level with the first two.

Put boning blocks on the sinkings, and rest a straight edge on A and B. A second straight edge on block C is sighted through from the first and adjusted until the two are parallel. This gives the height at which the boning block at D must be. Work the sinking at D, and check with the straight edges until the four blocks are in the same plane. This method of producing a plane surface is known as 'boning'. Always sight along the bottom of the straight edges to allow for them not being parallel.

The sinkings give the level of the marginal drafts, which define the plane surface. Join the sinkings, as well as can be with a pencil line on the rough surface of the block, and work the drafts through in turn, beginning with AB.

Take a hammer and pitcher, and remove the surplus stone above the line. Set the edge of the pitching tool about 2 mm above the line, with the shaft held just below the horizontal. Cut in along the length with a ½" chisel (Figure 8.2), finishing the draft with a 1" chisel. The width of the draft should be as near the horizontal as can be judged by eye and must be straight.

Next, work the draft CD and bone through with the straight edges again, adjusting as necessary. Then join the first two drafts with AD and BC, so that all the drafts are in the same plane. This point must again be checked with the straight edges before any further work is done and adjusted as necessary.

When working softer stones, or very short drafts, the boning blocks can be dispensed with, and the drafts cut straight in but following the same sequence: A–B, B–C, C–D, D–A.

Working the surface

To remove the stone in the centre of the face, the punch and the claw are used in succession. The punch should not be used at random, but in a series of rough drafts, working down to within about 3 mm of the surface and leaving no more than about 5–6 mm standing

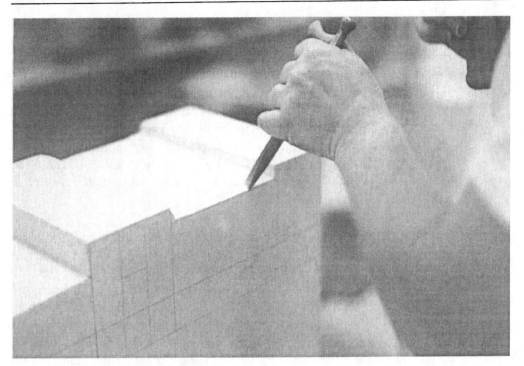

Figure 8.2 Cutting down to the line.

proud; the exact amount will depend on the particular type of stone and on experience. As far as possible, the punch should not be driven into solid stone but across the bulk so as to remove the surplus with the least effort. Driving into the solid will take more effort, remove less at each blow, and increase the risk of the stone 'plucking' or going below the surface.

The surface is further reduced with the claw, used with the mallet in regular drafts across the stone, leaving perhaps 2 mm above the finished surface. Each draft should be checked with the straight edge to ensure that it is reasonably straight from end to end and is not rising towards the centre. Each draft is used as a guide for working the next one, and should be reworked if needed before continuing.

The next stage will depend on the nature of the stone. Softer stones can be finished directly with the boaster, working in a series of drafts over the whole surface of the stone. This time, the drafts must be worked accurately and each one checked and made straight before going on to the next. Each draft acts as a guide for the next, which should overlap slightly. For the harder stones, it may be necessary to follow the claw with a 1″ chisel, working in drafts that are only just above the finished surface before finishing with the boaster. Pneumatic tools are particularly useful for cleaning large surfaces as seen in Figure 8.3.

After the surface has been cleaned with the boaster, it must be checked by using the straight edge diagonally from corner to corner. If the stone is either hollow or round it must be taken 'out of twist' by reworking the marginal drafts until a true plane is obtained.

The stone is then turned so that the worked face forms the vertical front of the block. Drafts are cut along the right- and left-hand edges of the new upper surface of the block, from front to back and square to the first face. These are joined by two further drafts and the second face worked. If this operation is repeated very accurately on all six sides, a perfect cube should be the result. In practice, there is rarely need to do any work on the back of the stone, which may be left rough.

USING TEMPLETS

Assuming that the stone has come to the mason sawn six sides, the first step is to check it with a square. Almost certainly it will not be completely accurate, and, where the shape of the stone allows any choice, the side selected for the face is the one most nearly square to the beds and joints. If the stone is to be worked on more than one face, these faces must be square to each other. If the stone is so far out as to make this impossible, it must be squared up before work begins.

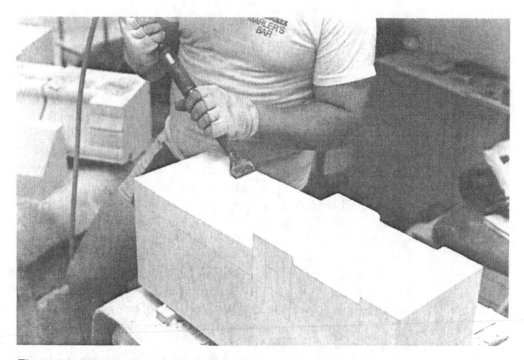

Figure 8.3 Using a pneumatic-powered boaster.

If there is a bed mould, set this in position, setting it first to the edge(s) which are to be worked. If the stone is too small, it is a matter of judgement whether it can still be used. If too large, mark on the excess to be taken off.

Scribe around the templet, if appropriate, or mark on very carefully any points which relate to the joint or face moulds. Holding the templet firmly in place, take the scriber and mark around the edges. The resulting line should be sufficiently deep both to be easily distinguishable and to take the point of a pencil. In hard stone, considerable pressure may be needed. In soft stone, it is unnecessary to carve a trench. A thin accurate line is called for. Remove the templet and, with a sharp 9H pencil, follow the scribed line to make it show up clearly.

For a straight run of moulding, place the section templet on the one joint, set to the bottom bed of the stone, so that any small discrepancy in the bed height will be adjusted in the same way at each end. *Do not* do this by having the stone resting on the banker softening and letting the templet find its own level. Raise and prop the end of the stone clear of the banker so that the lower edge of the templet can be set accurately. Hold a drag or similar item firmly to the bottom bed, and allow the templet to rest on it. Make sure that the templet is not tilted. At the same time, set the front edge of the templet to coincide with the face of the stone. It should preferably be set a fraction behind the face, sufficient to allow the scribed lines, which will be a little bigger than the templet, to be drawn completely. This set-back should be extremely small: half a millimetre may be too large.

When dealing with large templets, help may be needed to hold them firmly in position. If a templet moves during scribing, scrape the surface clean and begin again.

When satisfied, apply the templet to the second joint and repeat the operation. With complex templets, it is often best to use the square to run the wall line or other distinguishing feature from one side to the other, to ensure that the templet is correctly located on the second joint.

If the templet is symmetrical, it must be applied so that the same edge of the templet is to the front of the stone at both ends. This is done by placing it so that the markings on the templet are visible at one end and hidden at the other – 'lines up' and 'lines down'. The same applies with bed moulds; it is usual for them to be applied lines up on the top bed and lines down on the bottom bed, if the same templet is used for each.

Face moulds, which might, for example, show blank tracery, are set so that the relevant points match points on the bed and joint moulds. If there are any reference numbers on the templet, identify the stone by cutting them into the top bed. This is not a letter-cutting operation; roughly stabbing in with the chisel is all that is needed, so long as they can be read by others at a later date. Then put the templet aside carefully, preferably hanging it up by the hole provided. Leaving a templet lying about on the banker or on a shelf invites damage.

Returning to the example, all points where angles on the templet touch the edge of the stone should be joined from joint to joint by scribing against a straight edge. It is essential that these lines run exactly from the marked points – near enough is not good enough. The points at which rounded parts of the moulding touch the edge of the stone are ignored for the present.

WORKING MOULDINGS

Each mason has his own methods but the following gives the general principles to be followed.

Circular mouldings

Working a roll moulding is based on the working of drafts and is done entirely with ordinary chisels.

This example takes a simple, large semicircular moulding, as for a coping (Figure 8.4). Work the marginal drafts along the lower edges of the two long sides, checking them with a straight edge as usual. These drafts will be curved across their width. Next, take a sliding bevel, set the stock on the upper surface and the blade at a tangent to the curve as shown, and draw a pencil line. This should just touch the scribed line. Pitching some of the rough out of the way, cut in along this line to form a draft. It must be straight and square to the joint; check with the sinking square.

With a square, run lines from the ends of the draft through to the other end of the stone; a line joining them must touch the scribed curve just as on the first joint. If the stone is of small section and known to be square, it may be easier to transfer the line to the second joint by using the bevel. Whichever method is used, the two end drafts must be at the same angle. Join these to form a draft running from one end of the stone to the other. If the radius of the curve is very large, the draft will be very wide, and it may be necessary to work it as a plane surface in a series of small drafts.

Repeat the operation around the curve as often as is necessary, in a series of smaller and smaller drafts to give a multi-faceted polygon. The drafts should just touch the scribed line; they should be close enough to leave the minimum to be removed to form the curve, but

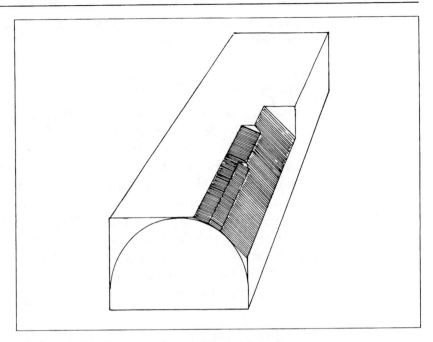

Figure 8.4 Working a circular moulding.

not so close as to leave flats on the finished curve. This is a matter of careful judgement, which can come only with experience. Each draft is used to draw the lines of succeeding drafts and, if they are not worked straight, the lines and thus the drafts will be curved in one direction, resulting in a barley sugar twist, which can be very difficult to get out of.

Now, work each end of the curve down to the line with the 1″ chisel, with the blade parallel to the axis of the curve. If the drafts have been correctly worked, their centres should now be just, perhaps 1 mm, above these curved marginal drafts. With the boaster, clean the curve by working drafts parallel to the marginal draft. When finished, check with a straight edge and correct as needed.

Circular-circular mouldings and sunk work

Circular mouldings, which themselves follow a curve, are worked in a similar way but it is often not possible to apply the templet directly. Instead, the moulding is first worked to a square shape and the chamfers worked by reference to the templet, which may be marked on the top bed for convenience. Finishing must to a large extent be judged by eye and checked frequently with a reverse.

Sunk work on the face of a stone, for example blank tracery panels, is worked in a series of square sinkings beginning with the most widely separated mouldings and stepping down to the final sunk face.

The mouldings are then worked as above or, if they cross one of the joints, worked from one end.

Working a hollow moulding

A surface which crosses the hollow is worked to the straight edge, and the line of each side of the hollow projected with the bevel, at identical angles at each end of the stone, to meet this surface, and drafts worked down each side from end to end. Each end of the hollow is cut in to the line and the rough taken out with punch and/or claw as appropriate. Depending on the size of the moulding, this should be done in drafts with a straight edge, as for a flat surface. Next, drafts are worked with a gouge or bullnose, and the final cleaning done with a boaster, working a little way in and then moving along to form a draft. Check the finished profile with the straight edge or, for a circular sunk moulding, with an appropriately curved edge.

Working a column

It is now rare for columns to be worked by hand, but the principle should be understood. The stone is assumed to have been sawn six sides; it is very important to check that it is square.

A small column will have parallel sides, with top and bottom diameters the same. If the column has an entasis, the bottom bed will be larger than the top, with its diameter the same as the section of the stone. In both cases, find the centres of the upper and one vertical edge on the bottom bed, and set the two diameter lines on the templet to these points; scribe round the templet. At the other end, trammel lines from the same two surfaces to find the centre and bone in the two diameter lines. Use these to set the top bed templet. By this method, any small discrepancies in the squareness of the stone will be reduced and will be taken out in the working.

A tangent is now drawn on at one end, as with any circular work, and either boned through to the other end or set with the bevel. It is now simply a matter of working the draft through and repeating as often as required. For a column with an entasis, an edge cut to the reverse of the entasis must be used instead of a straight edge.

Working a complete moulding

If the stone is to have a moulding run across it, the templet is applied to the right- and left-hand joints. A simple form of string course moulding, shown in Figure 8.5, will be used to explain the method of working.

As a general principle, the larger elements of a moulding are worked first. It is common sense to begin with the heavier work to avoid damaging more delicate parts; in this case, begin with the splayed weathering. Wedge up the stone so that all the surface will be horizontal. It is often necessary on large stones to work at an angle, or even vertically, but it is easier to work in a horizontal plane.

The method is the same as that for working any flat surface, except that, in this case, the positions of the marginal drafts are given by the templet and the lines joining the two ends of the stone. Roughly cut in the two long sides of the splay with a ½" inch chisel, a little clear of the line. This is quick work, giving a rough V-shaped cut, the purpose of which is to prevent stone breaking away below the line (Figure 8.5). The depth of the cut will depend on the nature of the stone, and can only be determined by experience. Take the pitching tool and pitch in the ends, again just above the line. Next, use the pitcher to remove as much of the bulk as possible. Hold the

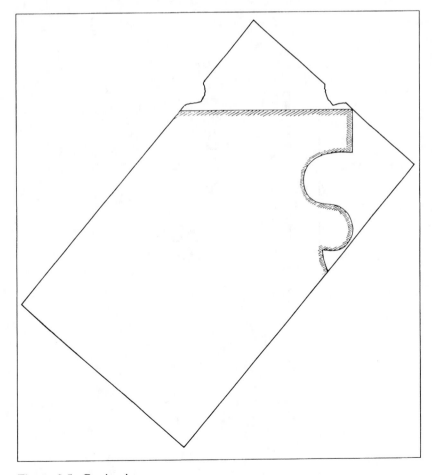

Figure 8.5 Cutting-in.

tool against the steepest of the long sides, working back from one end, holding it so that the edge is at about 30° to the horizontal. The reason for this is that pitching horizontally might take out large pieces below the surface, especially on a return, where the stone is on its natural bed. Complete the working of the weathering as described above for working a plane surface.

Next, turn the stone over so that it lies on its back, with the fillet uppermost. With a straight edge and a pencil, extend the line of the fillet at both ends of the stone a little way over the hollow moulding (Figure 8.6) and work this through until the line of the inner edge of the fillet can be drawn on the stone from joint to joint. Take the sliding bevel, set the stock on the bottom bed and adjust the blade

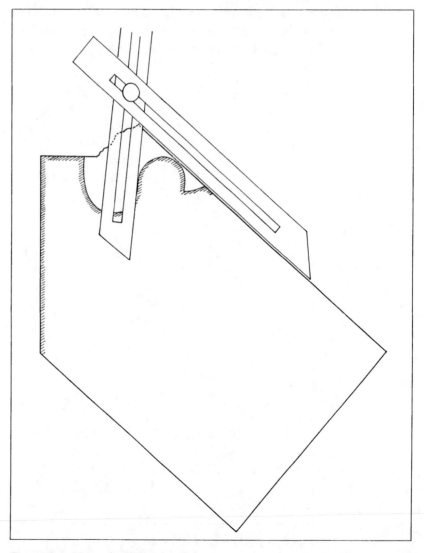

Figure 8.6 Using the sliding bevel.

so that a line can be drawn extending the line of hollow as shown (Figure 8.6). Transfer the bevel to the other end of the stone and repeat this line. Using the bevel ensures that the lines at each end of the stone are at the same angle.

Work a surface to this line, to the point where the hollow begins to curve. With the bevel, draw a line across the roll at each end at about 45°, and work through. With most of the excess stone out of the way, work the hollow moulding as described above. Next, by extending the line of the roll, cut in the quirk on the bottom bed and then complete the working of the roll.

During these operations it will have been necessary to tilt the stone to give the best access for the chisel, being careful not to damage those parts already worked. Great care must be taken to avoid catching worked arrises with the shank of the chisel while working other parts; nothing looks worse than a chipped and damaged arris.

This completes the moulding, which should fit the templet to within ± 0.5 mm at most, chisel marks showing, but nowhere too deep, and with clean, undamaged arrises. If a rubbed finish is called for, remove the toolmarks by rubbing with a piece of carborundum or sandstone, being careful not to rub any part hollow or to damage the arrises.

Most masons will at this point cut their banker mark into the top bed to identify their work.

The working of this simple moulding involves most of the principal techniques used in working stone. Multiple mouldings are approached with either a large chamfer, or by separate sinkings, or a combination of the two.

WORKING RETURNS

If the mouldings change direction, as at a right-angled return, the mitre is worked on the stone. The mouldings on the face are worked through as usual, with the exception of any hollow mouldings, which must be left unworked.

Turn the stone onto its top bed, scribe the section on the return and square the wall line through until it meets the wall line on the main moulding. The mitre will run from this point to the outermost point of the moulding (in this example, this will be the outer nose of the fillet) and then back to the wall line on the weathering.

The mitre line is obtained by holding a straight edge against a square on the upper surface of the stone. Adjust the position of the straight edge until a pencil held flat against it will run through the three points given above. An alternative method, if the return is at 90°, is to set a mitre square on the outermost moulding and proceed as above. The mouldings are then worked through from this line to the section on the return. The hollow moulding is worked last. If the hollow moulding on the face is worked before the return, it will cut through the mouldings on the return, an operation known at 'cutting its throat'.

WORKING COMPLEX STONES

It is neither possible nor realistic to discuss every type of more complex stone. Once the basic techniques described above have been mastered, all other work is simply a development which comes with experience and first-hand tuition.

REPAIRS TO NEW STONE

From time to time repairs to new stone may be needed for a number of reasons. The stone may have a natural fault or the mason may have made an honest mistake.

It may be argued that repairs to new stone are unacceptable and that any damaged new stone should itself be replaced by new work. This point is debatable and would depend on many issues, which cannot be discussed here. The fact is that they can be done well as they frequently were on mediaeval buildings by the original masons.

The requirement is to produce an 'invisible' repair as far as possible. The process is generally known as 'piecing in'. The damaged area is removed in such a way so as to leave a hole or slot of regular shape with flat bottom and sides. A piece of stone (preferably from the same original block) should be cut to fit the area of repair. If the surface has been worked, the repair should project slightly to allow for paring-in afterwards.

Time should be spent to make certain that the repair will fit into place precisely. A hairline joint is required on any exposed face of the stone when fixed.

Only when certain that the piece will fit perfectly, and that there is no movement or rocking when in position, is the repair ready to be glued into position. The stone must also be thoroughly dry and free of dust. A thin resin adhesive such as 'Akemi' or 'Fidal' should be used, and lightly spread on the surfaces which will come into contact, leaving an area within the stone free of glue. The purpose of this last point is to allow any moisture in the stone to travel between the main block of stone and the new piece. If this is not done, repairs can look unsightly as the colour match will be lost owing to differential drying.

The piece of stone should be pushed into position and held or weighted down until the glue has set. Any excess glue which is squeezed out when positioning the stone piece can be left to go hard, unless there is an excessive amount, which should be carefully removed without smearing or spreading onto the finished surface of the stone.

Once satisfied the glue has set, the repair should be worked into the finished desired profile of the stone, a process which will remove any excess glue from the surface. All that should be visible on the finished surface of the stone is a hairline joint, and from any reasonable distance no repair should be visible.

In some circumstances, it may be necessary to dowel the repair, especially if the repair relies solely on the glue to remain in position. An example is where the repair is on the underside of a projecting stone.

MOVING STONE ON THE BANKER

It will be useful here to look at the way in which large stones may be moved on the banker with the minimum of effort. As pointed out elsewhere, stone is a very heavy material, which can easily cause injury if care is not taken. It is worthwhile spending a little time considering how best a particular movement may be made without undue strain.

There are some basic principles to remember. Never place anything hard under the edge of a stone, unless you are certain that that part of the stone will be hidden in the wall, as damage to the arrises will result. Always brush off the top of the banker before moving a stone; if small skelps are left on the softening they will inevitably get under an edge where damage will be visible. Never take risks, either with the stone or with yourself; get help *before* emergencies arise. Remember that even small stones can be awkward; do not lift them by hand if they can be moved in some other way.

Lifting one end of a stone

Long stones may be too heavy to lift conveniently at one end. Raise one long side from the banker, either by pulling or pushing, and place something on the centre line near to the end to be raised. Lower the stone and the end will be lifted; this is invariably easier than trying to lift half the weight of the stone. What is put under it will depend on what is to hand and the weight of the stone. For comparatively light stones, a small skelp will be sufficient. For larger stones a small piece of wood, which does not come within 25 mm of the edge of the stone, will be better. If a skelp is used, be sure to brush out the remains of it before lowering the stone back onto the bed or the stone will be unstable.

Rotating or spinning a stone

It is often necessary to turn a stone so that the part to be worked is at the most convenient side of the banker. Again, raise one side of the stone and, under the centre of the stone, place a miller. This is ideally a disc of wood perhaps 75 mm across and 25 mm thick, but a skelp can often be used just as successfully. Lower the stone onto the miller, with some care as it will be unstable, and rotate it as desired. One person can easily turn a half tonne block in this way, but remember that help may be needed to tilt the stone safely.

Turning a stone

This means turning the stone over so that a different face is uppermost. First move the stone to one end of the banker, which may be done in one of two ways. If the stone has to be moved only a small distance (a few inches), placing a miller off-centre and rotating through 180° may move it a sufficient amount. Rotate again with a miller at the centre if necessary to get the right face to turn down onto the banker. If more movement is required, raise one side of the stone and put a small roller under it. Make sure that the roller is well clear of the edges and lower the stone onto it. If a heavy stone is being moved, be very careful, as the action of lowering the stone will cause it to roll towards the edge still resting on the banker. Help from a second mason is essential if a heavy stone is being moved.

When the stone is in position, remove the roller and turn the stone by pulling it up to the point of balance and then *gently* lowering down onto the new face. It is best not to use lewises to take the weight when turning a stone – the pull on the lewis will be sideways, for which it is not designed. If the help of lifting tackle is essential, use a webbing sling lashed tightly in position.

Lowering a stone

In order to work conveniently on a large stone, it may have to be lowered to the floor to work part of it. Use lifting tackle to lower it to the floor (on softening) and do any turning from there. It is possible to lower large stones by hand, sliding off the edge of the banker using wooden skids and plenty of softening, but it is rarely possible to get enough hands to the stone in a position to exert any real force. If a stone gets away it moves in an instant, and fingers and toes can be smashed beyond repair.

Using a combination of the above methods, most stones can be moved about the banker with little effort and small risk of damage so long as care is taken. Remember that there is always some risk of injury when stone is being moved.

9

Mortar

When fixing dressed stonework, the mortar is used to keep the stones apart rather than to stick them together. If the stone is carefully worked and properly bonded, almost any building could be put up without the use of mortar.

Mortar is needed to take up slight inequalities in the bed, to relieve pressure on the arrises, to keep out rainwater and frost, and to allow minor settlement and thermal movement of the building to take place without cracking the stones. The mortar must be strong enough to resist being washed out by rain and to resist frost damage. It must also retain a degree of flexibility over a long period, and be sufficiently permeable to encourage any moisture within the walls to evaporate through the joints rather than through the face of the stone.

It follows that the choice of mortar must be a compromise between the various requirements. A hard, dense mortar will resist weather, but will also make the building too rigid and risk damage to the stone. Too soft a mortar will wash out and lead to unequal stresses on the masonry. The correct choice of mortar is of major importance to the life of the stone and of the building.

From Roman times onwards, mortar has been a mixture of sand and lime. In the middle of the nineteenth century came the invention of cement, generally known as Portland cement as it was said to resemble that stone. Unless mixed with additives for specialized use, it is generally known as *Ordinary Portland Cement (OPC)*. Its popularity grew until it began to supersede the use of lime mortar. Warland recommends the use of lime mortar for bedding but neat cement grout for filling the joints, something which should not be tolerated today. Since the 1970s, a new appreciation of the qualities of lime mortar has led to its increasing use, although it has not yet succeeded in displacing cement mortar altogether.

LIME

To obtain lime for mortar, limestone is heated (burned) in a kiln at a temperature of around 1000°C. This is now carried out in highly efficient rotary kilns, but formerly the burning was in either flare kilns or draw kilns. The former was an intermittent process, the kiln being loaded with limestone over a hearth. When the burning was complete, the kiln was emptied and reloaded, the whole operation taking about a week. In the draw kiln, alternate layers of coal and limestone were loaded from the top, and the burned lime raked out of the bottom, after taking about a week to pass through the kiln. It was thus a continuous process, but the lime was rarely as well burned or as white as that from the flare kiln. In both types, coal or charcoal was likely to become mixed in with the lime and can often be seen when cutting out old mortar.

The process of burning drives off carbon dioxide, changing the calcium carbonate ($CaCO_3$) to calcium oxide (CaO) or quicklime, sometimes referred to as lump lime. The next stage in the process is slaking, which converts the calcium oxide to calcium hydroxide [$Ca(OH)_2$]. The quick lime is added to water, producing a violent reaction rather like boiling, with the production of heat and steam. Protective clothing is essential if this is carried out on site. Sufficient water must be used and the mass thoroughly stirred to ensure that all the lime is fully slaked. Any lumps of unslaked lime remaining must be sieved out, as they will later cause disruption of the mortar. The slaking of the sieved lime should be continued for at least one month, or longer if possible, to ensure that slaking is complete; it improves with keeping (but see below for hydraulic limes). The resultant plastic material, which has something of the consistency of solid emulsion paint, is known as *lime putty*.

For many years slaked limes have been dried and ground, and sold as a powder *hydrated lime* (bag lime) but, in recent years, lime putty has become available, and should be used in preference to hydrated lime.

The setting of lime mortar

Non-hydraulic lime

The choice of stone for burning to make lime governs the type of lime produced. Pure limestones, such as chalk, and also marble and shells, give a lime which sets very slowly by reaction with carbon dioxide in the air; the process can take many years to reach the centre of a large mass of masonry. The sand in the mortar increases the permeability and allows the setting to proceed more quickly than would otherwise be the case, as well as reducing the shrinkage which occurs with the setting. Lime of this type is variously known as *white, rich, fat* or *non-hydraulic* lime. The slaking rate is relatively quick.

Most limestones contain impurities, of which clay is the most significant in relation to mortar. The clay, and to some extent other impurities, has the effect of increasing the setting rate by reaction of water with the burned clay. The proportion of clay affects the setting rate. Those with up to about 10 per cent of clay are variously known as *feebly hydraulic, stone* or *grey lime*. (Grey does not refer to the colour of the lime, which still looks white.) Much of the setting is still by absorption of carbon dioxide.

Fresh, non-hydraulic lime putty may be well mixed with sand after slaking, and left to mature as *coarse stuff* for several weeks under damp sacking or in airtight drums. It is then remixed with any additives immediately before use.

Hydraulic lime

Limestones with up to 20 per cent clay give a stronger lime, which sets more quickly, and was formerly used in damp conditions where the use of OPC is more likely today. It is usually known as *moderately hydraulic* lime.

Where the clay content exceeds 20 per cent the setting of the mortar is almost entirely by the reaction of water with the impurities and so will set under water. The mortar is quick-setting (as little as 1 hour), has considerable strength and yet considerable elasticity. It is known as *eminently hydraulic* lime.

Hydraulic limes take longer to slake than non-hydraulic but will begin to set if slaked for too long a period. If these limes are slaked on site it is advisable to break down lumps to powder to speed up the slaking process. While non-hydraulic lime improves by being knocked up several times while in its putty form, hydraulic limes are like OPC in that, once they have begun to set, they must not be remixed.

The so-called Roman cement introduced in the early nineteenth century was a strong, dense form of hydraulic lime, usually of a distinct brown colour, which in practice has proved too hard for repair work and should generally be removed whenever encountered. Its name derives from its supposed resemblance to Roman mortars.

Hydraulic additives

The builders of ancient Rome discovered that mixing lime with volcanic ash from Pozzuoli, near Naples, gave a quick-setting mortar, which, like hydraulic lime, sets by reaction with water rather than with air. Brick and pottery dust gave the same effect but it is as *pozzolanic additives* that all such materials are generally known.

The principal pozzolanic agents used now are low-sulphate *PFI* (pulverized fuel ash, or *fly ash*), *HTI* (a ceramic powder used for high-temperature insulation) and brick dust. Red brick dust will, of course, have a noticeable effect on the colour of the mortar. Considerable research is now being carried out on mortars and additives, and at the time of writing, there are some objections to the use of HTI powder.

PORTLAND CEMENT

The ingredients for OPC are basically similar to that of hydraulic lime but the proportion of clay to limestone (usually chalk) is about 33 per cent. The raw materials are finely ground, fired at around 1400°C and the resulting clinker ground to a fine powder. It sets in two stages: the alumina in the clay crystallizes first to give an initial set after 1½–2½ hours. The final set may take 3 or 4 weeks to complete.

The use of OPC mortar has disadvantages from the point of view of its high strength and impermeable nature, which can cause damage to masonry for reasons given in the section 'The weathering and decay of stone' (p. 18). In general, the use of Portland cement mortar in the repair of stone buildings should be avoided unless there are very good reasons for its use. The addition of plasticizers, which improve the working of the mortar, gives what is sold as masonry cement. This does have advantages in the repair of those sandstone buildings where lime mortar is thought to have encouraged the decay of the stone. However, the very small area of mortar presented to the air does, in fact, rarely pose a threat to the health of sandstone buildings.

White cement contains fewer potentially damaging salts than OPC and its use may be preferred for some applications.

SAND

Lime and cement are mixed with an aggregate, usually sand, which is the largest ingredient of mortar. It is used to increase the bulk, to reduce the tendency to crack, to reduce shrinkage and to increase the permeability. This last attribute aids the setting of non-hydraulic mortars by allowing the passage of CO_2 into the interior of the wall. The voids between the sand grains usually amount to about one third of the whole, and should be filled by the binder. The ratio of sand to binder, whether lime or cement, is therefore usually 3:1.

Quarried sand (pit sand, sharp sand) is generally reckoned to be best for masonry work, as it tends to have angular grains. River sand (soft sand) has rounded grains, which make for a more workable mortar, but it is more difficult to mix uniformly and may have a greater tendency to crack. In modern practice, soft sand is more often used for brickwork and sharp sand for stonework. The size of the grains is important: very coarse sand has large voids between the grains which the binder will not fill. The best sands have a range of grain sizes, and the addition of soft sand will improve the workability of a very coarse sharp sand.

Sand must be clean, that is free of harmful salts, and earthy or clayey material. When obtained from reputable suppliers, sand comes ready-washed as necessary to achieve this end. As a simple site test, a sample is shaken with water in a jar. The sand should settle within about a quarter of an hour, with only a small proportion of silt on top of the sand. If clay is present, this will remain in suspension for some hours. Damp sand, which remains in a ball when squeezed or which stains the fingers, contains an excess of silt or clay. The range of grain sizes and the presence of lumps of foreign matter are easily checked by eye.

There has been something of a fashion for including large grit in the aggregate, especially for repointing on older buildings. This has to be used with care: in rough rubble work it may not look out of place but its use in ashlar work is not good practice. Any hard material in fine joints may lead to spalling of the faces should there be any settlement.

THE MIXING OF MORTAR

Hand mixing should take place only on a clean surface, free from old mortar and organic matter. When using dry ingredients – sand, lime, cement – the materials must be thoroughly mixed together before water is added. To this end, the sand should be stored dry as far as possible. It is reckoned that turning the mixture three times from one side of the mixing area to the other should give a good mix, but it is better to mix more rather than less.

The sand should be measured out first, and the lime and/or cement added on top. It is important that the measuring is carried out carefully to give not only accurate proportions but also consistency. Shovelfuls may be adequate for rough work but it is much better to use a gauging box, which, filled and levelled off, will give an unvarying mix throughout the work. A single box, equal to the smallest part required, e.g. cement, may be used and filled the appropriate number of times for the larger parts, e.g. sand. Alternatively, several boxes, each one equal in volume to the proper quantity of sand, lime and cement, may be made up. When adding cement or pozzolanic additives to a lime putty/sand mix, it is better to make them into a slurry before adding to the well-chopped mix.

The use of the ordinary rotary mixer is to be preferred to hand mixing, as it does the job more thoroughly. Better still is the mortar mill which, with its heavy rotating wheels, is the most effective when mixing mortars based on lime putty.

Water should be added gradually, using as little as possible to give a workable mix. All lime mortars are much improved by beating with a rammer, which gives a better mix and reduces the quantity of water required. Here again, the mortar mill has the advantage as it is effectively beating as it mixes.

MORTAR MIXES

It is not easy to lay down hard and fast rules about the proportions for mortars, as everyone has their favourite recipe. When dealing with historic buildings it is always worth taking samples of the existing mortar for testing. Laboratory analysis will give a good indication of the original mix, which, if it has proved generally satisfactory, can be repeated. If unsatisfactory, then the same mix can be avoided in the repairs. Samples should be taken from deep in the wall, to avoid sampling later repointing, and from an area that can be identified with reasonable certainty as original work rather than repairs.

The following are suggestions that have been found satisfactory in use; the basic rule to remember is that the mortar must be softer than the stone. The use of brick dust or other pozzolanic agent in the mix in addition to cement may result in a mortar which is too hard.

The use of cement in the mix is criticized in some quarters, but a little OPC does give an initial set which helps to minimize the effects of weather until the lime has begun to set. If cement is not used, even more care than usual must be taken to protect the face from rain and from drying out too rapidly until a set has been achieved.

In the following list of mixes used for particular stone, the lime is non-hydraulic lime putty, the cement is OPC and the sand is assumed to be largely sharp sand:

♦ Hard, durable stone in very exposed conditions (i.e. wall tops of ruined buildings) – 1:1:6 cement:lime:sand.
♦ Softer stone, or in less exposed conditions (i.e. elevations) – 1:2:9 cement : lime :sand, or 1:1:3 brick dust:lime:sand.
♦ Softer stone, which is beginning to show signs of surface

degradation – 1:3:12 cement:lime:sand, or 1:1:4 brick dust:lime: sand.

If the use of OPC is not insisted upon, a general purpose mix for bedding stone is 1:3 lime putty:sand.

If grouting of stone is required, this must never be carried out in OPC, which is too hard and carries the risk of introducing sodium salts into the wall. A suitable mix for general purposes is one part lime putty:two parts pulverized fly ash:eight or nine parts fine sand.

10

Fixing

Fixing is the art of laying stones in place on the building. In large companies it is often possible to specialize as either a banker or a fixer mason, but each should have a good working knowledge of the other's work.

SCAFFOLDING

Most fixing work calls for a scaffold. All permanent scaffolding should be erected and maintained only by a qualified person and not used until a certificate has been issued declaring that it is safe for use. The use to which a scaffold is to be put must be specified. A light scaffold for inspection and repointing is not suitable for the hoisting and fixing of heavy masonry.

Scaffolding on stone buildings must be independent, that is, the putlogs must be supported by standards and ledgers at their inner as well as outer ends; putlogs must never be cut into the wall. Whilst it is essential that the scaffold is tied in to the building, this should not be done by means of expanding bolts (Hilti ties), if it is at all possible to avoid their use. Ties through windows, around buttresses and around the corners of the building will usually enable the responsible scaffolding contractor to avoid this type of interference with the wall face.

All scaffolds move a little and, to reduce the risk of damage to mouldings and other projections, no standard should be closer than 50 mm to the stonework at any point. All tube ends within 50 mm of the building should be protected with plastic end caps and, where ties bear on the stone, there must be protection by means of boards or suitable softening.

Where large stones are to be hoisted and fixed, the point loads on the scaffold can be considerable and the scaffolding contractor must be made aware of this before the scaffold is erected. The movement of large stones calls for a wide scaffold.

Invariably, some scaffold tubes and fittings will be in the way of repair work. These must *never* be moved by the mason but only by a qualified scaffolder. It may seem a simple business to move a tube temporarily out of the way but, if another mason on another lift has done the same thing, problems can multiply very quickly. All scaffolding must be inspected at least once a week by an approved person. This need not be a scaffolder, but can be someone who has had formal training in identifying possible points of danger.

Working on a scaffold

Working at any height is potentially dangerous. A fall from 5 m can kill almost as easily as a fall from 50 m. Equally, materials or tools falling from a scaffold can kill or injure those below. Care is always needed.

Protective headgear should always be worn when working on or near to scaffolding; severe injury can be caused when straightening up under a low scaffold clip. Even on the topmost lift, where there is little or nothing overhead, it is quite easy to hit one's head on a standard or brace while fixing, and even momentary dizziness can be dangerous: the gap between the guard rail and toe board is quite large enough to allow the passage of a semiconscious mason.

Materials should be stacked to one side of the scaffold as far as possible to leave a clear gangway and all tools should be kept off the boards; stepping on a chisel left lying about is an easy way to lose one's balance.

Fooling about on a scaffold should never be permitted and, on a properly run site, is a serious offence. The perpetrator should at the very least be sent off to work on the ground.

HOISTING

Care of stone from the banker shop
to fixing on site

Stone is an awkward material to move, owing to the ease with which it can be damaged. During all hoisting and transport operations where stone may touch or rub against any other hard material, softening must be provided. A variety of materials can be used – straw, polystyrene, pieces of carpet – and each stone must be separated by one or more of these materials, especially during transport.

If slings are used to hoist individual pieces of stone, arrises must be protected from the slings as they stretch under tension. Even the simplest ashlar block risks damage unless these precautions are taken.

There should always be a supply of softwood laths, at least 25 mm thick, for stacking stones on. This spacing provides protection for the stone, room for fingers or for slings to be inserted for lifting.

If split-pin lewises are used for fixing on site, extra care must be taken where the stone has not been stored under cover; green algae may grow in the hole and this will seriously reduce the grip of the lewis. The hole must be very thoroughly cleaned. When in use never touch the legs or ring of the split-pin lewis. Steering the stone by gripping the legs will reduce the grip of the lewis and may allow the stone to fall. This is not just a theoretical possibility – it has happened.

On large contracts there will often be a fixed platform hoist onto which the stone can be loaded directly, either on a pallet using a fork-lift or on a trolley. The latter is usually easier for unloading on the scaffold.

Smaller contracts will usually rely on a rope and pulley, whatever the motive power may be, with the stone lifted in a timber or steel basket or the rope hooked onto a lewis in the stone. The power for a simple hoist is usually provided by an electric motor on a swinging jib attached to the scaffolding. Petrol hoists of this type should be avoided. Apart from the fire risk, these hoists have a greater tendency to jerk when stopping and starting, and are generally difficult to operate with precision.

If available on site, a better source of power is compressed air. For small works, simple, air-powered chain hoists are available. These can be hooked onto a scaffold jib and moved with ease as work progresses. There is no danger of fire or electrocution, and the connection is easily made simply by plugging the flexible hose into a quick-release fitting.

Secondary hoists may be needed to set large stones in their place on the building. The most convenient is usually the chain hoist, either manual or air-powered. They are normally slung from putlogs, doubled and properly braced as necessary. A travelling block can be used on a steel beam, as in the banker shop; a chain traverse allows for greater precision than the push–pull type of trolley.

GENERAL PRINCIPLES AND
PROCEDURES FOR FIXING

Removing old stonework

On restoration work the first task for the fixer is to chop out the old
stone. This sounds relatively straightforward but, where stone being
cut out is adjacent to stonework being kept, great care should be
taken not to damage surrounding stonework, especially when tools
such as angle grinders and power chisels are being used.

Generally, cutting out the first stone should begin in the centre,
working out towards the joints. Any hard cement pointing should be
nicked with a chisel to reduce the risk of spalling adjacent stones.
Joints must never be cut out using a disc cutter, as damage to adjacent
stones is almost inevitable. Old stonework should be cut out only to
the depth of the new stone to be fixed. Enough room must be left
in the depth of the wall for the part of the bedding mortar that may
be pushed back by fixing the new stone, but not too much. Trying
to fill large voids behind the topmost stones of the repair can be
tedious and uncertain.

Chopping out may reveal cramps and dowels of either iron, copper,
lead or slate. They offer a potential threat to the tips of chisels, so
care should be taken by removing stone from around them before
either removing them or cutting them back. If at all possible, iron
should be removed and substituted by a non-ferrous material.

Local cracking of stone, perhaps with rust stains on the surface,
may indicate the presence of an iron dowel, and a lead-filled pour
hole above a joint will indicate either a lead dowel or joint, or an
iron dowel run in with lead.

Features such as finials and pinnacles will almost certainly have
been fixed using some sort of dowel, and great patience and care must
be taken in removing them if any of the stones are to be saved. It
often involves painstakingly sawing through the bed joint and dowel
with a hacksaw blade held in the hand.

Chopping out is also likely to reveal oyster shells, which were very
commonly used for packing stones during fixing. If an archaeologist
is working on site it can be helpful to make them aware of the
presence of oyster shells, for their records.

If stonework is cut out in spring and left for some time before fixing
begins, it is worth blocking off the hole to prevent birds nesting.

It is always unwise to remove large areas of stone before fixing
begins. Many stone walls have cores of rubble and it is not always
possible to predict the depth of stone back into the wall. If there is
no appreciable variation in the bonding, weakness caused by over-
cutting out may cause an adjacent area of stone to bulge and lose its
bond with the core.

Fixing new stone

Once a stone has been removed, all surrounding joints should be cleaned of old mortar using a claw tool, and dust and debris brushed off. Wherever possible a dry fix should be undertaken, that is, the stone should be placed in its intended position without mortar. Wood laths or lead pads are used to give the intended thickness of the mortar bed. The dry fix can be very helpful for a number of reasons: the mortar bed thickness can be ascertained; the correct depth of cutting out can be checked; the bed height of the new stone may need reducing; and the final positioning for a run of moulding can be checked. There are so many problems that can arise during fixing that the time taken to dry-fix pays off.

At this point, it is worth mentioning an all too common practice on unsupervised sites. The dry fix takes place, the joints are all pointed up, and grout is poured all around the stone. The end result is a cosmetic finish. To all intents and purposes the stone appears to be a sound repair in the wall but, unless a lot of preparation has taken place, it is very unlikely that the grout will have filled the bottom bed joint, especially if this is only 2 or 3 mm.

Before fixing, both new and old stone should be thoroughly soaked on the beds and joints, using a sponge or a wet-brush (two-knot lime brush). Clean water should always be used to minimize the risk of discoloration of the stonework. Where a dowel is to be fixed using resin or lead, water should not be allowed to run into the hole.

If new stonework has beds and joints left off the saw, these should be roughed up by stabbing in with a punch.

Stone should always be laid on a mortar bed which has been spread on the wetted top bed of the stone below. Once a stone has been laid, it must be adjusted to the correct position. Time is limited, as water is absorbed out of the mortar into the stone even though the beds have previously been soaked.

Height and plumb/level are the first checks. If the stone is too high then twisting back and forth may reduce the mortar bed (being careful of the arrises of the joints). If there is access above the new stone, a heavy rubber mallet can be used to tap the stone to reduce the bed. A hammer can also be used, but only in the centre of the stone and with a block of wood interposed.

It is not sufficient to lay any new stonework only to a builders' line; it must be checked in all directions with a long straight-edge. Mouldings must be checked on the top and bottom beds, and along rolls and other prominent parts of the profile.

Where the stone has dropped at the front but is otherwise in position, a trowel inserted in the bed joint can be used to lift the stone, and more mortar packed into the joint. The use of slate or other hard material to prevent a heavy stone settling too much onto sloppy mortar is bad practice and should be avoided. If such packing is necessary, it should be pushed well back from the arris to avoid the risk of spalling.

If at this stage the stone is not sitting in its correct position, although its height and level are acceptable, wait a few minutes and remove any loose mortar which may have worked its way up the side joints. Side adjustment can now take place, as the bed will be very unlikely to sink further. The condition of the mortar at this stage will vary with differing stone types.

If the stone cannot be made to sit correctly, then it must be removed, all the beds cleaned off and the procedure begun again, and repeated if necessary. Side joints should now be packed with mortar, after rewetting the joints if needed. Whether a trowel or pointing key is used, the joint must be solidly packed with mortar. Both sides of the stone may need to be pointed at the same time, as pressure from the mortar whilst packing one side could move the stone sideways. Finally, the top bed should be similarly packed, pushing in plenty of mortar to fill the void at the back.

Excess mortar should be cleaned from the stone with a damp sponge being drawn along the edge of the stone into the line of the joint, so as to eliminate all trace of staining on the stonework. Clean water and frequent rinsing are essential. Any mortar that may have run onto stonework below should be cleaned off before it sets.

Grouting single stones

There may be a very few occasions when laying a bed or packing a bed joint are impractical, and there may be no substitute to using grout. If this is the case, particularly when there is a thin bottom bed joint, every effort must be made to ensure that the grout will flow under the stone and fill all voids. Very thorough pre-wetting is essential, and cutting channels in the beds and joints will aid the flow of grout. A conscientious mason will check, using a hacksaw blade or welding rod, that every void has been filled.

To aid the pouring of grout, a nest of clay can be moulded against a joint to allow a continuous flow. The grout must be stirred continuously to ensure that the heavier particles are kept in suspension. The grout will normally be of a similar mix to that used for fixing and *not* neat OPC.

Infilling with corework

In some projects it may be necessary to infill a void between outer skins of stone; for example, the shaft of a pinnacle may have only facing stones with a central core of infill. Here rough blocks of old stone which have been discarded may be used with mortar to make the infill and skelps used to pack in any gaps where excess mortar would have to be used.

Always make sure the stone for the infill is wet and, if grout is used, it should be as thick as will flow to fill all the voids. Again, the grout must be a similar mix to that used for bedding and not neat OPC.

POINTING

The quality of the pointing has a significant effect on the appearance, quality and longevity of the work. A full description of the requirements can be found in Chapter 12, Supervision and Specifications (p. 220, 234).

FINAL FINISHING

As a decorator is responsible for the quality of finish within a building, so a stone mason is also responsible or the final appearance of the stonework. When fixing is complete, the mason should closely check all details of the run of consecutive courses of moulding. There are occasions when, for example, one stone may have a slightly larger roll than its neighbour. The difference when measured may be negligible but any slight variation can look out of place, so the mason should pare the stone to improve the flow of the moulding. If more than minor paring-in is required, the working or fixing has not been up to standard.

Old walls rarely form a plane surface, and the face of new ashlar may have to be twisted in to match.

There are instances where paring-in may be planned during the setting-out stage. A shaft stooling on a string course may have to be finally worked once the stone has been fixed in position, since accurate prediction of the fixed position of the string course is often impossible. The stone is set-out with a larger amount of stone left for the stooling than required and the stooling worked after fixing.

Once finished in a given area, all stonework should be brushed down with a soft handbrush to remove all dust and debris, and mortar smears cleaned off with a damp sponge. Finally, if further work is in progress in the vicinity of any finished work, all carving and areas which might be damaged by falling stone or other materials should be adequately protected.

REPAIR BY LETTING-IN

Where a small but significant area of damage has occurred to a stone, repairs are often made by cutting out just the damaged area and letting-in a new piece of stone. The method is also known as a dental repair, from the resemblance to fillings in teeth. It is often the best way of preserving the major part of the original fabric of a historic building but, in excess it can become more unsightly than complete replacement.

The technique is similar to that recommended for piecing-in small repairs on new stone in that the recess must be cut square to accept the new piece with a fine joint. However, as the new stone will be larger in surface area (dental repairs of less than, say, 100 × 100 mm can look worse than the damage, especially if there is a large number) and deeper into the wall, the stone is usually best secured with a dowel fixed into both parts with resin. The joints should be unobtrusive, no more than 2 mm at most, and bedded in fine mortar or lime putty.

LEAD JOINTS

Molten lead can be used to form a joint between stone in certain circumstances where the use of mortar might be difficult or perhaps unsuitable. This is sometimes held to be an unnecessarily old-fashioned technique but the following case history will illustrate its modern relevance.

During the restoraton of the Great West Window at York Minster in the 1980s, it was found that the original tracery had been fixed using lead joints. The lead filled the joint completely except for the outer inch, which was pointed with mortar.

The original tracery had decayed so much that it was becoming dangerous and unable to withstand any more repairs. The decision was taken to renew the window tracery completely and also to fix it using lead joints. The method was as follows.

Preparation

Each piece of tracery had its joint joggled and a 25 mm (1") dowel hole was drilled to a depth of about 100–125 mm in the middle of each joint face. Pouring holes of 12 mm diameter were drilled from the glazing groove into the upper dowel hole of a joint. These holes were drilled in the appropriate position to ensure the complete filling of a joint, taking into consideration the eventual fixed position of each stone. A second hole was drilled for air release.

Fixing

Stones were set in their correct position using 25 mm square pads of lead to give the required thickness of joint. Where stones would not rest by their own weight, scaffolding was erected to support the stone. Several stones at a time were set up and positioned correctly by reference back to the full-size setting-out drawing.

The outside edge of each joint was dampened slightly with a wet sponge and clay was used to seal the outer 25 mm of the joint. Clay 'nests' were built around the pouring holes to assist in the pouring of the lead. Finally, loose sand was poured into any nooks and crannies in the tracery where any spillage of molten lead might afterwards have been difficult to remove.

The lead pourer, wearing face mask and protective gloves, then took a large ladle of molten lead and filled the joint in one pour, so that the lead within the joint and dowel holes would solidify into one unit.

Almost immediately, the clay could be removed, any excess lead cut away and the next stones set in position. The joints were left to cool for 24 hours before being pointed.

Advantages

A total of 129 pieces of tracery weighing up to 400 kg were fixed over an area of 28 square metres (300 square feet). There were definite advantages in using lead to fix this tracery. There is bound to be some movement over a period of time; lead joints give some flexibility and help prevent cracking of the stone around the joints, if any appreciable movement does occur.

The speed of this method of fixing was of great advantage. Once the lead had been poured, the next stones could be put in position immediately. If mortar had been used, time would have had to be given for it to go off.

HALF-SECTION REPLACEMENT OF TRACERY

It is sometimes possible to replace only the outer face of tracery, thus preserving the inner, usually undamaged, half.

The outer part must be cut away carefully to the glazing line; it is generally best to cut to the back of the glazing groove. To avoid damage, care must be taken to limit the effects of vibration on the inner half. To this end the disc cutter is invaluable. It is in any case advisable to support the rest of the window with timber struts. The dressed-back surface must be as flat as can be achieved.

It is particularly important that each new stone is exactly the same height as the half it is to match, so that the joints match in both position and width. The new stones are secured to the old one-by-one, using dowels and resin so that the two halves become one stone. The horizontal joints must be packed very solidly with mortar to avoid the old stone carrying the weight of the new. As always, any resin used in the joint between the two halves of the stone must not cover more than half the surface, to allow migration of moisture.

It can sometimes take less time to remove the tracery, saw the face off, and join the old and new halves in the workshop. Rebuilding is then as straightforward as with all-new tracery.

When taking out tracery, it is not normally necessary to provide any support for the stonework above as there is almost invariably an arch which is quite separate from the tracery.

CRAMPS AND DOWELS

Correctly bonded masonry normally needs no additional fastenings but, in some situations, greater security must be provided by cramps, which join stones across the joints in the same course, and dowels, which are straight fastenings securing stones in (usually) successive courses. They should be used only where necessary; too much rigidity in a building is a bad thing. Pinnacles, finials and other free-standing features usually have a single dowel passing though several stones to ensure stability. Cramps and dowels must be rigid enough for their purpose and be capable of surviving unchanged for the life of the stone.

Historically, the most popular materials have been wood, slate, and iron. Wood is unsatisfactory, and slate is acceptable but not convenient and is variable in strength. The disastrous consequences of the use of iron are all too often evident.

There are two metals acceptable for use as cramps and dowels: stainless steel and manganese bronze, the latter usually known by its trade name Delta metal. Both are said to be virtually incorrodible, and are obtainable as round bar, square bar and flat strip. Both Delta metal and stainless steel cramps can be purpose-made, or made on site. Making on site as required is advantageous, especially when dealing with unpredictable historic buildings, as each cramp can be made specifically for each individual situation. In this respect, Delta metal is a little easier to use than steel as it is more malleable. It also carries no risk of rusting.

There is still much debate about the best material to use for securing cramps and dowels. Any of the following may be used: a normal mortar mix, epoxy resin or molten lead. A neat OPC grout should not be used. Epoxy resin is becoming the favoured material, owing to its ease of use and great strength but, as mentioned above, great strength is not always the most desirable property. There is also no way of knowing how well it will perform over hundreds of years. There have been suggestions that it can deteriorate, becoming brittle over the years. Mortar is quite acceptable, although when dowelling it is not always easy to ensure that the voids around the dowel are filled. Lead, on the other hand, has been employed with success for at least 2000 years. Even in situations exposed to the atmosphere for 500 years, lead continues to do the job for which it was designed. Its use has a higher labour content but, in terms of the life of historic buildings, this is negligible.

Cramps

Cramps are commonly of flat bar 25 × 3 mm with each end turned down 25 mm or more depending on the nature of the work. For small work, cramps may be of round bar 2–4 mm diameter, with the ends turned down an appropriate amount. Whatever the form of the cramp, it must be fixed a reasonable distance from the edges of the stones being secured. If the beds are large enough, at least 100 mm is recommended.

The holes to take the ends of the cramps should be drilled or cut with a chisel. The use of a disc cutter to form the cramp hole is bad practice because in order to achieve any depth, a large gash has to be cut in the bed. A slot joining the holes and deep enough to take the full thickness of the cramp is cut across the joint.

Dowels

Dowels are made from square or round bar, usually 3–25 mm in diameter, depending on the situation. It is important to make the dowel long enough and of equal length in each stone – it is of little value to have 90 per cent of the dowel in one stone.

When using mortar or epoxy resin, the dowel is secured into the upper stone, the hole in the lower stone is partially filled with mortar or resin, and the stone is lowered into position on a mortar bed. The joint must not be disturbed until the mortar or resin has set. When using molten lead, the stone is laid on lead pads, as described above under 'Lead joints' (p. 188).

Where a new stone is to be dowelled into existing stones above and below, the dowel holes in the bottom beds are drilled to a depth which will take the full length of the dowel. Pour holes, for whatever material is to be used to secure the dowels, are drilled into the faces to connect with the dowel holes. The dowels are pushed into the upper holes and held with a slip of card or zinc until the stone is in place, and then allowed to fall into the lower holes and secured with lead, grout or resin. The dowels must not be released until there is complete agreement that the stone is correctly positioned – there is no second chance.

If horizontal dowels are used in a similar situation, the dowel is inserted into the deep hole with a loop of twine (known as a mouse) under its end. When the free end of the twine is pulled the dowel will slide across into position.

LEADING-IN

It is often part of the fixer mason's work to secure railings or other metalwork into stone. One of the oldest and best methods is to use lead, which has a long life and allows for thermal movement of the metalwork. It will also not stain stonework, if spilt.

Setting railings into a coping is usually best done by pouring molten lead into the hole. Everything must be bone dry, as the slightest hint of moisture will cause spitting of the lead. A face mask, gloves and protective clothing should always be worn. When the lead has solidified, it is tamped down with a leading-iron, using sharp blows of the hammer. Any excess lead is easily cut away with a sharp chisel.

Metalwork set in horizontal holes is best fixed with solid lead. It is advisable, but not essential, to rag the end of the bar. The hole, which should be wide enough to take the leading-iron down the side of the bar, is packed in stages with small pieces of scrap lead sheet formed into tight rolls. Each piece is tamped well down before the next piece is put in; the hammering of the leading-iron tends to weld the lead into a single mass. Care must be taken not to injure the surrounding stonework.

When the hole is filled and the metalwork tightly held, the surface of the lead can be tamped flush with the stone to give a neat finish or cut off flush using a sharp chisel.

Removal of a leaded-in bar is best done by carefully drilling out the lead using a sharp twist bit in a power drill. A slow drilling speed is recommended, as the lead tends to jam the drill bit.

REBUILDING ARCHES

An arch is an extremely strong and stable structure, provided the loads around it are more or less equal, and that the foundations and the abutments (those parts of the structure which take the sideways thrust at the base of the arch) are solid. The loading of an arch within a wall does not usually cause any problems, and minor work to the walls above and around it can be carried out without undue concern. In the case of flying buttresses, the arch must remain loaded in order to contain the thrust and prevent it buckling. If work involves removal of the stone strut above the arch it is wise to take the thrust on a steel strut between wall and buttress. This must also be done if the arch is being dismantled. Before replacing any stone in an arch, the rest of the arch must be supported.

Centres

The timber formwork used to support an arch during building or dismantling is known as a centre. It is easily made by a carpenter and, whilst it must by rigid and capable of bearing the load of the arch, excessive elaboration is unnecessary – a good proportion of the weight of the voussoirs is carried by the pier or wall from which the arch springs. The voussoirs rest either on short lengths of wood known as laggings or, more commonly with small spans nowadays, on plywood bent around the framework of the centre. Especially when dealing with complete replacement of an arch ring, the profile of the centre must be given by the setter-out.

The centre must be wide enough to carry the voussoirs without risk of them tipping but it is usually a little narrower than the soffit of the arch. It is important that it is held rigidly in place during building, and able to resist sideways adjustment of the individual voussoirs. The centre is supported on struts running either to the ground or to the scaffold. In the latter case, extra bracing may be needed to prevent any movement of the scaffold. In some cases the centre can be supported on the capitals. The centre should rest on *folding wedges*, which enables precise adjustment of the height to be made and allows for easing of the centre when the arch is complete.

Folding wedges are made up of a pair of long, slow (i.e. shallow) wedges set in opposite directions. It may be necessary to pin them with a nail to prevent movement.

Dismantling an arch

The centre must be wedged firmly into position beneath the arch, yet not so tightly that it tends to push the arch upwards. When taking out a small arch in an ashlar wall, the bonding of the ashlar above the arch ring will very often be self-supporting. In other cases it may be necessary to insert needles to carry the load of the wall.

If any of the voussoirs are to be replaced, they can be chopped out in the usual way, thus releasing the remaining ones. If all are to be reused, it should be possible to release them by carefully sawing out the joints. When the arch is out, the centre can be adjusted in form or position as necessary before rebuilding begins.

Rebuilding the arch

Depending on the size and access, the voussoirs may be lowered onto the centre by lifting tackle, or placed by hand. Where tackle is used, attachment is with the lewis, which should be set in the voussoirs so that each one hangs at the proper angle.

The voussoirs are fixed in the normal way, with solid beds. Care must be taken to keep mortar from getting between the centre and the stones, which would prevent them being set in the true position. Frequent checks must be made with both the spirit level and straight edge to ensure that the arch is plumb, and in the right relationship to the existing walls. Unless there are strong structural objections, if the walls are out of plumb it will be necessary to rebuild the arch out of plumb to match. In this case the centre must be set to the correct angle before work begins, and the plumb line cannot be used.

It is good practice to ease the centre as soon as the arch is complete, to allow any settlement to take place before the mortar has set. This allows each joint and voussoir to take its full share of the load without cracking of the joints. Once eased, there is no reason to keep the centre in position; there is no danger of the arch falling as it locks itself into position as it settles. Care must be taken when building up the surrounding walling to avoid cracking the mortar joints, but there is no reason why work on the walling cannot begin immediately.

REPAIRS TO VAULTS

As arched structures, vaults are normally very stable, but a vault can crack and show signs of collapse, usually as a result of movement of the abutments. Provided the abutments have ceased to move or can be stabilized, the only satisfactory method of repair is to take it down and rebuild it. While this perhaps appears daunting, the work is quite straightforward. However, it is necessary to understand a little about vault construction.

Vault construction

Simple vaults, whether semicircular or pointed, are merely very deep arches; they are often known as *barrel vaults* from their shape. Where one vault crosses another (usually when the main vault meets a short vault over a window opening), the vault changes direction without any change in material: the small stones of which it is made up turn into the cross-vault in the manner of a return on a vertical wall. This junction, straight on plan but curved in elevation, is known as a *groin*, and the vault as a *groined vault*.

In a ribbed vault there is a structural framework of arches (ribs) which take the place of the groins. They are usually constructed in bays, each bay being a section of the main vault and a pair of cross-vaults. The ribs, known as *diagonal ribs*, form a cross on plan. It is common for each bay to be divided from the next by a rib running across the main vault, at right angles to its length. These are known as *transverse ribs*. Later vaults often have additional ribs between the diagonal and transverse ribs, springing from the same point but running to a point on the ridge. These are known as *tierceron ribs*. The junction of vault and wall is marked with a further rib, built into the wall, called the *wall rib*.

All these ribs normally spring from one point and, in order to accommodate nine (or more) ribs meeting at one point, they are merged before they come down to the springing. It is usually only when the ribs are fully separated that the vault proper begins; the first three or four courses of the springing are built into the wall as corbels with horizontal joints. The first radiating joint marks the beginning of the arch and it is not normally necessary to take down below this point.

If the vaults are pointed, the continuous line formed at the crown is sometimes masked with a further rib, the *ridge rib*. This is more common in English vaults than in French owing to the method of constructing the *webs*, or panels infilling between the ribs. A glance at Figure G.19 will show that the diagonal rib is longer that the transverse rib and therefore, if the courses of stone in the web are parallel, the crown of the vault will be reached soonest against the transverse rib, with shorter and shorter courses used to complete the web. This gives an unsatisfactory junction between the two halves of the vault and the English designers tended to mask this by using the ridge rib. The French builders, who designed many English churches in the early mediaeval period, preferred to use tapered courses so that the final course was parallel to the axis of the vault and dispensed with the ridge rib. If any part of the web has to be replaced, as opposed to rebuilt, the original form of web construction must be followed faithfully.

The exception to the general description of vaults is the *fan vault*, often used in the Perpendicular style. Here the ribs and webs are all worked on one stone and each of the stones, which are in fact thin panels, is a voussoir. Pendant vaults are constructed with voussoirs which project a long way below the vault to form the pendants.

Taking down the vault

The vault must be supported by centring before any part is stripped. A simple rubble barrel vault is a straightforward continuous arch and only the length to be stripped needs to be supported. The support must be complete from springing to springing. If the vault is very distorted, the simplest way of achieving this is to use sheets of plywood, 12–25 mm thick according to the size of vault, cut part-way through on the upper surface to allow them to bend more easily and held in place by Acrow props. These should bear on lengths of timber nailed to the back of the ply and be tied to each other with scaffold tubes to form a rigid structure. The props must be tightened only sufficiently to give support without giving a positive upward thrust to the vault.

Ribbed vaults must be treated as two parts, the rib and the web. If only the web is to be taken down (usually only when individual stones of the web have perished), they are dealt with as above. There is one difference – the web is likely to be curved in two directions and this must be taken into account when constructing the centre.

If one or more ribs are to be stripped, the web must be taken out first and the ribs individually supported by purpose-made centres. Clearly, every rib which takes support from the damaged one must be supported. Even before any deformation owing to movement, in elevation the ribs are generally not simple arches, but compound curves, because of the need for ribs of differing lengths to rise to the same height. It is likely to be a matter of trial and error to get the centre to support each voussoir in a displaced rib, and wedges may be needed during the stripping. Special provision must be made for bosses, which are the voussoirs onto which is worked the junction of two or more ribs, and which usually have carved decoration project-ing below the line of the rib.

All stones must be individually numbered according to their course and position as they are taken off, so that they can be replaced as they were found. It is useful to take careful note of the distance from the ridge to several of the courses of the web to assist in rebuilding.

Rebuilding the vault

Barrel vaults

The centre for the barrel vault has to be restored as closely as possible to the original profile, which is done by taking up the props until it runs in a straight line between the two standing parts of the vault, or from standing part to wall line.

If the whole length of a vault has to be rebuilt, it is better to take out the temporary centre and put up a new, purpose-made one. A long vault can be rebuilt in sections, moving the centre as each length is built. It is preferable to use two centres, moved alternately so that the edge of the rebuilt vault is never unsupported; it would be subject to damage when the centre is raised to its new position.

The centres can be supported on timber rails on a rigid scaffold framework against the side walls. The rails must allow for the centres to be carried on broad folding wedges with a total thickness of at least 100 mm. The centres themselves may be made in two halves, bolted together for location, and supported in the middle on a trestle or securely braced props. When moving the centres, the greatest care must be taken not to strike the underside of the vault. A vault or arch, even newly constructed and with the mortar not yet set, can carry very high superimposed loads but is very susceptible to damage from below.

Barrel vaults are usually built in coursed rubble and were originally supported on centring made of boards and wickerwork, giving a relatively uneven soffit. If the use of a smooth plywood centre might give an obviously different finish, a spread of 25 mm of sand over the centre will introduce a slight degree of unevenness. If, on an ancient monument, it is archaeologically desirable to differentiate between original and rebuilt work, it is easier to use a thick bed of sand (50–75 mm) to raise the new work above the level of the original than to use additional timber laggings.

Rebuilding is quite straightforward, so long as it is treated as building a wall. Each stone must be firmly bedded on the one below, and not laid dry and then grouted. Check the course heights against the control measurements as the work proceeds. When complete, it is usual to apply a thick spread of mortar over the whole.

Ribbed vaults

Depending on how far the rib was deformed, it may be necessary to make a new centre before rebuilding, to reflect the true profile. If the displacement was small, it may be sufficient to add fresh laggings of varying heights to suit but this must be done carefully to avoid sudden changes. It is usually possible to obtain the correct profile for the centre from adjacent ribs, so long as they perform the equivalent function in the vault.

Rebuilding a rib is like building any arch; the voussoirs must be solidly bedded and it is unwise to use dowels in an attempt to strengthen the arch. If the rib will not stand without dowels, it is certain to be structurally unsafe. It is probably best to ease the centre only slightly and leave it in place while rebuilding the web to reduce the risk of accidental movement of the rib.

Re-forming the centre for the webs is more difficult than in the case of the barrel vault. Not only may the web be curved in two directions, but the centre must fit exactly the curve of the two or more ribs against which it abuts; the web goes over the ribs, either completely or onto a rebate. It is best to take several profiles from an existing web, fix these in their correct positions on the centre and cover the whole with ply. From this point, rebuilding is the same as for the barrel vault.

Striking the centre

As with building arches, it is best to ease the centre from the barrel vault or the web as soon as the work is finished, to allow the mortar to take up any minor movement before it is fully set. While it is unlikely to cause problems, it is probably best to avoid walking on it as far as possible before the mortar has had a chance to set.

GROUTING OF RUBBLE-FILLED WALLS

Many walls have outer skins of facing stone with the centre filled with broken stone. Where very little mortar was used in the infill or where the lime has leached out because of water getting into the wall, it is necessary to consolidate the core. This is usually done by filling the voids with grout.

There are differences of opinion on whether grouting is a really effective method of dealing with the problem as, however much care is used, there is no satisfactory method of determining either the extent of the voids or whether they have all been filled. Whenever practicable, it is better to take down the wall in sections and rebuild it. This is not always possible and, in the case of ancient monuments, very undesirable. Once a wall has been dismantled it is archaeologically 'dead', however much care is taken in rebuilding. At times, grouting has to be resorted to.

The wall must first be pointed or the joints filled with tow (teased out hemp fibres – pronounced 'toe'). Weep holes must be left every two or three courses, both to assist in flushing out dust and debris, and to prove the effectiveness of the grouting.

Flush out the interior thoroughly using a hose pipe. If the wall is unstable, this should be done in stages of a few courses at a time beginning at the bottom, and each stage grouted and allowed to set before proceeding. Grout is introduced through holes left in the joints, either by pouring into a clay cup (for small voids), by gravity grouting from a tank on an upper lift of scaffolding, or under pressure from a grouting machine.

A careful watch must be kept in case any joint bursts and releases grout, which must be flushed away immediately; in extreme cases, whole stones have been forced out of a wall. The pressure used must relate to the condition of the wall. A watch must be kept on the surrounding parts of the building, as grout has been known to travel many metres and emerge in unexpected places.

When grout is seen at the proving holes, grouting must stop until the hole is firmly plugged with tow. Tow must be taken out as soon as the grout is no longer liquid or it will be impossible to remove.

Mix for grouting

A general-purpose mix is one part lime putty:two parts pulverized fly ash:eight or nine parts fine sand. Neat OPC must never be used – see Chapter 9, Mortar.

While grouting, the mix must be stirred constantly to keep the heavier particles in suspension.

PLASTIC REPAIRS

Plastic in this sense means repairs made in a soft material, usually a mortar, which sets hard to resemble the stone. This type of repair is used either as an economical alternative to replacing all or part of the stone with new stone, or to reproduce the original profile while preserving as much of the original fabric as possible. It is never a permanent solution in the way that repair with new stone is but it should not be seen as a cheap alternative. It has its place as one of the methods of repair available to the mason.

Material for repairs

Resin-based materials have been used for many years, but they are usually impervious and do not change colour with changing humidity, which makes them difficult to match. Also, they do not usually weather at the same rate as the surrounding stone and, in time, will stand proud to form a lip, which will hold water. However, resins are changing all the time and permeable resin-based compounds, some of which can be graded to weather with the surrounding stone, are being developed, and a resin-based material may soon be produced which will satisfy all requirements. In the meantime, mortar-based repairs are normally preferred by most interest groups.

The choice of mortar for the repair is of the first importance – too hard a mix will result in a dense, impervious repair which will be liable to break away from the background, perhaps causing further damage. The mix must therefore be somewhat soft, which will cause the repair to weather away at a slightly faster rate than the surrounding stone. The repair will thus eventually have to be redone but this is kinder to the building than using a hard mortar.

The choice of mix for the repair depends on both the type of stone and its condition, and trials will be needed to establish what is best. As a guide, a mix of 1:3:10, white cement:lime putty:aggregate may be tried. The aggregate should have a good range of grain sizes and may include up to 20 per cent stone dust to improve the colour match. As with all mortars, only the minimum quantity of water should be used and the mixture well beaten to improve the workability.

On sandstone buildings, it may be best to avoid the use of lime and instead make the repair with masonry cement. A mix of 1:10, masonry cement:aggregate may be tried.

Techniques

It is always wise to carry out a trial repair on the building in question rather than in the workshop before the work proceeds. The colour of the repairs may need changing to suit different parts of the building to allow for minor changes in stone colour. Any cleaning must be carried out before repairs are made. There are many examples of blackened repairs that have been put into a dirty building which was subsequently cleaned, leaving the repairs to stand out. Even if no cleaning is anticipated, the repair should match the true colour of the stone rather than its present condition.

Any decayed stone should be carefully cut away to give a sound surface. The top and sides of the area should be undercut slightly to increase the hold of the mortar, but the lower edge should, if anything, have a slight outward slope to avoid creating a water trap. Feather edges must be avoided.

Projecting detail and large, deep areas may need the support of an armature. For this, copper or annealed stainless steel wire 20SWG (1 mm) is secured into drilled holes with epoxy resin; thicker wire may be needed for larger areas, perhaps in conjunction with dowels. Reinforcement should be kept 15–20 mm back from the surface.

All dust and debris must be cleaned out, and the cavity and surrounding area well wetted with clean water. The mortar must be tamped solidly into the cavity leaving no voids. Holes of greater depth than 15 mm should be filled in stages, each stage being left to go off for at least a day. The repair should be finished a little proud of the stone as overworking the surface can cause cracking.

When the mortar has taken an initial set, the surface should be scraped with a fine hacksaw blade until flush with the surrounding stone. The surface of the repair must not be reduced below the level of the stone. Where repairs to a run of moulding are carried out, it is important to maintain the moulding profile throughout the length, using a straight-edge and, if necessary, a zinc reverse mould to ensure accuracy.

To avoid staining, care should be taken to keep the mortar off the surrounding stone; use polythene sheet secured with adhesive tape where possible. Any staining which does occur should be removed as soon as possible using a clean sponge and sufficient clean water, without introducing further water to the repair. The emphasis must be on avoiding stains in the first place.

To prevent over-rapid drying out of the mortar in warm, dry weather, or in drying winds, it may be necessary to cover the repair with damp sacking or similar protection until it has fully set. In cold weather, mortar repairs should not be carried out unless the temperature, actual or anticipated, is at least 3°C above freezing point.

To sum up, mortar repairs should not be regarded as a quick, cheap alternative to replacement, but as a long-lasting and carefully carried out option, which is appropriate in some circumstances.

11

Cleaning

Owing to the highly technical nature of many of the cleaning processes and the continuing development of methods, it is only possible to give an outline of the various techniques in the space available. However, this will give the stone mason some insight into processes often carried out by specialist contractors. Further details are given in the books listed in the bibliography, but it is always sensible to take specific professional advice.

The cleaning of stone buildings is surrounded by controversy concerning both the method and necessity. There is no doubt that to restore a building to something like its original colour and appearance is visually beneficial and can be an aid to preventing, or at least reducing, chemical decay. As discussed above under 'The weathering and decay of stone' (p. 18), the accumulation of salt-bearing deposits is damaging to stone and it follows that reducing these deposits should lengthen the life of the stone.

It is not, however, quite as straightforward as it may appear. Objections to cleaning are often raised on the grounds that removal of dirt removes a part of the history of the building. Other objectors base their views on the undoubted damage caused by inappropriate methods and unskilled staff, and it is true that both factors have at times caused more damage to a building than pollution could achieve.

Cleaning is one of the treatments of historic buildings which is constantly under review. It is a highly specialized area of work for which independent professional advice should always be taken. Subject to this advice, it may be that some of the work can be undertaken by stone masons with appropriate training and direction; some work must be left to professional conservators. All that can be given here is a general outline of current methods.

As with any intervention in an old building, one must always ask whether the action is necessary and to what extent it should be carried out. A light cleaning can enhance the appearance of a building and prolong the life of the fabric. Trying to clean an old building until it looks new, on the other hand, is likely to be impossible without causing some, and perhaps a great deal of, damage.

A first step is to survey the building to establish: the cause and nature of the soiling; the precise type and composition of the stone ('limestone' and 'sandstone' is not enough); the nature and extent of any protection to vulnerable areas such as windows and open joints (both of which must be sealed to prevent flooding); and the likely effect of the cleaning method in the short and long term. It may be that the last point can only be answered by carrying out a trial cleaning on selected typical areas, which will also establish the standard of cleaning to be aimed for. Another aim of the survey must be to identify any carved or other significant detail which may be damaged by the general cleaning process, and must therefore be protected and treated separately. Each part of the building must be separately assessed, taking into account, among other factors, variations in the type of stone, and treated according to its particular circumstances and requirements.

When using any cleaning system, disposal of the detritus or effluent must be carefully considered, especially with regard to contamination of water courses and drains. Full consultation with the local water authorities is essential.

MECHANICAL CLEANING

Redressing

Traditionally this was done manually with mallet and chisel, but more recently with pneumatic tools and with grinding discs. It will be successful, in that removing several millimetres from the surface will remove most if not all the dirt and stains but it is a desperate measure, which effectively takes all trace of history from the building. Mouldings, unless recut, will remain dirty, and, if recut, at great cost in labour, will be reduced in size and the design will be changed. Grinding the surface almost invariably results in swirl patterns and arrises which are far from straight: enormous damage has been caused to major buildings in recent years.

Whilst it is true that, in some cases, redressing has been carried out successfully, it is not to be recommended as a method of cleaning.

Air abrasive

Abrasive particles are directed onto the surface using compressed air, breaking up both the dirt and the surface of the stone. This will remove surface dirt but very often at the expense of damage to the masonry. In the hands of a highly skilled operator the damage may not be great but smooth surfaces will show a lightly abraded finish at best, and, at worst, will lose material from softer areas of stone and show a shaded effect. The method can achieve rapid results but, if used carelessly, serious damage can be done in a short time; craters can be dug in the surface of the stone. Arrises and carved detail are particularly vulnerable. The operator may be unable to see the surface once the blast has been started and has to rely on memory.

Advances are being made in the development of both the cleaning medium and the means of application. Considerable success is being achieved with calcium carbonate used at low pressures, which not only reduces the possibility of damage to the stone but enables the operator to have a better view of the work.

In one type of gun the abrasive medium is forced out of the reservoir under pressure from the air blast. In another, the abrasive is not forced out by the compressed air but the fine particles are drawn out of the reservoir by the suction of the air passing across. This gives better control and is better suited to work on small details. The dry abrasive process does not of itself introduce the risk of staining, or of flooding, but the surfaces must be washed down to remove all trace of the abrasive particles.

Wet abrasive cleaning adds water to the air/abrasive blast. The principal benefit is that the nuisance and possible health hazards of dry abrasive dust are much reduced. However, the mist around the operator and the slurry on the surface can make observation of the cleaning process even more difficult than dry abrasive. A new system of low-pressure blast mixes the water and medium before it reaches the nozzle, giving much better control and a good view of the work.

There is no doubt that very effective and economical cleaning of suitable surfaces can be achieved with an abrasive system. It is essential that the work is carefully specified, and carried out only by highly trained and conscientious personnel.

Pencil abrasive cleaning

This is a dry abrasive system on a small scale, using a gun little bigger than an ordinary pencil to direct very fine abrasive particles. With careful selection of the abrasive medium and in the hands of an experienced user, very good results may be obtained, but its small size and delicacy of operation means that it is best suited to fine detail and carvings. It can be used to remove a layer of dirt and yet leave in place traces of colour beneath. Even with a pencil gun, it is possible to cut right into the stone rather than merely clean it, and it must be used only by trained operators.

When using any air abrasive system, the potential health hazards must be borne in mind.

Scrubbing

Using a scrubbing brush is the simplest form of mechanical cleaning but this will remove only loose dirt from the surface. If used with a bucket of water, a certain amount of ingrained dirt may be loosened. Steel wire brushes must never be used, only natural or synthetic bristle, or soft bronze wire. Any brush can damage the surface of a soft or decaying stone, so care must be used in their selection.

Scrubbing with carborundum may serve to remove stubborn surface dirt, but is liable to damage the surface of the stone.

WATER WASHING

It is the deposition of sulphates which causes the greatest damage to stone. Deposits on sandstone are not water soluble and water will, at best, remove only a small amount of surface dirt. Sandstone buildings are typically cleanest in those parts sheltered from rain, where water-borne pollutants do not reach. Most of the pollutants on limestone, on the other hand, are water soluble, which is why those areas which are regularly washed by rain stay cleaner than the sheltered areas where deposits are allowed to build up. Washing with clean water will not only remove the visible dirt, but will also remove some of the damaging salts and extend the life of the stone. The washing must be done with care; connecting a hose pipe to the mains and aiming it at the building is not the way to proceed.

Relatively small quantities of water are needed; the aim is to soften the dirt, which is best achieved by maintaining the surface in a moist condition. Soaking the surface is liable to give rise to staining, as dirt and salts are drawn to the face. The ideal is an intermittent mist spray, which softens the dirt without either soaking the stone or causing heavy run-off.

A variety of fine nozzles are available, some mounted on rigid booms and some on flexible hoses; the individual nozzles may be fixed or swivelling. In some cases, agricultural spraying equipment can be utilized; nozzles and rigid pipes can be obtained from agricultural suppliers as individual units and assembled as required. Interchangeable heads for the nozzles allow the weight of the mist to be varied; it is normally the finest sprays which are called for.

It is standard practice to use mains water for large-scale cleaning. The water should be fed through a ball valve into a clean plastic tank to avoid any risk of contaminating the mains supply. Water is delivered to the nozzles through an electric pump, controlled to give an intermittent spray. This is most simply achieved by means of a clock which can be set to give a fixed on–off cycle. Typical cycles might be 5 seconds on and 5 minutes off, or 10 seconds on and 5 minutes off. The pre-contract trial will establish the optimum pattern but the minimum on-time consistent with maintaining a lightly moist surface should always be aimed for.

To reduce the risk of staining, surfaces below the part being cleaned must be protected from run-off. Horizontal divisions are often obvious in the form of string courses, below which temporary plastic guttering and fall pipes can be used to divert the waste water to the ground. In the case of large vertical areas, polythene sheet should be battened and sealed to the building, conducting the water to the guttering, allowing the building to be cleaned in stages.

The water sprays must be carefully monitored and, as soon as the dirt is softened, it must be gently removed by brushing, if it is not running off naturally. Brushes should be of natural or synthetic bristle. In the case of stubborn dirt a soft bronze wire brush may be used with care, but even these may damage the surface of soft stone. Steel wire brushes must *never* be used on stone. Brushes of a variety of sizes and shapes must be available, so that there is no danger of the brush-head bumping mouldings or carvings.

Cleaning ashlar and simple moulded work in this way should present no great problems but, where delicate work is being cleaned, the very greatest care must be used, and the work closely monitored. Owing to the risk of frost damage, it is inadvisable to carry out water washing during the winter months. The use of water is not a simple, safe process; very fine carvings on at least one cathedral have been badly damaged by the careless use of water in recent years.

CHEMICAL CLEANING

The use of chemicals for stone cleaning has led to a number of problems in the past, caused partly by their careless use and partly by the danger that salts, which are harmful to the stone, can be deposited. The problems are lessening as cleaning contractors have become more professional, and steps have been taken to prevent or neutralize salt residues. It may be necessary to remove any previously applied water repellent (see below) before beginning any chemical cleaning.

The most commonly used cleaning agent for sandstone, hydrofluoric acid, is one of the oldest and, if used with care, one of the safest. When the dilute acid is sprayed or brushed onto the pre-wetted stone, it acts by dissolving the silica, bringing with it the surface dirt. After a suitable interval, between 20 minutes and 1 hour, the stone must be thoroughly washed down, with special attention being paid to any water traps. Failure to do this will result in the formation of stains that may be almost impossible to remove. The acidity of the wall should be checked after washing down, which must be repeated until a satisfactory value is achieved. Scaffolding and other associated equipment must also be thoroughly washed.

If carried out under properly controlled procedures, the use of hydrofluoric acid on sandstones with a siliceous matrix can be very successful. Its use on ferruginous sandstones can cause brown staining, which is impossible to remove effectively. Calcareous and dolomitic (magnesian) sandstones are at some risk, as the matrices are soluble in the acid; used carefully, the loss from the surface may not be significant.

A long-standing method of cleaning marble headstones is dilute hydrochloric acid ('spirits of salts'). It is effective but, as it dissolves calcium carbonate, it is very likely to remove the surface from the stone, leaving a saccharoidal (sugary) finish and its use for this is, therefore, not recommended. Conservation-grade soap and water is a good first approach to the cleaning of marble. Be very sure that the 'marble' is not alabaster, which is soluble in water and can, in general terms, be cleaned only with white spirit.

Alkaline-based (caustic) cleaning agents can be effective for removing stubborn dirt, but all carry the danger of leaving salt residues in the stone. They have, however, proved very effective when properly used, especially where they are applied in poultice form. Very thorough washing off is necessary, and the use of a mild acid in the wash may be recommended to neutralize any remaining alkali. The use of a cleaning poultice (see below) may be needed to draw salts to the surface.

OTHER CLEANING METHODS

Poultices

In principle, the poultice is a thick paste applied to the stone, the purpose of which is to loosen and draw out the dirt. Poultices can be very useful for drawing out soluble salts, which migrate from the stone to the poultice and can then be removed. The usual base for the poultice is a type of clay, such as sepiolite, or acid-free paper.

Poultices must be used only on sound stonework, as friable stone will lift with the poultice.

Lime poultice

This was developed for use on limestone and marble. Fresh lime putty is applied to the surface of the stone, and allowed to dry slowly, absorbing surface dirt and salts as it does so. On removal, the surface is rinsed with water and brushed to remove remaining dirt.

Chemical poultices

These may be specially developed proprietary cleaning agents or they may be made up according to established formulae. They are normally kept moist by wrapping in plastic film immediately on application, after which they are kept in place for anything from a few hours to a day. They have in some cases proved extremely successful, and are likely to become a more important part of the cleaning armoury in the future. They can be much more carefully controlled than other chemical methods and they have no mechanical action on the surface of the stone.

Laser cleaning

Cleaning by means of lasers has been used successfully in the laboratory for the treatment of museum objects. At least one organization has now developed modern portable equipment for use on scaffolds and this has great potential. The rate of cleaning is at present very slow, as the beam is narrow and covers a spot only a few millimetres in diameter, and is thus more suitable for specific sculptural or decorative features. However, future developments may make this of practical application for large-scale cleaning.

Graffiti

There are a number of proprietary agents developed for the removal of graffiti and paint. Many of them are specific in their effect, and it is necessary to establish the nature of the paint or ink used, as well as the type of stone. If paint is involved, a methylene chloride paint stripper (Nitromors) can be used without risk of damage to the stone and may be successful. Low-pressure calcium carbonate slurry has also been used with success.

This is a specialized area and it is wise to seek professional advice.

SURFACE TREATMENTS

It has been the intermittent practice for centuries to treat stone in order to arrest decay. The principle seems to have been to keep the stone dry, on the assumption that water was the greatest enemy. Linseed oil and beeswax were the principal constituents; weathered linseed oil on limestone can give an appearance of a crazed, dull varnish. Both tended to discolour with age to give a yellow/brown appearance and, while stones which appear to have been treated (records are understandably lacking) have survived, their use can be harmful in the trapping of salts beneath the surface. Anecdotal evidence suggests that the waxing of Purbeck marble used both internally and externally may have been beneficial (damp Purbeck decays more noticeably than dry) but the trapping of salts beneath the surface is an ever-present risk. The continued use of oil and beeswax cannot be recommended.

More sophisticated water-repellent treatments are now available. Those based on silicone are colourless, do not give rise to darkening of the stonework and are generally held to be among the most effective. Their effectiveness depends on the depth of penetration. The question may be raised as to whether a newly cleaned building should be coated to preserve its appearance.

During the period for which the surface of the coating remains intact, visible soiling will be reduced but the life of the coating is negligible compared to the life of the stone. Even silicone-based treatments which have penetrated satisfactorily and continue to form a water penetration barrier will lose their surface coating within a relatively short time. The non-uniform breakdown of the repellent surface can lead to uneven soiling and, even where the surface remains sound, the resulting increase in the rate of run-off may lead to changes in the appearance of the building with uneven streaking. In general, water-repellent treatments cannot be recommended for maintaining the newly cleaned appearance of a building.

Water repellents may have a place in reducing the effects of decay but they may also exacerbate the problems. They should never be used without professional advice from a consultant who fully understands the chemistry both of the treatment and of its interaction with the stone in the specific circumstances of its use.

12

Supervision and Specifications

THE ARCHITECT AND THE STONE MASON

The architect

Since about the 1950s there has been a reduction in the number of architects and other supervisors of masonry work who have direct working experience of masonry. Ironically this trend is occurring at a time when more money and effort than ever before are being spent on repairs to historic buildings. The fault is not that of the individuals but of the system, which trains architects in their role as designers but does not inform them in detail about the work of the stone mason. This is understandable, for many architects will never deal with stone buildings throughout their professional life.

It is also the fault of the masonry trade itself, because its members have been reluctant to put pen to paper for the education of outsiders. Instead, this has been left to others who have had some contact with the trade. Architects, archaeologists, conservators and others have all dealt with the subject in varying detail over recent years, and almost all have failed to do justice to the subject.

It must be said that the view commonly held in the UK, that the theoretician is superior to the practitioner, has not helped the interchange of information with a trade regarded as the second oldest in the world, and one traditionally as recalcitrant as its material. Stone masons may have become a comparatively rare breed, but treating them almost as exhibits in a zoo does not help to gain their confidence. Under these circumstances, it is very easy for suspicion to turn to hostility and this obviously does not promote good working relationships.

This chapter is written to assist architects in their supervision of masons. The term 'architect' is used from this point on as a convenient shorthand for all supervisory personnel. A thorough reading of the technical chapters of this book together with what follows should help to give a better understanding of what the skilled stone mason can and cannot achieve. This can only help to raise the general standards of the trade, which in some respects have fallen off in recent years.

This is not intended to suggest that the tradesman expects the architect to have a complete and full understanding of every process – that would be quite impractical. The architect is there as designer and co-ordinator as much as supervisor, and cannot be expected to share all the technical knowledge of every trade. However, questions asked on the basis of a reasonable understanding will not only limit the possibility of skimped work but will also increase the respect of the mason for the architect.

One of the problems is that most architects have some personal, practical experience of the work of other trades. They may not be very good at painting windows, putting up shelves, building garden walls, or wiring up a security light, but they have some idea of what is involved and at least know what the job should not look like. Very few non-masons have even seen stone being worked, much less had any first-hand experience, and this is a barrier which both sides must work to overcome. Many architects are prepared to ask questions and to seek advice on aspects of work that are unclear, and these questions are usually welcomed. The issuing of impossible instructions based on little direct knowledge of the trade merely increases any divisions which already exist.

The stone mason

A word of warning is necessary before going on to discuss particular aspects of supervision. The word 'mason' or 'stone mason' can cover a wide range of skills.

Bricklayer-masons are used, to whatever degree, to fix stone dressings or features in a brick building. This may be dressed stone or it may be walling, but they are very unlikely to know anything about the dressing of stone other than knocking the corners off walling stone. They may be accustomed only to walling stone, which is not a good training for fixing dressed stone.

Dry-stone wallers are likely to describe themselves as such, rather than as masons. Pavior masons are street masons, used to laying flags and kerbs, and having the skill to dress these as required (not merely butchering the stone with a disc-cutter). Fixer masons deal only with the fixing of dressed stone which has been worked by others. They may well have a fair knowledge of working stone if they have served a formal apprenticeship.

Banker masons have the skill to dress almost any stone to any form required, from a simple moulding to a nodding ogee arch. They are also likely to be accustomed to fixing as well but this should not be assumed. Good banker masons will usually make a better job of fixing than anyone else because they are more aware of what is involved in dressing the stone.

Obviously, skills may overlap within the several branches of this trade and the practitioners range from excellent to abysmal. The ability to differentiate between them depends on having a reasonable working knowledge of the principles and practices of the trade.

REPAIRS: THE PHILOSOPHY, NATURE AND EXTENT

The nature and extent of repairs to masonry is often a matter of judgement rather than of science. The course chosen will be influenced by, among other factors, the budget, the views of the client, the function of a particular stone, the nature of the stone, the type of building and the views of interested third parties such as planning departments, heritage organizations, etc.

Decay in stone is not of itself necessarily harmful. The simple weathering of a few millimetres from the face of an ashlar wall merely reflects the age of the building and is best left alone. The rapid decay of a single voussoir in an arch presents a structural danger and must be replaced. Severe decay in a single ashlar in an otherwise well-preserved wall is not aesthetically pleasing, drawing the eye in a way that was never intended, and also has the potential for allowing water to penetrate the wall. Likewise, the decision to replace a piece of string course which has weathered away, allowing water to run down the face of the wall and cause staining, can be a relatively simple one.

A weathered feature which presents no structural threat poses a different problem: is one justified on economic grounds in leaving it for later repair if a 70 m scaffold will have to be re-erected in 20 years' time? At lower levels, it may be feasible to erect a relatively low, light scaffold in order to carry out repointing and perhaps some mortar repairs to a feature, which, with such care, will last another 50 years before major repairs are essential. There will very often be constraints imposed by Listed Building or Scheduled Monument Consent, which may have to be the subject of negotiation. It may here be worth pointing out to the mason, who is often not aware of this, that owners of historic buildings are not free to do as they wish. Statutory constraints are imposed, which, quite rightly, force careful and detailed consideration of proposed repairs. There is no point in complaining to the owner or anyone else concerned because the regulations must be obeyed, and grey areas are best dealt with by discussion rather than confrontation.

Most cases are not straightforward, and involve considerations of the philosophies of preserve-as-found or repair-as-designed. More often than not, it is the philosophy which determines whether to renew stonework. It is not possible to lay down rules by which the decision can be made on practical grounds, other than structural stability or the safety of the public. A summary of the choices may help, but first the philosophy behind the decision must be addressed.

The philosophy of repair

This subject, above all, has been bedevilled by controversy and strong disagreement for over a hundred years. The nineteenth century saw restoration of countless churches, many of which had been allowed to fall into a state of disrepair which would amaze the modern visitor in the present 'heritage-aware' climate of opinion. Many mediaeval churches were demolished and rebuilt, or so thoroughly repaired that little of the original fabric remains. Very often, churches were revamped to convert them to the Victorian idea of what was 'proper' for a mediaeval church. Usually this meant 'restoring' the Early English features which were assumed to have been there – and sometimes this happened in churches not founded until the Decorated or Perpendicular period. Sometimes the church was remodelled to what the patron of the repairs felt was appropriate – St Albans cathedral is probably the most notorious example.

Out of all this arose a movement to act on behalf of the lovers of ancient buildings to preserve what was left before it was too late. Undoubtedly this saved many more ancient buildings from suffering wholesale reconstruction and the climate is now such that, in general terms, old buildings are regarded as a valuable part of what is so often called 'our national heritage'. However, it cannot be said that all is well, or even that all those seriously interested in historic buildings think alike.

With some it has become an article of faith that no stone should ever be replaced, on the somewhat specious grounds that the original fabric is sacrosanct. They consider that to put in new stone is an act of deception on the public, if not of the present, then of the future. It is the view of this school of thought (speaking of the general tendency of this school rather than of any specific interest group) that, if any part of a building has to be replaced for structural reasons, then the replacement should be in a foreign material such as tile or brick. Thus, the reasoning runs, there is no deception so far as the public is concerned as the replacements are obvious. One may ask what is being achieved by the insertion of tile, brick, or other foreign materials into an ancient building. Structural stability, obviously, but at the expense of the visual satisfaction which the public is entitled to expect.

Repairs carried out in brick 200 years ago to a stone-built house because the then owner could not afford, or did not care sufficiently, to use stone, are a part of the history of the building. To make repairs in brick today for philosophical reasons serves simply to advertise that philosophy, and tells future generations nothing about the way in which the building was used in the last half of the twentieth century. English Heritage, the guiding guardian of historic sites and buildings, indulges in the academically suspect practice of 'improving' the appearance of achaeological sites by inserting stone where none existed at the time of excavation, so why should the owner of an historic building in current use, which also happens to be a scheduled ancient monument, not be encouraged to make repairs in the original material in order to preserve the original design?

Part of the responsibility for the 'preserve-as-found' viewpoint lies in the belief that the 'integrity of the craftsman' is all-important. This is a strange notion, held largely by those who have never worked as straightforward craftsmen, and is rarely reflected by those who handle tools throughout their working lives.

The present authors have both worked and fixed everything from ashlar to mouldings and tracery which were replacements for medi-aeval work, and are prepared and content for these stones to be cut out and replaced in their turn when they have reached the end of their useful life in 200, 300 or 500 years. There is nothing sacrosanct about a piece of worked stone, merely on the grounds that it once had a face or some detail on it which has long disappeared or become unsound. It is very clear to the authors, who have examined and measured historic masonry in far greater detail than the average architectural historian, that the mediaeval mason was very like his present-day counterpart. He varied from idle and drunken to dedi-cated and hard-working, from conscientious to slapdash, and from highly skilled to barely fit to sweep the scaffold.

A good deal of nonsense has been talked about our great cathedrals being built by men working for the glory of God. The mediaeval mason was working for largely the same reasons as the mason of today. Some, no doubt, were motivated by religious feelings, and others not. Some came into the trade because they saw it as an easy option, and some because they felt an affinity with the work. The intricate detail of mouldings set 50 m above ground was not the responsibility of the individual mason but was carried out as part of the design set down by the master mason. The care often, but not always, put into working these stones was partly a matter of pride and job satisfaction, and partly that they were not worked at high level but on the ground. The critical and often very vocal opinion of fellow masons can be a significant spur.

This has been something of a digression, but it is important to set historic buildings and their workmanship in proper context, something which is rarely done. It should not in any way be read as a dismissal of the importance of historic fabric; the authors have remained in their occupations because of the care and appreciation they have for the work of their predecessors.

Conservation of buildings by means of replacement has been the philosophy for several hundred years and, while some of the work is open to very serious criticism in the light of modern views, the buildings are at least still standing. The overriding consideration must surely be for the integrity of the original design. It seems extraordinarily arrogant to say that no future generations shall see historic buildings in the form in which they were designed, but will instead see only weathered and barely recognizable features in place of the crisp outlines which were intended. It is not unreasonable to take the art world as a parallel. When an old master suffers damage, it is repaired to recover the original appearance, and rightly so. It would be unthinkable to see the Mona Lisa with her nose flaking, and a missing eyebrow made good with a flat wash. If the same policy were applied to art as to historic buildings, there would hardly be an art restorer left to earn a living.

There seems to be an inability to discriminate between the various types of historic structures. The foundations of a Roman fort, the roofless remains of an abbey, and the chimney of an abandoned tin mine are archaeological monuments and, as such, should receive only the absolute minimum of work carried out in order to preserve them. There is no good reason to do any more. Once a single stone has been taken out and rebedded, the monument is on the way to being archaeologically 'dead' as far as future study is concerned. On the other hand, a mediaeval building, still roofed and in use, is a living building, and must be kept in good repair so as to maintain not only its structural integrity but also the integrity of its design. Only by doing so can due respect be paid to its designer and builders. Such buildings were put up not only for utility, but to impress and delight the observer. They were built for the people and to the glory of God, or for reasons of civic pride, as the case may be, and not for the historian, and should be maintained in the same way. To do any other is to break the continuity of purpose.

The modern move to preserve a roofed and usable, but not currently used, building for its own sake and not for some specific use, is relatively speaking so new that we have yet to come to terms with it. Is it solely a piece of archaeology? Or is it something to be altered, as it will have been throughout its life (but this time as sympathetically as possible) to suit some practical and useful purpose? There is no convincing evidence that these questions have been satisfactorily resolved. And do we have the right to say that this or that building, repaired, altered and adapted over 500 years, must now be frozen in time in the condition in which we now find it?

Having said all this, it must also be emphasized that there has certainly been too much 'restoration' in the past, and much beautiful and important work has been destroyed in this way – often to satisfy the philosophy of the moment, as with the 'Victorianizing' of churches, mentioned above. The present tendency to leave alone at almost any cost has come about as a reaction to past horrors, and to that extent is both understandable and to some extent necessary. However, signs of a reaction and a nostalgic desire for the free-for-all of the past are appearing.

The answer is, as in most things, a happy balance, weighing the practical considerations of preserving the integrity of the building with aesthetic considerations. Extremism in any direction is rarely a good thing.

There is an argument that future generations will not be able to study the original features of the building which is conserved by replacement and can never be sure whether replacements follow the original form. The solution is relatively simple. First, all replacement must be carried out to the highest standards, from the setting-out onwards. To this end, all architects should read closely the chapters on setting-out in order to have a proper understanding of the immense care and time required in the process, and to take an active interest in this side of the work. Secondly, the following procedure should be adopted: the best example of each moulding due for replacement should be carefully removed, labelled and put into permanent store. It is then available for study and comparison at any time in the future.

So far, we have been discussing the masons' work on the building, which, with the appropriate time and care, can be reproduced without difficulty. It is a different matter with carvings, be they figure or foliage. Here there are fewer set rules, the work being influenced by the imagination and ability of the individual craftsman, and so replacement carries the seeds of greater controversy.

In every period of architecture there has been a contemporary style which the craftsmen followed, either by inclination or direction. Within this style, they carved according to their manual skill and artistic abilities. The individuality of the carver can often still be recognized within a group of carvings carried out by a number of carvers. (The work of individual masons on a run of moulding also can often be recognized, but it is less obvious and less easy.) Many of the mediaeval carvers were run-of-the-mill craftsmen, while some showed significant artistic talent, but in all cases a degree of artistry is there for all to see. A case in point is the carvings in the chapter house at Southwell Minster, where the work varies from the competent to the superb.

Where carved work on the exterior of the building is decaying to a shapeless form, or where there is imminent danger of this at high levels, which will not be worked on again for perhaps a hundred years, some course of action has to be taken. A hundred or even twenty years ago, the decision was usually simple; chop it out and start again. Now that there is a better appreciation of such work, we are faced with multiple choices. Chop out and replace is still an option in some cases, for example, a capital or a statue which has weathered to a formless lump with no trace whatsoever of the previous form. There is little archaeological, artistic or architectural historic justification for keeping it. Once it has been recorded and properly measured for replacement (and there will almost always be some trace to be found by the setter-out of the original size), it can be discarded. Where there is still some visible and meaningful indication of form and subject, it becomes a matter of subjective judgement as to whether it should be carefully removed from the building for storage and display, or whether there is sufficient left for specialist conservators to save *in situ*.

This raises several questions. First, removal and display, which is probably practised more widely in the rest of Europe than in Great Britain, has the merit of greatly reducing the risk of further decay and allows the public, who pay for much of the work anyway, to have a close view of ancient craftsmanship and artistry.

Secondly, conservation *in situ* raises the question of the method to be employed, and whether that method is truly proven to have an economic life and be beneficial in the long term. Conservation is an academic solution to a very practical problem, and may involve the spending of a great deal of money for work which has to be redone at a later date, often requiring very expensive scaffolding. The application of a thick 'shelter coat' might protect the work, but that work can then no longer be seen and the building can take on a 'fuzzy' appearance.

Conservation definitely has its place in the maintenance armoury but it must be looked at from the practical point of view. It is an area where specialist advice is essential at an early stage. It must also be remembered that 'conservation' can cover a range of options, from stabilizing what is there to building up missing areas that can be restored with certainty. Again, the philosophy must be settled first.

The third question is, what should take the place, on the building, of objects removed to a museum? There are three possibilities: nothing, reproduction of the original and contemporary work. To leave a gap is to destroy the integrity of the building; to make a copy is to 'deceive' the public; to put in contemporary work is to change the style of the building. This last can be acceptable if seen as a development of the history of the building, but great care must be taken if it is to harmonize with the surrounding structure. If a reproduction is the preferred course, it should be carved in the original stone, but need not be a direct copy of what was, or might have been there. It can be very difficult to reproduce with certainty the original design of a weathered statue but, so long as the style is faithfully copied it can be acceptable. Again it is a question of philosophy, and there are no absolute rights and wrongs.

Whatever philosophy is behind a particular repair programme, the team of masons, conservators, carvers, or whoever, carrying out the work must understand that philosophy and the reasons for it. With a good team of masons, well briefed and motivated, there is nothing in the field of masonry repairs which cannot be undertaken. There still exists within the masonry trade the skill and experience to rebuild an entire cathedral if that is what the philosophy calls for. Equally, the most minute and painstaking repairs can be made if the situation and aims are clearly explained.

The nature and extent of repairs

A careful survey of the building, at close quarters, is an essential prerequisite for establishing the extent of problems and the likely solutions. It may be possible to do much of the work from a hydraulic hoist ('cherry picker'), at least sufficient to produce a reasoned assessment, but working from the scaffold will give a more accurate result.

The following list of options will give a guide to the possible courses of action.

1. *Do nothing*
   This is very often the best course, especially if the work is at low level and can easily be inspected at frequent intervals. If mouldings are decaying it may be wise to have them set-out in full against the time when work is necessary, at which point the profiles may have become irrecoverable.

2. *Make mortar repairs*
   If this work enhances the appearance of decaying stone, helps to prevent further loss of detail or defers until funds are available for a full repair programme, then this should be considered. It will only be temporary but can have a life of several decades. It

is less likely to be of use at high levels, where inspection at intervals will be expensive or unlikely. Again, setting-out against future repairs may be wise.

3. *Make dental repairs*

    This involves letting-in small pieces of stone to restore specific, small areas of decay. This is one step on from mortar repairs and should last much longer. If carried out with care, they should last as long as the original stone, but a large number of small repairs, however carefully done, will almost always stand out against the original stone to some extent. This has been compared to an outbreak of measles. If limited in number and carried out sympathetically, the dental repair can be a useful option.

4. *Conserve*

    This involves carrying out an intervention which maintains, more or less, the appearance of the stone, while consolidating it to reduce the rate of decay. This is likely to be expensive and will have a limited life, but may be the only way to preserve *in situ*, more or less intact, interesting or artistic detail. Again, the effect will be temporary but, by the time further work is necessary, techniques of preservation may have changed. At present, the injection of chemical consolidants into the stone is irreversible and their long-term effect is based on prediction rather than experience. This is not to say that they do not have their place, however, and they must be considered as part of any repair programme. The scope and nature of this work is outside the limits of this book.

5. *Replacing the decaying part with new stone*

    All other considerations apart, this is the ideal course for the long-term health of the building. If this course is decided upon, the greatest problem is knowing where to stop; only the philosophy and the budget will determine this.

It is by no means easy to decide what course of action to take, even within a clearly determined philosophy, unless that philosophy is very restrictive. In any case, the philosophy can often only be finalized in conjunction with the results of the survey. Only first-hand experience in the repair of masonry, whether practical or supervisory, can provide the answers. Only with a good understanding of the techniques of the mason, as explained in the previous chapters, and of the conservator, can an informed judgement be made.

It should be noted that, in the case of a scheduled ancient monument, which can quite easily be a building in current use, Scheduled Monument Consent may well include a requirement for a full archaeological recording of the elevation under repair, and for the archaeologist to be responsible for making a record of all work carried out. The cost of this falls on the owner, subject to any grant-aid available.

A summary of various aspects of the trade follows. Some aspects are repeated in abridged form from the earlier chapters to provide a convenient reference.

Repointing

It should not normally be necessary to cut out old pointing with a chisel. If it cannot be raked out, then it should be able to withstand many more years of weathering. Two exceptions can be made: when the work is being carried out at high levels, which are not likely to be re-scaffolded for many years, and there is any doubt about the longevity of the pointing; and where hard cement pointing is causing damage to the stone.

If chisels are needed, only small, sharp ones should be used, preferably of the quirk variety, that is, where the shank immediately behind the cutting edge is reduced so that the shank does not bear on the arrises. This is especially important when dealing with dressed stone. Cutting out old cement pointing from narrow joints carries a high risk of damage to the arrises but, if sufficient time and care are taken, there should be little or no damage. This part of the work can be very expensive in labour. On no account should the use of disc cutters be permitted. The use of a mortar pick may be appropriate when taking out decayed pointing from rubble walls.

Any vegetation must be cut out and remaining roots killed off with a suitable herbicide. Every effort should be made to remove large roots and the space they occupied in the core of the wall filled with rubble/mortar. Small plants will almost inevitably begin recolonizing a rubble wall within a year.

Old pointing should be taken out to a depth at least twice the width of the joint, and all dust washed out with a water spray. It is essential that the stone and the old bedding material, and adjacent old pointing are well damped before repointing begins.

It is argued by some that only a pointing key should be used whatever the nature of the work, but the skilled mason will use whatever tool seems best in the circumstances.

When the pointing has taken an initial set, the surface should be brushed over to take off the polish left by the tool. Brushing must always be along the joint rather than at right angles to it, and should not leave a smear of mortar on the stone or the visible brush marks caused by hard brushing when the pointing has taken too great a set. The weather conditions and the nature of the work will usually dictate the rate of progress but pointing may have to cease half-way through the last working day of the week to allow the initial set, as it may become too hard if left over the weekend. Too-rapid drying out of the pointing must be prevented (using wet hessian or similar) and the pointing must be protected from the rain until the danger of rain washing it out has passed. White stains of lime leaching from the joint are very disfiguring, to say nothing of the possible resulting weakness of the pointing.

The fullness or otherwise of the joint is a matter of judgement. With ashlar/moulded work the pointing must be flush with the face but not covering the arrises. Where the arrises have weathered to a rounded profile, the mortar should be kept back to preserve something like the original joint width.

Rubble walling normally has rather wide joints and, in the past, it was the practice to apply pointing rather liberally. Current practice is to keep the pointing back to show the edge of the stones, without leaving ledges to hold water. Any small stones, slate and pebbles, used to wedge the stones during the original building, should be preserved or replaced to avoid the stones being lost in a sea of mortar. Pointing of wide, deep joints is particularly liable to crack as it dries, especially at the junction of mortar and stone. When fully set, such cracks can often be detected by the hollow sound produced when tapped with the head of a chisel, but a similar sound can often be the result of adjacent stones which, while sound enough to be retained, have loose beds. Much depends on the nature of the stone.

Replacing dressed stone

Dimensions

If it is necessary for the architect to give stone sizes, the dimensions must always be given in the correct order: length of face × depth into the wall × bed height. To avoid confusion this order must never be changed. Note that where the beds of the stone are not horizontal, e.g. in a coping or voussoir, it is the natural bed of the stone which remains the bed height. A coping is thus given as height × depth from front to back × length. This is not just an arbitrary rule. When stone sizes are listed, the bed height required is always the last figure and thus easily identified. It is normally the bed height which is the most critical when ordering or sawing stone. If only two dimensions can be given, the standard order must be followed and the dimensions annotated to prevent misunderstanding.

Bedding planes

It is convenient to repeat here the exceptions to the general rule that stone always goes on its natural bed: *sills, copings, cornices, stone ridges,*

and *string courses* must be *edge-bedded*. This is based on the principle
that a free surface, either on the top or the bottom bed of the stone,
is liable to delaminate as it weathers. A cornice stone, or any other
stone, at the corner of a building, must be carefully selected for
soundness and laid on its natural bed, otherwise the return would be
face-bedded. *Voussoirs* should be cut so that the bedding planes are at
right angles to the direction of thrust, that is, they must lie on
the radius of the arch. *Monolithic columns* were usually edge-bedded
owing to limitations of bed heights available, and will usually have to
be replaced in the same way, despite the fact the two sides of the
column will be face-bedded. In all other cases, face-bedding must be
forbidden.

Setting-out

Here the architect is very much in the hands of the practitioner, and
must rely on the latter's skill and sense of responsibility for what is
due to the building. It is very difficult to check what has been drawn
except by occasional physical comparison of templets to original
mouldings. The use of CAD can give greater overall accuracy than
might be achieved by the drawing table. However, mouldings and
other details must be drawn out to full size and pasted into the CAD
program. They should not be drawn at small scale on the screen and
then enlarged through the plotter.

However the setting-out is done, mouldings must not taken from
a bank of records and used without alteration as being 'near enough'.
Also, mouldings must not be simplified to reduce the cost of working,
or to make possible what would otherwise be impossible to work by
machine. An example of this is an actual occasion where a new section
of hood mould at the head of a large Gothic window was worked to
a straight line on a simple profile saw on the grounds that the very
slight curvature was an economic extravagance. If replacement is
called for, it must be as accurate a reproduction as possible.

As noted in Chapter 4 on setting-out, all mouldings to be replaced
must be checked individually by the setter-out. Figure 4.15, which
shows the left- and right-hand jamb mouldings of one doorway, is an
example of how misleading a casual glance can be.

A decision must be made at an early stage whether errors by the
original setter-out are to be reproduced (which is the authors' preference and practice), or whether they are to be rectified. Identifying the
precise reason for the error, let alone reproducing it, can take a little
time but is worthwhile.

The person taking off the moulding profiles should have a basic
training as a stone mason and should be further trained in the
discipline of setting-out. Achieving accuracy is slow and painstaking.

Using photogrammetric elevations enlarged to full size, together with a profile gauge, is about as useful as working from a sketch. The level of detail taken by the architectural historian or archaeologist for record purposes is equally unsatisfactory. Setting-out is done for practical rather than theoretical purposes and has to achieve very different results.

Properly organized setting-out will provide a good and accurate record, for the future, of the stones that have been replaced. However, an archaeological recording of work on a scheduled ancient monument is still needed.

Setting-out is the heart of any repair programme and, if not properly carried out, the effectiveness of the masons' work can be largely nullified. It is essential for the architect to have an understanding of the work of the setter-out, and to appreciate fully the standard to which he should be able to work. It is not recommended that the architect takes on any of this work.

The working of new stone

Traditional handworking of stone is being replaced to an increasing extent by computer-controlled mechanical production. This is not the place to discuss the effects of this on the level of skill likely to be available in the future but it has an important effect on the appearance of repairs. Gothic and earlier buildings show small but significant variations from total accuracy and signs of toolmarks are to be seen everywhere, all of which contribute to the overall effect. Replacement by dead-accurate mouldings looks just that – dead. However the stone is worked, it should always be finished by hand, a process which should preferably involve complete removal of the mechanical surface. A few toolmarks on a smooth surface are likely to give an appearance reminiscent of Olde Oake Beames applied to a hitherto unobjectionable public house in order to convert it to an Olde Inne. Masonry of this sort has been seen.

There is much less objection to mechanical finishing on repairs to later buildings. Renaissance and most nineteenth and twentieth century work was frequently very accurately worked, and left with a rubbed finish. It is important that any saw marks should be removed, whether straight lines of the profile saw running the length of a moulding or the swirl marks of a circular saw on ashlar. Whatever is replaced should have the appearance of the unweathered parts of the building. Short-cuts must not be taken to facilitate the production process. Mitres, for example, must be worked on the stone rather than straight runs of moulding being sawn at 45° and glued or otherwise jointed to form the return.

Both mechanical and hand working of stone must be carried out accurately within their limitations, the assessment of which causes many problems. New stone should be worked to the same standard as the stone it replaces, no better and no worse. An understanding of what is possible is essential for the architect. Always remember that working stone is *easy*, to a tradesman who knows what he is doing.

The hand working of stone is an accurate business. Surfaces meant to be straight should be so, with any slight undulations being of no more than a millimetre; if the stone is round, it will be impossible to check the accuracy of fixing with a straight edge. Similarly, faces meant to be at right angles should be so – if not, fixing will be made more difficult and the finished appearance will suffer. Curves should be smooth curves, subject to very minor undulations, and circular work must be circular, without the chamfers worked as part of the process remaining visible. If the work is left off the chisel, the toolmarks should be reasonably regular and of even depth, and all at about the same angle. There will be some variation but it should be minimal. A tooled surface specified at 8 batts to the inch should have just that. There should be no sign of holes plucked in the stone during roughing-out. Arrises should be clean and devoid of snips or other damage, all of which result from carelessness in sawing, working or handling.

None of this calls for remarkable skill; the training of the banker mason is, or should be, designed with this sort of accuracy in mind. Of course, no mason is perfect and there will be minor deviations from the ideal, but they should be minimal and should certainly not be obvious. As with all trades, any mason who is conscientious as well as skilled will leave his work looking right even if all is not exactly as it should be. Skilful doctoring of mishaps, without having recourse to fillers, is an essential part of training.

When a large amount of replacement work is being carried out, it may well pay to commission one or more samples to an approved standard, to use as a reference.

Fixing of new stone

Bricklayers on good-class work will be expected to build their walls so that all the bricks are in the same plane with only the most minor variations. Why then should ashlar masonry, the production of which requires much more investment, be any less well built? There is no reason at all. When building with large stones, with ashlars weighing anything from 10–30 kg and large moulded stones of perhaps half a tonne, handling is more difficult. Large bed heights and narrow joints exaggerate any discrepancy but it is perfectly possible to build accurately. It is no good trying to lay large ashlars just with a builder's line. Only a straight edge applied vertically, horizontally and diagonally at frequent intervals will reveal mistakes before it is too late to correct them. If one edge of an ashlar, especially with a rubbed face, is displaced by only $\frac{1}{16}''$ (1.5 mm), the effect can be horrible. The same is true of mouldings – near enough is not good enough.

All mouldings worked by hand, however carefully, will vary slightly and there will be a need to pare-in some of the variations before the work is finally finished. However, if the major elements are not in alignment during building, the true line will be lost; straight lines will be crooked and curves will be polygonal. It is a matter of judgement which variations must be corrected by rebedding the stone, which ones can be left for paring-in and which ones call for working a new stone to the correct profiles.

The most difficult stones to fix are probably those with mouldings in two planes, as in blank tracery panels on returns. Here, unless the stone has been worked with the faces square to the bed and to each other, it will be almost impossible to plumb both faces and to match the mouldings at all points. Even so, much can often be achieved by trial and error to find the best match. A pinnacle may have two or four stones in a course which are interchangeable and, while it is laborious and time-consuming to try all the stones in every combination, it may well pay off in terms of quality. Of course, this costs money and a tightly-priced contract may not allow for such luxuries; it is up to the architect to insist that the highest quality is achieved. Naturally, the height of the work above ground level is irrelevant.

As with all trades, there has to be give and take on all sides, and some compromise is always necessary. Two essential points must be borne in mind: working stone is not difficult and, if a better standard of fixing can be achieved by taking off a half-tonne stone and rebedding it, then this must be done.

ERRORS ANCIENT AND MODERN

Figures 12.1–12.13 show a number of examples of work which could have been significantly improved had a greater degree of skill and care been shown. It should be noted that they begin at around AD 1200.

SPECIFICATIONS

It may be useful here to give some general points which might be included in a specification for masonry repairs. It will be a matter of judgement whether some requirements may be omitted or amended to suit the particular case.

Figure 12.1 *Twelfth-century niche.* The head of the niche does not meet the centre line, and the arc on the right is excessively freehand.

Figure 12.2 *Fourteenth-century vault.* The stooling on the wall rib was worked (or set-out) in the wrong place. The left-hand side has been worked off to match the rib, leaving the rib overhanging the right-hand side.

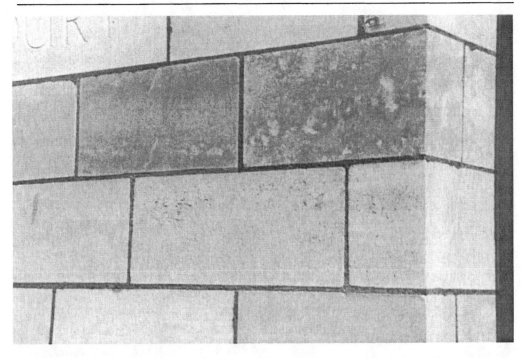

Figure 12.3 *Ashlar*. This ashlar work on a prestigious building shows tapering and uneven joints, snipped arrises and occasional saw marks.

Figure 12.4 *Base for window jamb*. When this left the mason it was in perfect condition. After fixing by bricklayers it shows a damaged corner, tapering joints and is fixed with strong OPC mortar.

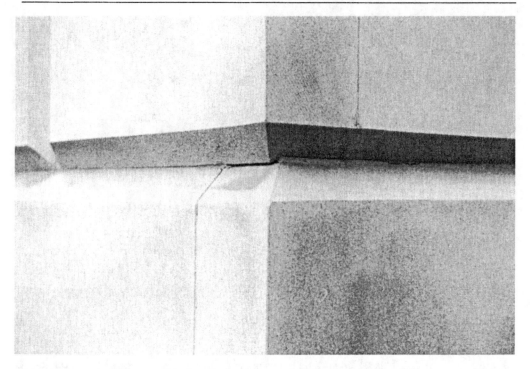

Figure 12.5 *Mitred returns.* No attempt has been made to make the mitres line up on repairs to a Grade 1 listed building.

Figure 12.6 *Renewal of an ogee arch.* These voussoirs are seriously misplaced, owing to the standard of the setting-out, the working or the fixing. The joint width is also excessive.

Figure 12.7 *Repairs to a mullioned window.* Neither the jamb nor the head line up with the return. They were pared-in satisfactorily before completion.

Figure 12.8 *Renewal of stone steps.* One or both stones of these stones should be reworked to give a parallel joint.

Figure 12.9 *Repairs to a squared rubble church.* The lowest of the new stones has been cut part through with an angle grinder and then snapped. Mortar has been smeared over the faces of adjacent stones.

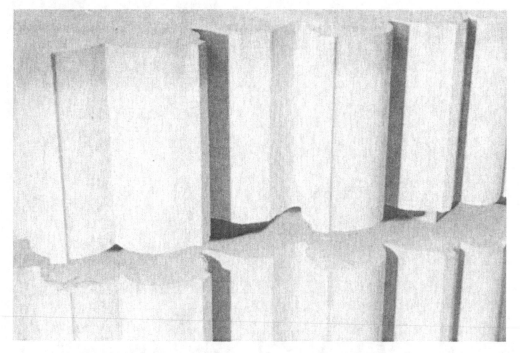

Figure 12.10 *Newly worked stone.* Mouldings worked by hand should still look as crisp as this example both before and after fixing.

Figure 12.11 *Repointing of a rubble wall.* The pointing is correctly set back a little to show the edges of the stones and maintains the joint widths in the dressings.

Figure 12.12 *Renewal of ashlar.* An excellent example of new ashlar work; even though 60′ above ground, this shows even joints, the old coursing matched precisely and sympathetic mortar. New stone always stands out, but since this photograph was taken it is beginning to merge with the original work.

Figure 12.13 *A new finial.* Although imperfections can be found, this shows crisp arrises, and a good finish to match its period. The pointing between the finial and the base needs a little attention.

Stone

New stone shall be from [specify the quarry and, if necessary, the particular bed], to a sample to be approved by the architect before any orders are placed. (Refer to Chapter 3 for the selection of new stone). It shall be free of any defects, such as shakes, vents or clay beds, which might detract from the performance of the stone.

All new stones will be laid on the natural bed, with the exception of sills, copings, cornices, stone ridges and string courses, which will be edge-bedded. Returns on these features to be natural-bedded in carefully selected stone. Voussoirs to be bedded at right angles to the thrust.

When delivered to site, the stone is to be stored carefully under cover, protected from accidental damage and not in contact with soil or other contaminants.

Templets

All mouldings to be replaced are to be set-out carefully, to be as close a copy as possible of the original profiles, and templets produced in zinc. The size and jointing of replacement stones must match the original, unless otherwise agreed with the architect.

All drawings and templets are to be retained for record purposes.

Chopping out and dismantling

Stone due for replacement is to be cut out without damaging adjacent stones. Disc cutters must not be used for this purpose (except in individually approved special circumstances). The stone must be cut out to full depth, and old mortar cleaned from the adjacent beds and joints. All ironwork must be completely removed.

Stones which are to be dismantled for re-use are to be numbered on the top bed before taking down, and must be taken down carefully so as to minimize damage. Joints are to be sawn out by hand first, if necessary to break the hold of hard pointing on the arrises. A disc cutter must not be used.

Any old cramps or dowels in stone which is to be re-used are to be cut out by drilling out the old fixing material, or by cutting with a chisel if suitable.

Dressing of stone

All replacement stone is to be finished to match as closely as possible the original finish. Machined stones to be left with an allowance for hand finishing and not tooled over the smooth surface.

Any sawn surfaces must be rubbed free of sawmarks/to be finished by hand chiselling/to sample (as appropriate).

All new stone is to be free of snips, spalling or other defects, which detract from the appearance of the stone, and worked to the highest standards within the requirement to match the original.

A sample stone, worked to an agreed moulding and to the satisfaction of the architect, shall be provided before work commences.

Fixing

All stones must be solidly bedded and jointed so far as possible. If grouting of any joints is essential, this must be carried out in the same mortar as used for bedding. The use of OPC grout is forbidden.

The stones must be thoroughly wetted before fixing.

No part of any stone shall project beyond another stone by more than 0.5 mm at most. All mouldings and ashlar to be pared-in after fixing, if this is necessary, but major paring-in is prohibited in favour of working a new stone or stones; the designed profiles must be maintained.

Fixing may not be carried out unless the temperature, actual or anticipated, is at least 3°C above freezing point.

Pointing

Old mortar is to be raked out with a sharp steel implement, which will not damage the arrises. Cutting out with chisels will not normally be necessary. If chisels are necessary, to cut out hard cement pointing, they should be fine quirks, narrower than the width of the joints. The use of a disc cutter is forbidden.

The joint is to be taken back to sound mortar, or a minimum of twice the width of the joint.

Before repointing, all dust and debris is to be removed by washing with a light water spray or other suitable means, and the joints well dampened, but not wet, right to the back.

New pointing is to be pressed fully into the joint, leaving no voids and the joint filled flush. Mortar must be kept off the face of the stone.

When the mortar has taken an initial set, but no more, brush lightly along the joint with a stiff brush to remove the hard surface and reveal the aggregate. This operation must not smear the face of the stone, nor leave brush marks.

At completion, the pointing is to be flush with the faces and with the arrises visible, without leaving ledges to collect water.

Any stains left on the face of limestone are to be removed using a clean sponge and sufficient clean water without introducing any more water to the mortar.

New pointing is to be protected from rain-water and from over-rapid drying until the surface set is complete. Mortar that has cracked will not be acceptable.

Pointing may not be carried out unless the temperature, actual or anticipated, is at least 3°C above freezing point.

13

Training into the Twenty-first Century?

by Kevin Calpin

Head of Stonemasonry and Brickwork,
York College of Further and Higher Education

REFLECTIONS OF PAST TRAINING

To begin with, a reminiscence. I entered the trade on a cool August morning in 1965 without due ceremony. A strange world of seemingly strange men, mostly of few words but overflowing with a gift I will always admire – the ability to fashion stone.

I was taken into the banker shop, introduced to the old stone mason with the banker nearest the coke-burning cast-iron fire, and instructed to 'do what he tells you!' This daunting situation was immediately defused when he opened a large metal box by the wall and proceeded to take various odd-shaped tools from it and talk about them as though they were sacred – and to him they were. My learning and five more years of training had started.

My reason for this reminiscence is simple: that learning process happened by doing and, more importantly, it was unrushed. I was treated to sessions of one-to-one instruction by a man who knew his craft intimately and who had time to relate his experience without the constraints of production schedules, bonus targets and the like. This was a time when a young person would join the company, be almost a part of a family and know at the point of joining that they would be figuring in the long-term plans of the company for at least the 5 year term of apprenticeship.

The apprentice was linked with his own mentor, his mason master, who would teach him the craft, guide him, pass on his own values and, not until he was satisfied that the apprentice was fully capable of carrying out a task, would he be allowed to partake in a 'real' job. The mason master was not penalized financially for teaching an apprentice, as allowances would be made for time spent in this way. Indeed, in some larger companies, he would be employed specifically for training and may have a number of apprentices to train.

As one matured, the actual training time was reduced and tasks became more complex, thus allowing the apprentice to become more confident, contribute to the work of the company and encourage him to think for himself. The apprentice would also be integrated with other craftsmen to enable him to gain skills of fixing, carving and lettering, giving him an all-embracing background of the industry.

During the indenture period of 5 years, the apprentice would be expected to achieve the internationally recognized qualification of City & Guilds Craft and Advanced Craft Certificates. Unfortunately, this was the highest craft-based qualification at that time and further study for the young craftsperson was the route to technician qualifications. The direction chosen by most stone masons at the conclusion of the apprenticeship was to gain experience in various aspects of the industry to widen their knowledge, I for my part chose the latter route.

PRESENT-DAY TRAINING

Training today consists generally of three modes:

1. Vocational training leading to a qualification.
2. Non-vocational, short training courses, offered by specialist institutions leading to no qualification.
3. On-the-job training during employment.

The first two modes are offered by specialist centres, for example, the Stonemasonry Department at York College of Further and Higher Education where all current national training schemes are delivered. In addition, a number of short courses relevant to the industry are available on demand. These courses include letter cutting, a basic introduction to carving, to more advanced carving techniques, setting-out and preparation of templets and moulds, and advanced stone cutting. Employers are also able to infill their craftspersons onto existing courses for short periods to learn complex stone-cutting techniques. Along with the above courses, there are specialist short courses aimed at providing architects, conservation officers and others with an interest in conservation, with supplementary training in the use of stone and other traditional materials.

The third example of training is generally carried out during employment, will normally be very limited and tailored to the specific type of work undertaken by the employer, and in some cases the actual training is non-existent. No formal recognition is available from this form of training.

The only craft-based qualification available until recently was City & Guilds in Stonemasonry. Since April 1992, however, National Vocational Qualifications (NVQs) have replaced the City & Guilds schemes in most of the craft areas of the construction industry. As a consequence, the last City & Guilds examination for stone masonry at York took place in June 1995.

National Vocational Qualifications

NVQs are awarded at five levels. At present, the highest stone masonry level available is level 3, although there is a possibility that there will be a level 4 Master Craftsman in the near future. The various levels cannot be compared with City & Guilds, but one can assume level 2 approximates to City & Guilds Craft Certificate and level 3 to Advanced Craft Certificate.

The NVQ system is a recognition of evidence collected by a candidate that will be assessed by a registered assesssor and is not a training scheme. The evidence collected will reflect the candidates' abliltly to achieve competency in a series of tasks to industry-recognized tolerances and standards. Unlike the training initiatives of the past that required study for a specific period of time culminating in external written examinations and a series of practical projects presented for scrutiny by an independent external assessor appointed by City & Guilds, NVQ training is, in theory, not linked to a time scale. It is now possible for a student to take anything from a few weeks to several years to gain an NVQ award.

The award of an NVQ is available to anyone who can satisfy the criteria by either assessment or evidence of competency in other forms. This is now particularly attractive to employees who have been in the industry for a number of years and have the experience, but are without formal qualifications; it also favours those trainees who are able to take charge of their own learning and achieve at a rapid pace. For most candidates, who are more likely to be school leavers with average learning ability, it is short period for them to prove their worth.

Unfortunately, industry-funded schemes are linked to time scales and outcomes are linked to funding. Therefore, the period of training 'off the job' for a stone mason on an industry-funded scheme is currently 28 weeks to achieve a level 2 qualification over a period of 2 years, and a further period of 8 weeks during the third year to achieve level 3.

'On-the-job' training

'On-the-job' training today is in the main unstructured and limited. There are some employers who genuinely care about training and the continuity of the craft, but there are also a number of employers who have little or no commitment to training. There are a number of factors that contribute to this apathetic approach, including:

- Reduced training budgets.
- An upsurge in self-employment.
- Effects of recession.

When an industry is in recession, one of the options open to a company to try to remain cost effective is to reduce the overhead cost; a simple saving can be made by reducing the training budget. This surely is the wrong strategy because, when confidence returns and new programmes of work are identified, a ready-trained workforce must be available to be able to react instantly to the challenge.

The cost of training is high. There are a number of reasons for this, although probably the most significant is the small number of centres offering training and their geographical locations. The major specialist centres are widely spread over England and Scotland in York, Bath, Weymouth, London and Edinburgh. It is unlikely that other centres will be made available because of the low numbers entering the industry and the difficulty of the existing centres to sustain courses running on low enrolment. This results in high costs for employers having to provide travelling and accommodation costs.

The recent increase in the already high number of self-employed labourers in the construction industry (approximately half of all construction operatives are now self-employed) has given rise to a great number of small contractors setting up. These contractors were probably victims of the recession, losing their previous job either through redundancy or business failure. This type of employer will have little committment to training in its wider sense and will concentrate on areas that are specific to him, and will possibly have a lack of expertise within their company. Companies in this category will almost certainly have less time to commit to training in order to survive and ensure continuity of work orders.

As already noted, the deep recession has been a significant factor in the decline of training. Only when the industry recognizes the need for a highly skilled, creative workforce, which is adequately rewarded and valued, to help it recover when confidence returns, will the industry become healthy once again. We are agreed that we need creativity and flexibility from a future workforce, but these will not happen with NVQ standards alone. It requires creative teachers and real support in the workplace to enable trainees to understand and transfer their knowledge and skills from the specialized to the mundane.

CURRENT TRAINING PROGRAMMES

The recent introduction of the NVQ has brought about a change in delivering training programmes. The NVQ schemes are unit based, these being a self-standing series of competencies that can be undertaken in any order, at any time, by anybody. Training institutions are being pressurized into providing 'roll on–roll off' programmes with trainees joining and leaving the courses at various stages. While this is seen as a continual training programme by some, I believe it will lead to poorer quality craftspeople. The only way to achieve roll on–roll off is by a large proportion of student-centred learning, where the trainees take charge of their own learning, supported by the tutor. As mentioned previously, this kind of learning is not entirely suitable for the type of trainee currently entering the industry.

As may be seen below from the titles of the units, the NVQ is not particularly user-friendly and does not indicate the scope of the training involved.

The scope of the units

Although level 2 has a large fixing unit (Unit 187), the main thrust is to ensure the trainee has completed the basic skills of stone cutting, thus allowing those trainees who wish to specalize in fixing to have some basic skill in working stone. This has been a problem area in recent years owing to the influx of unskilled labour, especially on cladding work. In contrast, level 3 has now two routes, Banker Mason or Fixer Mason, which give the trainee the opportunity to choose between more complex stone cutting or fixing of stonework at level 3.

Units 66 and 67 are common to all construction crafts at level 3 and are similar to the City & Guilds Site Procedures component of the Advanced Craft Certificate syllabus. These are two vast areas where the reduced training period is placing pressures on the lecturer and trainees. Unit 66, Contribute to the Planning, Organisation, Monitoring, Control, and Evaluation of Operational Activities, seeks to prepare the trainee to contribute to the planning of work activities and methods, plan for the use of resources, organize work and assist in evaluation of work, monitor and control resources, and provide feedback on work performance to teams and individuals. Unit 67, Maintain Working Conditions and Operational Activities to Meet Quality Standards requires the trainee to maintain operational activities, and maintain necessary conditions for an effective and safe work environment. To ask that a student fully understand and put the information into context is perhaps expecting too much. I believe the outcome is likely to be that the candidate will be able to demonstrate knowledge of these areas but not full understanding. These units are concerned with management training while, at this stage, trainees will still be training as craftspersons. They will clearly be unsuitable for those trainees who do not aspire to higher levels, and may well lead to confusion and despondency.

Along with practical training, there is a full programme of masonry technology and general knowledge relating to the stone industry. Past experience has proved that a split of 65 per cent to 35 per cent in favour of practical training to technology will cover the the course content fully.

The specific content of the NVQ scheme is outside the scope of this chapter but consideration is given to safety and regulations governing the industry. The trainee will know of their responsibilities under the Health and Safety at Work Act, COSHH 1989 Regulations, Accident and Emergency procedures, and the roles of others in relation to those Regulations.

THE WAY FORWARD

There are a number of areas we could explore that would enhance the quality of the trainees entering the industry, thereby raising the quality of the craftsperson on completion of training. We should look at the way new entrants are initially selected. In most cases trainees are placed by the Construction Industry Training Board with a sponsoring employer for the first 2 years, usually after undergoing a CITB written test. The applicant, who indicates the first and second choice craft they would prefer to train in, carries out a Construction Skills Learning Excercise that lasts for 50 minutes and comprises approximately 50 per cent calculations and 50 per cent aptitude and space relation. This is followed by an interview with feedback on performance. The result of the exercise may influence the particular craft area in which the applicant will actually train. Clearly this is not the best way to select future craftspersons. We need to approach selection quite differently.

As an industry we must look to early selection during the final school year. This is where a degree of marketing should be directed to make not only the prospective trainees more aware of our industry but also the careers officers, who are in position to guide and influence pupils. The employers must play a more active role in selection. There can be nothing more frustrating than spending 2 years training someone who does not have their heart in their work and who will ultimately leave the industry. The industry, schools and local TECs (Training and Enterprise Councils) must collaborate to investigate the possibility of implementing courses where school leavers can attend the local Further Education College during their final school year. This kind of vocational course would provide an ideal background for all future entrants to construction crafts, it could prepare those students in the core skills, for instance, geometry and setting-out, craft calculations, communication and safety. These areas could be assessed and the candidates awarded with units contained in NVQ level 1, if successful.

Another alternative could be for trainees to spend the first year in college before being placed with an employer. The trainee would be in a position to contribute much more and the employer would not need to spend a great deal of time on basic training. There is an obvious drawback in that employers would need to look critically at their future needs and to forecast their training requirements one year ahead. This could also form the basis of a pool of trained craftspeople, where employers who need to take on more staff could contact their local college, obtain a reliable report and arrange an interview with the prospective trainee.

The Construction Industry Training Board (CITB) is the industry-led body which is reponsible for setting standards, and the NVQ has been developed to reflect the skills most frequently carried out on site. The research was carried out by a mapping exercise target-ing employers nationwide. This method is not likely to give accurate results for, if the target group has a large proportion of new-build contractors, it will give different results from a target group with a majority of restoration or maintenance contractors, although it is likely to highlight areas of specialism or additional work. The surveys are ongoing and the research will be used to develop NVQs further and identify future training requirements. To provide a more flexible approach, a bank of units could be available with a set series of core units that all trainees must complete; the additional units could then be chosen to reflect regional variations or local specialism.

Employer and trainees alike must remember that training does not end at the conclusion of level 3 – learning and gaining experience continues. One great advantage of the old apprenticeship system was that this was clear for all to see. Those craftspersons who show an interest in further study of old materials, traditional methods, complex methods of working and the techniques of related crafts such as carving, lettering and conservation should be given support and resources to follow their studies. More emphasis must be placed on sponsorship, scholarships and bursaries to assist students to enhance their skill and knowledge to relieve the pressures on the finances of both student and employer. We should remember we are not just training for the present but to ensure a continuous supply of crafts-persons with the necessary skills to perform in future.

I find myself concerned about the compression of the training period over the past 20 years. Whereas, when the apprenticeship was the norm, the training was spread over 3 or 5 years, we now expect a school leaver to achieve a similar standard in 2 years. This makes a nonsense of the skills involved. Apprenticeships allowed for that now underrated element, experience. During the past 9 years, the 'off-the-job' period of training has been reduced from 36 weeks to 28 weeks a reduction of over 16 per cent, and at level 3 the reduction is a massive 33 per cent. This gradual erosion in 'off-the-job' training time has brought about a decrease in content and the range of knowledge within the scope of the scheme.

Are we to end up with bricklayers who can just lay bricks, carpenters who can just saw wood, and stone masons who can just cut stone, all at a basic level? No. The issue is much more important than just providing a workforce made up of tradespeople with only a basic understanding of their craft, who are able to carry out only those tasks that are currently in vogue. If we are to follow the current training philosophies, we must ensure we provide continuity and progress for those who wish to gain knowledge and experience, and give recognition to the effort involved. We need to accommodate the enthusiastic craftsperson, pass on the knowledge and experience that we still have and, when they have proved their worth, we must be willing to reward them in a proper fashion.

I have heard it said that the quality of trainee is not of the same calibre today as in the past. In my experience, I have had the pleasure of teaching many who are excellent, a great number who are very good, many who will be solid craftspersons and some who, as one would expect, are unlikely to make the grade. Most of the students I have taught have been motivated and enthusiastic during their training, but this enthusiasm has not been harnessed after training, resulting in a potential loss to the industry.

We have witnessed over the past 20 years highly experienced craftsmen, trained in traditional techniques using traditional materi-als, bowing out of our industry, and the last of this elite band will soon be lost to us. We must use their experience and ensure that the age-old craft of stone masonry is kept alive and not diluted. I am not so naïve as to believe that, in the present climate, the same system of training could be operated but, if we are to train what will be the craftsperson of tomorrow, then we should ensure that the training we give is of the highest quality.

The views expressed in this chapter are entirely the personal opinion of the writer and do not necessarily reflect the corporate opinion of his employer, York College of Further and Higher Education.

Glossary of Architectural Terms

(Words in italics have their own entry in the glossary.)

Abacus	The upper part of a capital, either square or round in plan and either moulded or plain, on which the arch or other feature rests.
Abutment	The mass of masonry, or solid ground, which resists the thrust of an arch or vault.
Acanthus	A plant with large leaves much used, especially in Corinthian and Composite capitals, for decoration.
Acroterion	Sculpture on the lower end of a pediment.
Aisle	The part of a church or hall flanking the nave or choir.
Annulet	A small semicircular moulding around a shaft or column, often used to link short lengths of circular shafts to the main pier, and as the lowest element of a capital.
Apse	The semicircular end to a chapel, chancel, or other part of a church or secular building.
Arcade	A row of arches supported on piers or columns, either free-standing or attached to a wall.
Arch	A self-supporting arrangement of wedge-shaped stones, which span an opening. For the varieties of arch, see Chapter 5, and for parts of an arch, see Figure G.1.
Arch ring	Each course of voussoirs in an unmoulded arch, e.g. single ring, three-ring arch (Figure G.1). See also *Order*.
Architrave	The lowest division of the horizontal member spanning an opening in classical architecture and resting directly on the abacus. Also, the moulded frame around a door or window.
Archivolt	The underside of a moulded arch; when unmoulded, it is known as the soffit.
Arris	The distinct line or edge formed by the meeting of two surfaces.

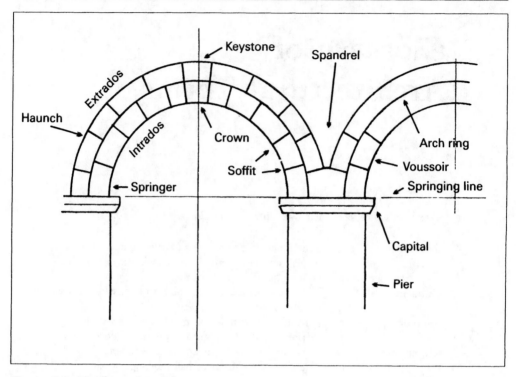

Figure G.1 The parts of an arch.

Ashlar	Stone which is carefully dressed or sawn to give a rectangular elevation with worked arrises. If the face is not plain, it is bounded by a marginal draft.
Ashlar stop	The termination of a moulding against an ashlar face within a single stone. A chamfer stop is where a chamfer reverts to the square quoin (Figure G.2).
Astragal	A small semicircular moulding (Figure G.3).
Ball flower	An ornamental feature consisting of a ball inside a

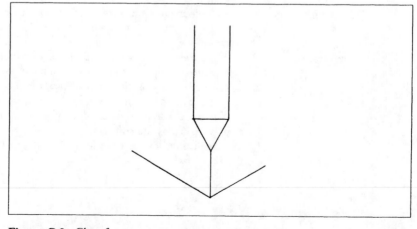

Figure G.2 Chamfer stop.

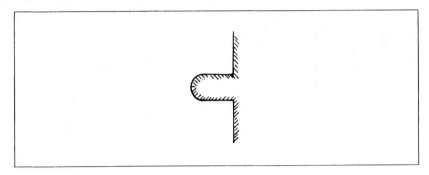

Figure G.3 Astragal.

	three-petalled flower, usually worked in a hollow moulding.
Baluster	A short pillar or shaft, usually swelling in the centre.
Baluster die	A half-baluster, worked on the ashlar at the end of a balustrade.
Balustrade	A row of balusters, capped with a coping.
Bar tracery	See *Tracery*.
Barrel vault	A vault which is semicircular in section. Sometimes known as a wagon vault.
Base	The lowest part of a pier; the foot on which it rests, usually moulded.
Batter	The gradual inwards slope on a wall deliberately built out of plumb.
Battlement	A parapet of upstanding parts, or *Merlons*, and openings, or *Embrasures*.
Beakhead	An ornament resembling a series of birds' beaks worked on the surface of a moulding.
Bell	That part of a Corinthian capital below the abacus, generally hidden by foliage or other carving. Often used to describe the same part of any capital.
Bevel	A horizontal sloped surface; usually, and incorrectly, called a *Splay*.
Billet	An ornament, usually circular but sometimes square, and supposed to resemble short lengths of wood. It may be worked in a hollow moulding.
Bond	The staggering of vertical joints so that joints in successive courses do not coincide.
Boss	A voussoir carved with foliage, etc., to disguise the junction of two or more ribs in a vault.
Bowtell	A round moulding, forming part or most of a circle; a roll moulding. When the roll is flattened to meet in a blunt angle, it is known as a pointed bowtell (Figures G.4 and G.5).
Bracket	A projecting stone, usually decorated, to support a figure or column. Similar to a corbel, but the latter usually supports horizontal members and is generally not carved.
Broach	A spire, which rises from a tower without a parapet.
Buttress	A mass of masonry projecting from a wall to provide

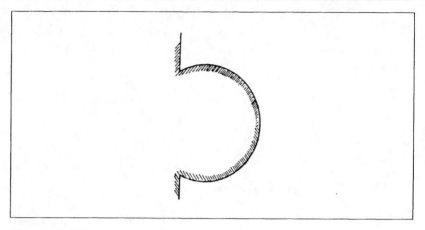

Figure G.4 Bowtell.

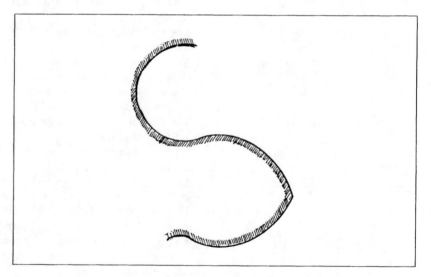

Figure G.5 Pointed bowtell.

	additional support. Early buttresses tend to be shallow and plain, later ones deeper and more highly decorated. Angle buttresses are set at 90° to each other, touching at the angle of the corner, a clasping buttress is square in plan, masking the corner, and a diagonal buttress is set at 45° to the corner. See also *Pilaster*.
Cable moulding	A circular moulding worked to resemble the twists of a rope.
Cabling	A round moulding sometimes worked in the lower part of the flutes of a classical column.
Capital (cap)	The head of a column or pilaster (Figure G.1).
Cavetto	A quarter round concave moulding (Figure G.6).
Chamfer	The angle of a stone cut away to a flat surface, usually at 45°.

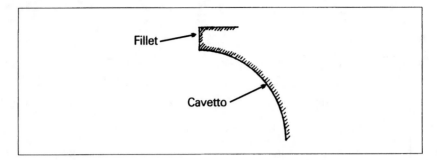

Figure G.6 Cavetto.

Chancel	The part of a church containing the altar. In a small church, the whole of the part to the east of the nave.
Chevron	A zigzag moulding.
Choir	The part of a church in which the service is sung. Strictly speaking, it is usually part of the chancel but, in larger churches, often used to describe the whole of the part east of the nave.
Cinquefoil	See *Foil*.
Classical architecture	The architectural styles of ancient Greece and Rome, broadly divided into Doric, Ionic, Corinthian and Composite.
Clerestorey	The upper windows in a church or hall, above the arcade and the aisle roofs.
Cloister	An arcaded walk surrounding an open space, found in monasteries and sometimes in larger churches in imitation of monastic buildings.
Cloister garth	The central area enclosed by the cloister; often used in former times for the growing of medicinal herbs.
Closer	The final stone in a course, often sawn oversize and cut to the precise length on site.
Coffer	A sunk panel in a ceiling, vault or classical cornice.
Colonnade	A row of circular columns.
Column	The support for an arch or lintel, usually circular in plan but often enriched with mouldings, or with smaller shafts clustered round it. See also *Pillar*.
Coping	The upper course of a wall designed to shed water. Ideally, the coping is wider than the wall and has a *drip* groove on the underside. There is a wide variety of forms, some of the more common being:

- Once weathered, where the upper surface is slightly sloped in one direction (Figure G.7a).
- Twice weathered, where the upper surface is angled to each side, either at a shallow or steep angle; the ridge may be central or offset to one side (Figure G.7b).
- Saddleback, which has a half round or segmental top; this type is often the same width as the wall (Figure G.7c).
- Pea top, which is the name sometimes given to the pyramidal coping to a pier (Figure G.7d).

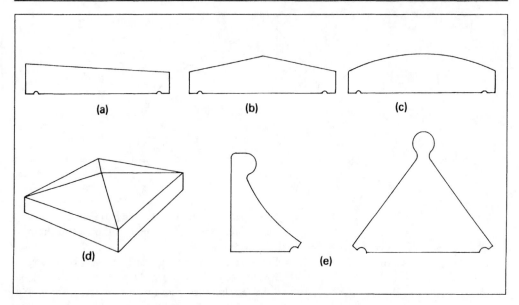

Figure G.7 (a) Once weathered coping; (b) Twice weathered coping; (c) Saddleback coping;
(d) Pea top coping; (e) Gothic copings.

	◆ Gothic copings, which may be of variety of forms, two of which are illustrated in Figure G.7e.
Corbel	A projecting stone, usually for the support of a beam or other horizontal member.
Corbel table	A series of corbels to support a parapet or cornice.
Core, corework	The rubble filling, which may or may not be mortared, between the two outer leaves of a wall.
Corinthian	One of the orders of classical architecture, characterized by fluted columns, a moulded base and a carved capital of acanthus leaves beneath a square abacus with concave sides.
Cornice	A projecting moulded course at the top of a building; originally confined to the upper part of the classical entablature, now used more generally.
Crenel	An alternative name for the *Embrasure* in a battlement, hence *Crenellation*. In military architecture: a loophole for the discharge of arrows, etc.
Crenellations	Another term for *Battlements*.
Crocket	In Gothic architecture, a projecting bunch of foliage ornamenting the angles of gables, spires, pinnacles, etc., and occasionally on jambs and mullions. The style varies according to the period, earlier forms being rather open, later ones being tighter and of more regular form.
Crown	The highest point of an arch on the intrados (Figure G.1).
Cushion capital	A form of Norman capital in which the lower part of a plain square block is tapered down in a curved chamfer to fit a circular shaft.

Cusp	An approximately triangular projection in Gothic tracery and beneath transoms. In general, the greater the number of cusps in one group, the later the work. See *Foil* and Figure G.8.
Cyma recta	A combination of reverse curves, the upper one being concave, the lower convex (Figure G.9).
Cyma reversa	The opposite to the cyma recta, i.e. with convex moluding at the top and concave below (Figure G.10). In Gothic architecture, known as the *Ogee*.
Dado	The part of a classical pedestal between the base and the cornice; also known as a *Die* (which see for an alternative meaning).
Decorated	See *Gothic architecture*.
Dentil	A small square block beneath the projection of the cornice in the Ionic, Corinthian and Composite orders of classical architecture.
Diagonal rib	In vaulting, the rib running diagonally across the bay between the wall and transverse ribs. See *Ribbed vault*.
Diaper	Surface decoration of an area of wall with repeated patterns in a square or diamond form, either plain or with flower ornament.
Die	See *Dado*. Also, a sunk panel on which an inscription is carved.
Dog tooth	An ornament worked in a hollow mould, consisting of a sharply pointed pyramid with each side split almost to the point. It was extensively used in the thirteenth century.
Doric	One of the orders of classical architecture, distinguished by a capital consisting of a pair of volutes with egg and dart moulding between, a fluted column with the flutes separated by fillets and a moulded base.
Drip	A downward projection on a moulding, designed to allow water to fall away. A groove cut on the underside of a sill or coping for the same purpose.
Drip course	Another name for a label or hood mould.
Drop arch	See Chapter 5.
Drum	One of the stones of a circular pier. The walls, either circular or square in plan, below a dome.
Early English	See *Gothic architecture*.
Echinus	A convex moulding, similar to an ovolo, forming the lower part of a Doric capital, beneath the abacus.
Egg and dart	A decoration, or enrichment, worked on an ovolo moulding in classical architecture, so called because of its resemblance to alternating eggs and arrow heads or darts.
Embattled	A wall or building with *Battlements*.
Embrasure	The open part of a *Battlement*.
Enrichment	An ornament carved on a moulding. It may be either continuous or occurring at intervals, but always consists of repetition of a single form or pattern; typical examples are egg and dart on an echinus

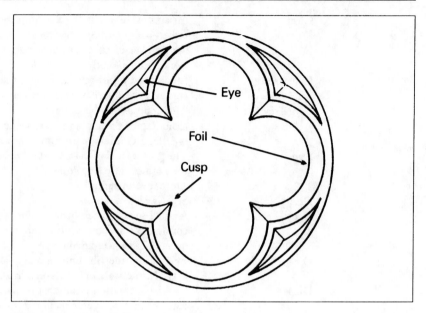

Figure G.8   Quatrefoil.

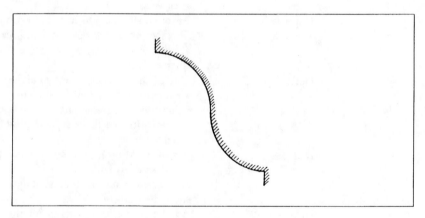

Figure G.9   Cyma recta.

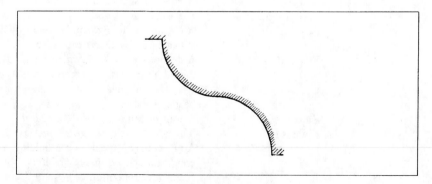

Figure G.10   Cyma reversa.

mould, and acanthus leaves in a scotia. Foliage is not an enrichment as it is a non-repetitive decoration.

Entablature	The horizontal part of a classical building above the columns. It consists of, from the bottom, the architrave, the frieze and the cornice.
Entasis	The convex tapering worked on large columns in a colonnade, without which they would appear to narrow slightly in the middle. The top of the column is smaller than the bottom, but the reduction is greater above the middle than below, giving the appearance of a slight swelling when viewed individually.
Extrados	The outer curve of an arch (Figure G.1).
Eye	The space in tracery formed by the outward curve of the cusp away from the main moulding (Figure G.8). If the cusp is large enough for the whole of the subsidiary moulding to separate from the main tracery, the eye can be pierced and is said to be open. If the cusp is too small for this to happen, the eye is blind.
Façade	The face of a building.
Fan vault	Vaulting in which both *Ribs* and *Webs* are worked on the face of large flat voussoirs, to give the appearance of a very elaborate ribbed vault.
Fillet	A flat band between two mouldings (Figure G.6).
Finial	The decorative termination of a pinnacle or other feature, usually carrying foliage carving, but sometimes carrying geometrical or architectural moulding.
Flamboyant	A form of tracery in which the bars form waving or flame-like patterns. Also known as curvilinear.
Flush pier	The support for an arch set flush with a wall and consisting of stones larger than the main run of walling.
Flute	An elliptical, semicircular or segmental channel, usually on a column.
Flying buttress	A buttress separated from the arch or wall it is supporting but connected to it by an arch which carries the thrust over the intervening space, often an aisle roof.
Foil	A leaf-shaped opening between two cusps. Trefoil = three foils; quatrefoil = four foils; cinquefoil = five foils (Figure G.8).
Foliage	The naturalistic representation in carving of plants, leaves, etc.
Frieze	The part of a classical entablature between the architrave and the cornice; it may be carved or plain. Any carved band, usually depicting a scene.
Gable	The triangular wall at the end of a pitched roof. A triangular feature on a wall or buttress often used for ornament.
Gablet	A small ornamental gable.
Gargoyle	A spout for discharging water from the roof of a

	building in the absence of fall pipes, usually carved as a weird or amusing figure. If plain, sometimes known as a spitter. See also *Grotesque*.
Glazing line	The plane in which glazing is fixed in a window opening.
Gothic architecture	The mediaeval form of architecture, coming after the Norman, or Romanesque and before Renaissance. It is commonly grouped into three separate styles: Early English (1190–1280), Decorated (1250–1330), Perpendicular (1330–1500), after which it gradually merged into the Tudor and Elizabethan styles. The dates given are very general; examples of each style occurred both earlier and later than the given range. See also Chapter 1.
Groin	The curved line formed by the intersection of two vaulting surfaces.
Groined vault	A vault built without the use of ribs, thus showing the groins.
Grotesque	Any weird or amusing figure carved on a building, usually projecting. A grotesque may also be a *Gargoyle*.
Guttae	Small cone shapes carved under the *Triglyphs* in a Doric entablature, and on the soffit of the *Mutules* of the cornice.
Haunch	The lower part of an arch ring, from the springing line to between one-third and one-half of the height (Figure G.1).
Head	The upper part of a window or door, whether arched or flat.
Herringbone	Walling of thin slabs laid diagonally, successive courses being set at opposite angles to give a herringbone pattern.
Hollow chamfer	A chamfer which is sunk in the centre (Figure G.11).
Hollow moulding	A concave moulding in Gothic architecture, approximately corresponding to the *Scotia* of classical architecture. Also known as a casement moulding (Figure G.12).
Hood mould	A moulded course running over an arched door or window. Also called a drip stone.
Impost	A projecting stone, usually with only a simple moulding, at the springing line of an arch when it springs from the wall or from a flush pier.
Intercolumniation	The space between two columns in a colonnade.
Intrados	The inner curve of an arch; it is the line of the arch, not the under-surface (*Soffit*) (Figure G.1).
Ionic	The simplest classical order, with sharp arrises rather than fillets between the flutes on the columns, which have no base, and a square slab *Abacus* over an *Echinus* moulding.
Jamb	The vertical sides of door and window openings. See also *Reveal*.
Joggle	A notched joint, to prevent movement. If worked on

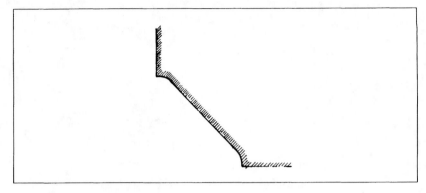

Figure G.11 Hollow chamfer.

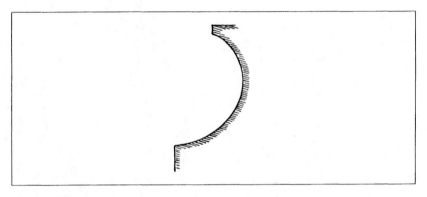

Figure G.12 Hollow moulding/scotia.

	the joint but not appearing on the face, it is called a secret joggle. A groove cut in a joint face to be filled with lead or mortar.
Jumper	A walling stone, which rises through two or more courses.
Keel moulding	A moulding made up of two ogees, which in section come to a sharp point, unlike a pointed bowtell, which has a blunt point forming more of a right angle (Figure G.13).
Keystone	The central stone in a semicircular arch, often more prominent than the others. In structural terms it has no more value than any other voussoir. The pointed Gothic arch never has a keystone but instead has a joint on the centre line (Figure G.1).
Label mould	A projecting moulded course running over a flat-headed door or window. Often used instead of *Hood mould*, which is properly the moulding over an arch.
Label stop	The decorative termination, often a head or foliage, at the end of a label mould or hood mould.
Lancet arch	See Chapter 5.
Ledger slab	A grave or memorial slab laid flush with the floor inside a church.

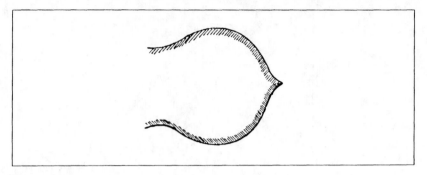

Figure G.13 Keel moulding.

Figure G.14 Mouchette.

Lierne	A vaulting rib which runs between two other ribs rather than beginning at the springing line. See plan of *Ribbed vault* (Figure G.19).
Lierne vault	A vault with *Lierne* ribs.
Light	The vertical divisions of a window, formed by one or more *Mullions*. Thus, a window with three mullions is known as a four-light window.
Lintel	The horizontal stone spanning an opening.
Lozenge	A diamond shape.
Merlon	The upstanding part of a battlement.
Metope	The stone slab between the triglyphs in the Doric order.
Mitre	The line formed at the meeting of two mouldings. In masonry, the mitre is always worked on the stone and the joint formed clear of the mitre.

Modillion	A type of bracket used beneath the upper part of a Corinthian cornice.
Mouchette	A outline shape with a curved centre line, formed in curvilinear tracery. Colloquially known as a ghostie, for obvious reasons (Figure G.14).
Mould	A templet.
Moulding	The profile formed by working stone to a set contour.
Mullion	The upright which divides a window opening into two or more *Lights*.
Mutule	The deep blocks in a Doric cornice, decorated with *Guttae*.
Nail head	A decorative feature consisting of a series of low pyramids, resembling the heads of a square nails.
Nave	The main body of a church or hall.
Newel	The central post on a spiral stair, worked on the end of each tread.
Nodding ogee	An arch of ogee form which in side elevation also takes the form of an ogee.
Nook shaft	A slender column set in an internal angle.
Norman architecture	The style introduced around the time of the Norman Conquest and lasting until about the middle of the twelfth century. Now often known as Romanesque from its slight similarity to the style of the Romans.
Nose	Outermost or most prominent projection on moulding.
Ogee	A moulding consisting of two reverse curves, as a *Cyma reversa*. In the Gothic style, it is sometimes used upside down, as a *Cyma recta*. An arch of this form, the lower half of the soffit being concave, the upper part convex (Figure G.15). See also *Nodding ogee*.
Order	One of the divisions of architectural styles, e.g. Doric, Ionic, Decorated, etc. In a moulded arch, or where successive rings are stepped out, each ring of voussoirs is known as an order. See also *Arch ring*.

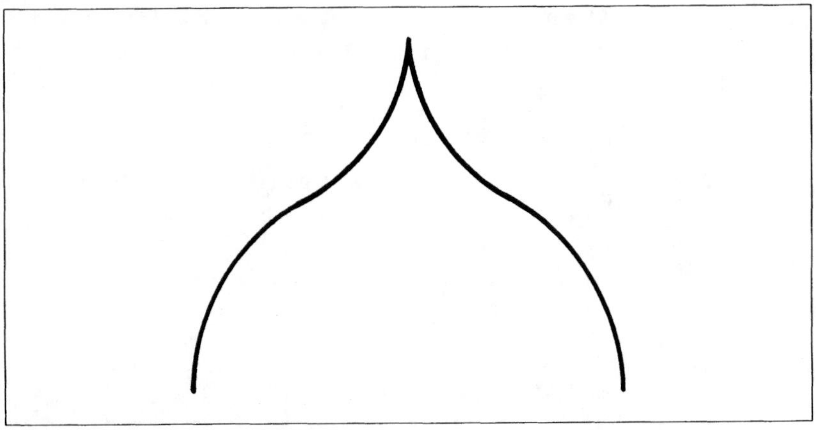

Figure G.15 Ogee arch.

Oriel	A projecting window, which is supported on a corbel or bracket rather than from the ground.
Ovolo	A quarter-round moulding (Figure G.16).
Panel	An area which is sunk, raised or otherwise framed for decorative purposes.
Parapet	A low wall on the outer side of a roof gutter.
Pediment	The low triangular gable on a classical building.
Pellet	An ornament worked on Norman mouldings, consisting of a series of balls or discs.
Pendentive	The masonry in the angle of a square base beneath a dome, by which the dome is supported across the angle. It is concave, resembling the web of a vault and is, in effect, a downward continuation of the dome. See also *Squinch arch*.
Perpendicular	See *Gothic architecture*.
Pier	The masonry between two adjacent windows, or the solid mass supporting an arch or the larger pillars in an arcade, especially in Romanesque architecture, where the very fat, round columns are often known as piers. The distinction between a pier and a pillar can be a little blurred at times (Figure G.1).
Pilaster	A very shallow buttress against a wall, often serving more for decoration than effect.
Pillar	The support for an arch, not round in plan but often light in appearance compared with a pier.
Pinnacle	The spire-like termination to a buttress, turret, or similar feature. The term is usually applied to that part of the structure which rises above wall-top level and may be square, round, pentagonal or octagonal, or any combination of these, on plan.
Plate tracery	See *Tracery*.
Plinth	The projecting course(s) at the base of a building, finished with a bevelled or moulded weathering.
Quadrant	A convex, quarter-round moulding.
Quatrefoil	See *Foil*.
Quirk	A narrow groove between mouldings, or between moulding and ashlar.
Quoin	The corner of a building. Also a stone forming the corner.

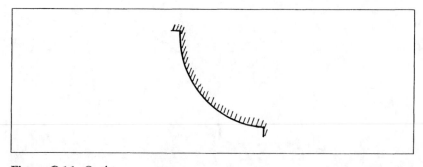

Figure G.16 Ovolo.

Ramp and twist	A wall, or other feature, which rises and turns at the same time.
Relieving arch	An arch, often roughly worked, set over a lintel to relieve the load by discharging the thrust to the sides of the opening.
Renaissance architecture	The return or rebirth of the style of the Greek and Roman period. See Chapter 1.
Respond	A half-pillar engaged with, i.e. part of, but projecting from, the wall at the end of an arcade or beneath a single arch.
Return	Any wall or moulding which changes direction, usually at 90°, either horizontally or vertically.
Reveal	That part of a jamb which is outside the glazing line or door frame. Also that part which is inside the glazing line or frame. If the reveal is set at an angle, whether inside or outside, it is referred to as a *Splay* or a splayed reveal.
Rib	An arched member forming the framework of a vault (see Figure G.19).
Ribbed vault	A vault built with ribs, in distinction to a groined vault (see Figure G.19).
Ridge rib	The vault rib, which runs along the crown of the vault on the axis of the vaulted space (see Figure G.19).
Rise	The distance between the springing line of an arch and the highest point of the soffit.
Roll	In Gothic architecture, a convex moulding which may be either of circular form or made up of compound curves. See also *Bowtell*.
Rose window	A circular traceried window. When the tracery takes the form of radiating spokes, it is often known as a wheel window.
Rubble	Stone used straight from the quarry or with simple dressing to bring it to a roughly square shape.
Rustic	Granite left with a natural face.
Rusticated	Stone where the joints are recessed behind the face, using either a chamfer or a sunk marginal draft, to give a bold effect with deep shadows. The face may be finished in any style.
Rock-faced	Limestone or sandstone with a natural face. Rock-faced ashlar will have a carefully worked marginal draft. Rock-faced rusticated ashlar will have either a second marginal draft sunk below the first one, or the rock face will return to a fillet before the sunk draft.
Scallop capital	A form of Norman capital which is decorated with inverted half-cone shapes.
Scotia	A concave moulding in classical architecture, part-elliptical in section. Often used for any concave moulding (Figure G.12).
Scroll moulding	A circular moulding in which the two halves are of different radii, producing a step resembling a paper scroll (Figure G.17).

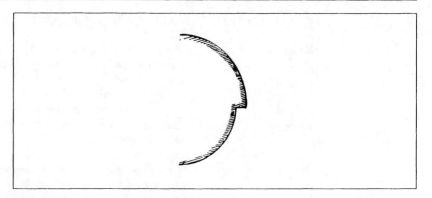

Figure G.17 Scroll moulding.

Shaft	A slender column used either singly or in groups.
Skewback	The stone which supports the bed joint of the lowest voussoir in a segmental arch.
Snecked joint	Where the bed joint of one stone is cut away to give an abrupt change of course height.
Snecked walling	Rubble wall, usually squared, where the coursing is interrupted by the use of jumper stones rising through two or more courses, in either a regular or an irregular pattern.
Soffit	The under-surface of an arch, lintel or other feature (Figure G.1).
Span	The width between the uprights supporting an arch or lintel.
Spandrel	The masonry between two adjacent arches, filling the space between the springer and the crown (Figure G.1).
Splay	A vertical run of masonry set at an angle, as in the jambs of a window. Often used for any angled surface.
Springer	The lowest voussoir in an arch (Figure G.1).
Springing line	The horizontal line from which the arch springs. This is normally the top bed of the capital, but see *Stilted arch*.
Squinch arch	An arch in the right angle of the walls supporting a dome. It is similar in function to the *Pendentive*.
Stilted arch	An arch in which the jambs are continued above the capitals in a vertical line before the arch proper begins.
Stooling	The seating worked on a sill to receive a jamb, mullion or any similar feature.
String course	A horizontal moulded course running across the face of a building.
Stylobate	The base of a classical building; that part below the columns.
Sunk chamfer	Another name for a hollow chamfer.
Tas-de-charge	The horizontal stones which are corbelled out from the wall to form the lower three or four courses of a rib. They have horizontal joints and are not part of the arch proper.

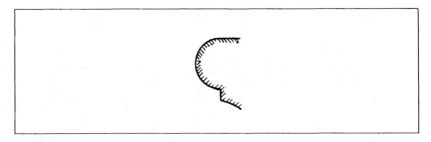

Figure G.18 Torus moulding.

Template	Stone slab set in a wall on which the beam-end rests. Also known as a padstone.
Tierceron	A rib running betwen the transverse and diagonal ribs, from the capital to a point on the ridge rib. See plan of *Ribbed vault* (Figure G.19).
Tierceron vault	A vault containing tierceron ribs.
Torus	A large semicircular moulding in classical architecture (Figure G.18).
Tracery	Ornamental stonework in the upper part of an opening. When worked on a decorative panel, it is known as blank tracery. The earliest type was plate tracery, in which a slab of stone was pierced to give a decorative effect, giving way to bar tracery in which slender moulded elements provide openwork decoration.
Transom	The horizontal division across a window.
Transverse rib	Vaulting rib, which runs from side to side of the vault. See plan of *Ribbed vault* (see Figure G.19).
Triforium	The space between the arcade and the clerestorey in a Gothic church. It usually takes the form of a second, smaller, arcade.
Triglyph	Panels with three wide vertical grooves in the frieze of the Doric order.
Tympanum	Semicircular panel between an arched head and transom over a doorway. It is often very richly carved.
Vault	An arched ceiling. See *Barrel vault, Groined vault, Ribbed vault.*
Vesica	A pointed oval window.
Volute	A spiral moulding resembling the end view of a scroll.
Voussoir	The wedge-shaped stone used in the construction of an arch (Figure G.1).
Wall rib	The vaulting rib which is worked on the wall forming one side of the vaulted space. See plan of *Ribbed vault* (Figure G.19).
Weathering	A sloping surface designed to throw off water.
Web	The masonry infilling between the ribs of a vault.
Wheel window	See *Rose window.*
Zig zag	A Norman moulding in zig zag lines.

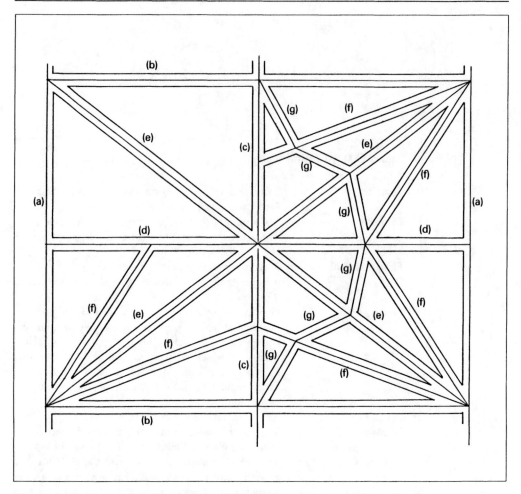

Figure G.19 Plan of ribbed vaults: (a) wall rib; (b) transverse rib; (c) ridge rib; (d) transverse ridge rib; (e) diagonal rib; (f) tierceron rib; (g) Lierne rib.

Glossary of Technical Terms

The definitions of those words particular to the masonry trade are based on current usage in masons' shops familiar to the authors and their colleagues and acquaintances. Owing to the many regional variations, it is neither possible nor even desirable to establish uniformity of usage.

Very few tools are defined here, as this would repeat the list given in Chapter 6.

(Words in italics have their own entry in the glossary.)

Acute angle	One of less than 90°.
Arc	A part of the circumference of a circle.
Arris	The distinct line or edge formed by the junction of two surfaces.
Axis	The line passing through the centre of a three-dimensional object.
	A line passing centrally along the length of a building or geometrical figure.
Banker	The solid stone bench at which the mason works.
Banker mason	One who is skilled in the art of working stone to templets.
Base line	The line from which all vertical measurements are taken.
Batted	See *Tooled*.
Bed	The top or bottom surface of a worked stone.
	The mortar forming the joint below the stone.
	The sedimentary layers in stone.
Boasted-for-carving	Roughly blocked out by the mason to the overall shape of a carving, where a worked stone includes carved detail.
Boastered	The finish on the face of a stone which has been dressed with the boaster, giving a series of broad drafts set at an angle to the vertical. Not to be confused with *Boasted*.
Brace	A scaffold tube running diagonally across the face of

	a scaffold, or from inner to outer standards, to give rigidity.
Centre	The temporary timber framework on which an arch is built.
Centre line	A line through the centre of a drawing or stone from which all horizontal measurements are taken.
Check	A sinking worked in a stone.
Chiselled	Worked stone with the chisel marks still visible, not rubbed. Also called off the chisel.
Chord	A line across a circle which does not pass through the centre.
Circumference	The boundary line around a circle.
Closer	The final stone in a course, usually worked over-long to allow for precise cutting on site.
Concave moulding	A sunken moulding, curved in section.
Concentric	Circles or arcs of circles struck from a common centre.
Convex moulding	A projecting moulding, curved in section.
Cope	To split stone with wedges, or (for thin slabs), to split by scoring and tapping with a hammer.
Datum line	Similar to a base line, not necessarily at the lowest part of a drawing.
Diameter	A line across a circle which passes through the centre.
Draft	A worked strip of stone. A marginal draft runs around the edges of the face.
Dragged	The finish to a stone resulting from the use of a drag.
Ellipse	An oval figure. An elliptical arch is in fact half an ellipse.
Face mould	The templet that gives the outline of the face of a stone and carries information about mouldings or other features on the face.
Fish belly	A nickname for the two-handed masons' and quarrymen's cross-cut saw. The name comes from the convex cutting edge.
Frigbob	A large, single-handed cross-cut saw, often made from a cut down cross-cut.
Hexagon	A closed figure bounded by six straight lines. A regular hexagon has all the sides of equal length.
Hypoteneuse	The side of a triangle opposite to a right angle.
Joint	The side of a stone abutting the next stone in the course.
	The mortar filling the space between adjacent stones in a course.
Laggings	Short lengths of wood connecting the two frames that form the side of a centre and on which the voussoirs rest.
Ledger	A horizontal scaffold tube running the length of the scaffold to support the putlogs.
Monolithic	Made from a single stone. Used for large stone objects which might otherwise have been made in several pieces.
Mould	A templet.

Moulding	The profile formed by working stone to a fixed contour.
Normal	A line at right angles to another. A line cutting a curve and which lies on the radius of the curve.
Obtuse angle	One of more than 90°.
Octagon	A closed figure bounded by eight straight lines. A regular octagon has all the sides of equal length.
Pentagon	A closed figure bounded by five straight lines. A regular pentagon has all the sides of equal length.
Perpendicular	A line set at right angles to another.
Plain ashlar	Ashlar that has a rubbed or dragged finish.
Plane	A surface that is straight in all directions.
Polished	A surface which is smoothed until it reflects light. A polished surface is only possible on certain stones.
Polygon	A closed figure bounded by any number of straight lines. A regular polygon has all the sides of equal length.
Putlog	A short horizontal scaffold tube carried on the ledgers and supporting the boards.
Radius	A line joining the centre of a circle and the circumference. It is equal in length to half the diameter.
Raking section	A section through a moulding which is not taken at right angles to the surface, or, in the case of curved mouldings, not lying on the radius of the curve.
Reverse	A small section of templet that fits exactly into one element of a moulding. The negative image of a moulding. A templet cut to a radius used where the moulding or other surface is curved.
Rhomboid	A figure bounded by four straight lines, the opposite sides of which are equal but in which the angles are not right angles.
Section	A templet that defines the profile of a stone. The outline of a solid seen from one end, or when cut through by a plane. For a true section, the cutting plane is at right angles to the axis of the solid, or lies on the radius of the curve.
Sector	A part of a circle, bounded on two sides by radii and on the third by an arc.
Segment	A part of a circle bounded by a chord and an arc. That part which is cut off by a chord.
Shiftstock	See *Sliding bevel*.
Skelp	A piece of stone removed by working.
Skid	A short length of timber used to chock up stone.
Sliding bevel	A tool for transferring angles, in which both blade and stock are slotted. Also known as a *Shiftstock*.
Spall	A piece of stone detached as the result either of mechanical, frost or other damage.
Standard	A vertical scaffold tube.
Tangent	A line touching, but not cutting, the circumference

	of a circle. It forms a right angle with the radius which meets the circle at that point.
Template	Stone slab on which beam-end rests. Also known as padstone.
Templet	A pattern made in a rigid material showing the shape to which a stone is to be cut.
Tooled	Finished with a broad chisel to show vertical grooves running from top to bottom of the face and set a specified distance apart (so many per inch). Also known as *Batted*.
Wall line	The general line of an ashlar wall to which a specified line on a moulding must be matched during fixing.

Bibliography

Some of the following list, especially those titles dealing with Gothic architecture, are long out of print, but are well worth seeking out in second-hand book shops for the quality of their illustrations if nothing else.

INTRODUCTION AND GENERAL

Addleson, L. and Rice, C. (new edn 1994) *Performance of materials in buildings* London: Butterworth-Heinemann.

Anon. (1991) *Natural stone glossary* London: Linked Advertising and Marketing (for The Stone Federation).

Ashurst, J. and Dimes, F., eds (1990) *Conservation of building and decorative stone* (2 vols) London: Butterworth-Heinemann.

British Standards Institution (1976) BS 5390: *Code of practice for stone masonry* London: BSI.

Conservation News London: United Kingdom Institute for Conservation. (A magazine of conservation matters, 3 issues per year.)

Davey, N. (1961) *A history of building materials* London: Phoenix House.

Feilden, B. (1994) *Conservation of historic buildings* London: Butterworth-Heinemann.

Harvey, J. (1972) *Conservation of buildings* London: J. Baker.

Natural Stone Specialist (formerly *Stone Industries Journal*). (The magazine devoted to the masonry trade, 11 issues per year.) Herald House Ltd, 96 Dominion Road, Worthing, West Sussex BN14 8JP.

Purchase, W.R. (new edn 1987) *Practical masonry* Builth Wells: Attic Books.

Warland, E.G. (2nd edn 1953) *Modern practical masonry* London: Pitman.

CHAPTER 1: HISTORY

Fletcher, B. (1991) *A history of architecture* London: Butterworth-Heinemann.

Knoop, D. and Jones, G.P. (3rd edn revised 1967) *The mediaeval mason* Manchester: Manchester University Press.

Murphy, S. (new edn 1976) *Stone mad* London: Routledge & Kegan Paul.

Parker, J.H. (1900) *An introduction to the study of Gothic architecture* London: James Parker & Co.

Salzman, L.F. (corrected reprint 1967) *Building in England down to 1540* Oxford: Clarendon Press.

Statham, H. H. (3rd edn rev. 1950) *A history of architecture* (edited by H. Braun) London: Batsford.

West, G.H. (1927) *Gothic architecture in England and France* London: Bell and Sons.

CHAPTER 2: HEALTH AND SAFETY

Building Employers Confederation (undated) *COSHH in construction* London: BEC Publications.

Health and Safety Executive (1992) *A guide to the Reporting of Injuries, Diseases, and Dangerous Occurrences Regulations 1985*, HS(R)23 London: HMSO.

Health and Safety Executive (1992) *Management of Health and Safety at Work; Approved Code of Practice for Management of Health and Safety at Work Regulations 1992* London: HMSO.

Health and Safety Executive (1992) *Personal protective equipment at work; Guidance on Personal Protective Equipment at Work Regulations 1992* London: HMSO.

Health and Safety Executive (1992) *Work equipment; guidance on Provision and Use of Work Equipment Regulations 1992* London: HMSO.

Health and Safety Executive (1992) *Workplace, health, safety, and welfare; Approved Code of Practice for Workplace (Health, Safety, and Welfare) Regulations 1992* London: HMSO.

Health and Safety Executive (1994) *Managing construction for health and safety: Construction (Design and Management) Regulations 1994* London: HSE.

Health and Safety Executive (1995) *Designing for health and safety in construction* London: HSE.

Health and Safety Executive (1995) *A guide to managing health and safety in construction* London: HSE.

Health and Safety Executive (1995) *Health and safety for small construction sites* London: HSE.

Pybus, R.M. *Croner's guide to COSHH* Kingston-upon-Thames: Croner Publications Ltd. (Annual publication.)

Secretary of State for Employment (1974) *Health and Safety at Work Act 1974* London: HMSO.

Stone Federation (undated) *COSHH information pack* London: Stone Federation of Great Britain.

Stranks, J.W. (1993) *The handbook of health and safety practice* London: Pitman Publishing.

CHAPTER 3: GEOLOGY

Anon. *Natural stone directory* Herald House Ltd. (Biennial publication.)

Blyth F.G.H. (7th edn by M.H. de Freitas) 1984 *A geology for engineers* London: Arnold.

Clifton Taylor, A. (4th edn 1987 by J. Simmons) *The pattern of English building* London: Faber.

Fletcher, B. (1991) *A history of architecture* London: Butterworth-Heinemann.

Hart, D. (1988) *The building magnesium limestones of the British Isles* London: Building Research Establishment.

Hart, D. (1991) *The building slates of the British Isles* London: Building Research Establishment.

Honeybourne, D. (1982) *The building limestones of France* London: Building Research Establishment.

Leary, E. (1984) *The building limestones of the British Isles* London: Building Research Establishment.

Leary, E. (1986) *The building sandstones of the British Isles* London: Building Research Establishment.

Shackley, M. (1977) *Rocks and man* London: George Allen and Unwin.

Schaffer, R.J. (1972) *The weathering of natural building stones* Watford: Building Research Establishment.

CHAPTER 5: SETTING-OUT

Rawle, J.S. (1896) *Practical plane and solid geometry* London: Simpkin, Marshall, Hamilton, Kent, & Co.

CHAPTER 10: FIXING

British Standards Institution (1993) BS 5973: *Code of practice for access and working scaffolds and special structures in steel* London: BSI.

Health and Safety Executive (1992) *Manual handling; guidance on Manual Handling Operations Regulations 1992* London: HMSO.

CHAPTER 11: CLEANING

Andrew, C. (1994) *Stonecleaning. A guide for practioners* Edinburgh: Historic Scotland/Robert Gordon University.

Ashurst, N. (1994) *Cleaning historic buildings* London: Donhead.

British Standards Institution (1982) BS 6270: *Code of practice for cleaning and surface repair of buildings, Part 1 Natural stone, cast stone, and clay and calcium silicate brickwork* London: BSI.

British Standards Institution (1984) BS 6477: *Water repellents for masonry surfaces* London: BSI.

Pybus, R.M. (1994) *Croner's Guide to COSHH* Kingston-upon-Thames: Croner Publications Ltd.

Stone Federation (undated) *COSHH information pack* London: Stone Federation of Great Britain.

CHAPTER 13: TRAINING

Full details of the cost and availability of the NVQ Candidates Assessment Evidence Record, which contains all the competencies mentioned, along with other CITB publications can be obtained from: Publications Distribution Department, CITB, Bircham Newton, Kings Lynn, Norfolk PE31 6RH (Telephone 01553 776677).

GLOSSARY

Ditchfield, P.H. (1947) *English Gothic architecture* London: J.M. Dent.
Fleming, J., Honour, H. and Pevsner, N. (4th edn 1991) *The Penguin dictionary of architecture* London: Penguin Books.
Parker, J.H. (5th edn 1850) *Glossary of Gothic architecture* (3 vols) Oxford: John Henry Parker.
Parker, J.H. (1866) *Concise glossary of Gothic architecture* Oxford: James Parker & Co.

Index

This index does not show items in the list of setting-out and templet-cutting tools (pages 41–46), the descriptions of masons' tools (pages 119–130), or the glossaries (pages 245–266). Methods of drawing particular features are indexed under Setting-out.